# Spreading the Word

# Spreading the Word

## A History of Information
## in the California Gold Rush

### Richard T. Stillson

UNIVERSITY OF NEBRASKA PRESS
LINCOLN AND LONDON

Manufactured in the United States of America

Library of Congress Cataloging-in-Publication Data
Stillson, Richard T. (Richard Thomas)
Spreading the word : a history of information
in the California gold rush / Richard T. Stillson.
p. cm.
Includes bibliographical references and index.
ISBN-13: 978-0-8032-4325-5 (cloth : alk. paper)
ISBN-10: 0-8032-4325-1 (cloth : alk. paper)
ISBN-13: 978-0-8032-1827-7 ( paper : alk. paper)
1. California—Gold discoveries—Information resources—
History—19th century. 2. Communication—Social
aspects—California—History—19th century. 3. Mass media—
United States—History—19th century. 4. California—Guidebooks
—Bibliography. 5. California—Maps—Bibliography.
6. Catalogs, Publishers'—United States—Bibliography. I. Title.
F865.S966 2006
979.4'04—dc22
2006004324

Set in Monotype Bulmer by Kim Essman.
Designed by R. W. Boeche.

# CONTENTS

ILLUSTRATIONS

**Figures**

**Maps**

**Table**

## ACKNOWLEDGMENTS

Like all serious scholarship, this project was a cooperative effort, impossible without the support and guidance of many people and institutions. My deepest debt goes to my mentor at Johns Hopkins University, Professor Ronald Walters, who suggested the idea of using the California gold rush as a case study for my interests in communications history, and then followed and improved each phase of the work. Professor Toby Ditz of Johns Hopkins opened what was for me a new world of the study of language, literary criticism, and reading. She then helped me relate my ideas about information assessment to this literature. This guidance, together with her detailed and helpful editorial comments, greatly improved my document. My wife Marion, in addition to providing support at home and forbearance for long research trips away from home, read most of the manuscript in various drafts and helped translate my ideas into readable English.

The archival research on which much of this study is based would not have been possible without the financial support and collections of many research libraries, particularly in California. I wish to thank the Western Historical Association for a Martin Ridge Fellowship that allowed a month-long study at the Huntington Library in Pasadena, California, and a Turner Grant from Johns Hopkins University that eased the financial burden of continuing my reading in California at the Bancroft Library at the University of California at Berkeley. At the Huntington, Mr. Peter Blodgett and Ms. Jennifer Martinez were particularly kind in helping me navigate the intricacies of that remarkable library. I continued my studies in California at the California State Library in Sacramento where Mr. Gary Kurutz also encouraged my focus on communications and information dispersal in the gold rush. In San Francisco, I used the archives of both the California Historical Society and the Society of California Pioneers, from which I obtained much of my primary material relating to the Lassen Cutoff.

Not all my archival work was done in California. Chapters 1 and 2, on newspapers and guidebooks, would not have been possible without the resources of the American Antiquarian Society (AAS) in Worcester, Massachusetts, and the help of the research and curatorial staff there. I wish to thank the AAS for the financial support of a Stephen Botein Fellowship to study there, but more importantly, I would like to thank Mr. John Hench and Ms. Caroline Sloat for their help and

*Acknowledgments*

support in using the library. The collections of the Newberry Library in Chicago, which also provided financial support, were extremely useful, particularly for their maps and guidebooks. In addition to the Newberry's maps, I used many maps from the Map Division of the Library of Congress and the Carl Wheat collection at the University of California at Berkeley. I wish to thank the staffs of these institutions for their help and for making excellent reproductions of their original maps. The Beineke Library at Yale University is the only library that has all of the copies of the *California Herald*, the study of which formed an important part of chapter 1. Finally, chapter 3, on the Missouri trailhead towns, could not have been written without use of the collections of the Missouri State Historical Society in Columbia and the Missouri Historical Society in St. Louis. I wish to thank the staffs of both of these institutions for help during my stay in their libraries.

Spreading the Word

## INTRODUCTION

This study is about how Americans from the East who went overland to California for the gold rush in the years 1849 to 1851 obtained, assessed, and used information. The principal findings are that the forms and constraints of communications, the mechanisms of information dispersal, and the perceived credibility of the content strongly affected how information was assessed and used. These aspects of communications and information influenced goldrushers' behavior and thus the magnitude, sequence, and timing of events. Communications and information dispersal provide a new lens through which to view the gold rush. This study looks through that lens and explains certain events that otherwise are mysterious. In doing so it contributes to both gold rush history and the historical analysis of communications and information.

### Why the Gold Rush? Why Information?

The gold rush provides a rich case study with which to examine many questions concerning U.S. social and cultural history. It was a founding event of California history and an important episode in the history of the West, including the occupation of the region by European Americans, Europeans, Latin Americans, and Chinese. It was disastrous to Native Americans. Hundreds of thousands of people left their homes and families throughout the world over about a five-year period to search out their "main chance," and they found some $300–$500 million in gold. These people were part of the largest internal migration in U.S. history. Many of the important effects of the gold rush on the country were due in large part to the magnitude and short time span of this migration. The scale depended on the rapid generation and dissemination of information concerning gold and how to travel west. Thus, information and the communications mechanisms through which it was disseminated are central to the study of the gold rush and, by extension, the study of nineteenth-century America more generally.

Potential goldrushers in December 1848, when news of California gold became widely believed, had a difficult information problem.[1] The majority were from the East and what is now the Midwest and had little or no knowledge of the West, much less how to travel there. Goldrushers, who were predominantly men with some resources and, often, families, had a lot to lose if the gold was a chimera or the trip a disaster. They had, however, some information. Many realized that speed was important and that, if they were to go, they had to make their plans and leave the East by March or at latest April 1849. The one thing that most knew was that the trip was dangerous and that how well one prepared could be a matter of life or death. They needed a great deal of information, and they needed it quickly as they attempted to make decisions about whether to go by land or sea, which route to take, what and where to purchase outfits and provisions, and what they needed to mine gold. Information on all these subjects was, in fact, produced quickly as newspaper editors, book publishers, and others tried to cash in on gold rush fever. The result was that much information was incredible, contradictory, and subject to frequent change. Credibility became a major issue for both goldrushers and their information providers. Also, the information available to goldrushers was different in different locations and, as the emigrants traveled, they frequently had to reassess what they thought they knew.

Many goldrushers realized the problem of inadequate and inaccurate information. They took with them multiple guidebooks and maps and hired guides who supposedly knew how to get to California. Even this was insufficient, so they purchased handwritten guidebooks and considered signs and advertisements along the trail, and importantly, they listened to rumors and the opinions of other goldrushers. After they got to California, they wrote letters home, many of which were published by newspapers in the East. These letters substantially changed the information available for the second year of the gold rush, in which there were even more emigrants to California than in 1849.

The drama and pageant of the gold rush have long been recognized by amateur historians and western history buffs. Within the past twenty-five years, academic historians have also begun to realize the complexity and importance of the event, and scholarly studies of it have multiplied.[2] Viewing the gold rush through the informational problems of the travelers, however, and how these problems affected their decisions, has not been explored in detail in gold rush historiography or communications history.

## Information and Credibility

It is fairly intuitive that good and widely dispersed information is important to effective markets, democratic politics, and a free and competitive society. There are aspects of information dispersal, however, that are less intuitive and need further thought and study. First, information is a scarce commodity that takes resources to generate and disseminate, and it is bought and sold in a market as other commodities; thus an analysis of the information marketplace is necessary for the study of information in an event like the gold rush. Second, information as a commodity is usually contained within its means of dissemination, or media, such as newspapers, books, radio, television, magazines, lectures, and education. Each of these media also sells other services such as news or entertainment. Conceptually, each of these services is a separate product; the fact that they are sold jointly means that the price of information alone is disguised. Third, information must be assessed and credible to be useful, and information assessment is also a scarce commodity that can be bought and sold; thus an analysis of the means of information assessment is necessary for the study of the information marketplace. These markets within markets and joint products and prices show that providing information and disbursing it is a complex activity.[3]

Possible problems with the information marketplace are well known to policymakers, and in the late twentieth century, many mechanisms were established by law, government regulators, private firms, and the press to improve information dissemination and assessment. For example, in the financial field the law requires formalized disclosure and publication of information and assessment of this information (external auditing). The information assessment market is also regulated, and standards of accounting certification provide information about the information providers and assessors. Further layers of information assessment are provided by financial regulators (the Securities and Exchange Commission) and the private sector (brokers, financial firms' research departments, and the financial press). Even with these safeguards, the information marketplace can break down with disastrous consequences as in the Enron and WorldCom scandals in 2001 and 2002.

Without any public or private mechanisms for information assessment, goldrushers had to decide how to judge the credibility of the news that proclaimed the gold finds, the guidebooks that gave advice on travel, the maps that showed the way, and the rumors that said almost anything. Providers of this information knew that establishing credibility was key to selling their product. In the case of guidebooks, if the marketing did not establish credibility, the book would not sell. In the case of newspapers, maintaining credibility was even more important because if the stories were too unbelievable the credibility of other news items might be affected and thus the future as well as current sales of the newspaper. No goldrusher wrote about what made one source of information more credible

3

than any other, but newspaper editors, guidebook writers, and map publishers did write in their advertisements and introductions what they expected would make their publications credible.

In analyzing what made various kinds of information credible to goldrushers, I distinguish between what I call credibility criteria and credibility markers. Credibility criteria are factors that people use to assess information. In the case of the gold rush, these criteria were usually an information source such as a government authority or an expert.[4] The concept of credibility criteria is broader than sources of credibility, however, in that it can encompass ways in which information is transmitted, such as print, handwritten documents, or speech. Credibility markers are ways in which credibility criteria are identified by information users. In the gold rush, this was usually some form of print, such as the name of a government agency on a report or on the legend of a map. Identifying credibility markers allowed someone to interpret the way information was presented in terms of perceptions of credibility. One of the themes of this study is how these credibility criteria and markers changed with the location, time, and the experience of the goldrushers.

This study of the informational problems of the goldrushers, and their solutions to them, begins with the information sources available to potential goldrushers in various parts of the United States in December 1848 through June 1849. Chapter 1 is about information available through newspapers, and chapter 2 is about guidebooks and maps. In these early months of the gold rush, the primary sources of credibility were printed documents, and the markers were references to government expeditions, maps, and military rank or political office. Printed documents were not equally available geographically. An analysis of bookseller catalogs shows that guidebooks written and produced in the West of the time (St. Louis, Cincinnati, Louisville, and Chicago) were not available in the East, although eastern guidebooks were available in the West. It was as if the market for information had a one-way valve, with books and information flowing east to west but not vice versa. This had important implications for goldrushers from the East because when they obtained new, different, and what they considered better, information as they traveled to the trailheads, their initial information sources lost credibility. They then reassessed not only the specific information in these sources but also the way they assessed it.

The study continues with a narrative that follows the activities of a selection of American goldrusher companies from a variety of locations in the East and the current Midwest.[5] Chapter 3 takes the companies to the trailheads, and chapter 4 along the trail to California. A key finding of this part of the study is that as the emigrants traveled farther into unknown territory, their trust in printed material, mainly guidebooks and maps, declined; and the credibility of handwritten, oral, and unverified information increased. Sources of credibility changed from official information to local expertise. Ultimately, this change led thousands of travelers to choose an unwise route on which many died and most suffered greatly.

In spite of the hardships, most of the goldrushers reached California where the informational problems changed. Chapter 5 focuses on these problems and their solutions. There was almost no communications infrastructure in California in 1849 to 1851; in particular, the Post Office Department was inadequate and mistrusted. Express companies filled this communications gap. These companies ranged from individuals and small partnerships forming a "pack mule express" to international express companies providing transportation and banking services for miners sending packages and gold back home. The chapter describes each of these types of businesses as well as the cooperation and conflicts among the competing information-distribution services, both public and private. These descriptions show that the private endeavors, along with the Post Office, formed an unplanned network of communications and information dispersal.

Chapter 6 analyzes the content and influence of communications from California and the implications of these informational flows for the gold rush of 1850. Goldrushers' letters back East had a widespread influence. Private letters that were published in newspapers and books written by returnees provided important sources of public information. These sources of information were particularly credible because they came from people who had survived the trip and had firsthand experience in mining or merchandising in California. Personal experience trumped official credentials and local expertise as the most important source of credibility. Letters were also the primary method of communications for merchants and businessmen in California who had to order goods some eight to nine months in advance.

This study is a beginning to systematic research on communications and information problems in the California gold rush and, more generally, in the mid-nineteenth-century United States. It focuses on goldrushers from the eastern United States, who were almost entirely English-speaking white men. Focusing on this group is justified because miners from the East formed the large majority of goldrushers. Other groups, however, were also important and numerous, particularly miners from Mexico, South America, Europe, and China. Also, the non-English-speaking miners from other parts of the world had different and more difficult communications and information problems than did easterners because of language differences and greater distances from the gold fields.[6]

The Californios, former Mexican citizens who lived in California in 1848, had different communications and informational problems: they did not have to hear about the gold finds through newspapers nine months after James Marshall's discovery, but misunderstandings due to differences in language and culture exacerbated racial repression and strongly impeded their ability to profit from the gold. Finally, various groups of Native Americans, those found living both near the trail and in California, suffered from communications and information problems in their attempts to cope with what was happening to their traditional lands and to deal with the massive influx of non-Indians. The repression and near extinction of many Indian groups, particularly in California, is one of the most tragic aspects of the gold rush.[7]

### Imagining the West in 1848

Before beginning the story of the goldrushers and their search for credible information, it will be useful to review the kind of information they had before they heard of California gold. Easterners did not learn of the gold finds with a blank slate in regard to the West. The context of their prior knowledge of the history, economics, and geography of the region is important to understanding their perceptions of the flood of information they began to receive about California in December 1848.

The potential goldrushers in late 1848 had a picture in their minds of the lands, mountain men, Indians, and Mexicans that inhabited the territory. Their views of the West were mostly obtained from print, particularly books including histories, government reports, novels, adventures, and travelogues. In Joseph Sabin's comprehensive catalog of antebellum books about America, there are several hundred books about the American West published between 1806, when the first books about the Lewis and Clark expedition came out, and 1848.[8] Although there is little information from this time period about the size of print runs, many of these books were bestsellers as indicated by the large number of editions over many years. The impressions created by these books varied, but there were some consistent themes, including the vastness of the region, the majesty of the scenery, the exoticism and danger of the Indians, and the supposed laziness

6

and wantonness of the Mexicans. Perhaps the most important theme in terms of influencing the goldrushers was that the trip west was possible for those with determination and the appropriate knowledge and preparation.

Bookseller catalogs show what books were sold in various markets and years. It is reasonable to assume that if prospective goldrushers would consider traveling to California at short notice, they would probably have had an interest in such literature. Four catalogs from 1845 to 1848 from different types of publishing and bookselling companies in New York and Philadelphia, give a good indication of the nature of publications about the West available to readers in the East.[9] They reveal some consistencies in their lists: versions of Lewis and Clark's *Travels*, books about the army explorations of the West, histories and travelogues about Oregon, the popular books of Washington Irving and Henry Dana, and picture books from Catlin and Maximilian were carried by two or more of the booksellers. The full list of entries about the West from these catalogs is in appendix A.

The first and possibly the most influential books about the American West were those that stemmed from the Lewis and Clark expedition, some of which had been reprinted many times and were listed in booksellers' catalogs in the mid-1840s. One of the most important ways in which books about the expedition set the stage for later literature about the West was framing the epic nature of the story in which determined men, with the help of an Indian woman, were able to overcome hardship and great distances to cross the wilderness and return home safely. In fact, there was only one death during the expedition, from a ruptured appendix, which could have occurred anywhere, and not a great loss of equipment or property. The alien land was hard and required organization, knowledge, and skill to survive it, but crossing it was possible. This theme was likely to have formed part of the mindset of potential goldrushers as they contemplated challenging the wilderness themselves.

Lewis and Clark's journals were not published in full until the twentieth century, although there were many books published in the nineteenth century about the expedition. The first was Jefferson's report to Congress, which was published in Washington the year the expedition returned, 1806.[10] The first publication based on Lewis and Clark's journals was compiled, paraphrased, and edited by Nicholas Biddle in 1814.[11] By this time members of the expedition had published their own versions; other authors had also published both unauthorized versions of the report and their own histories of the expedition.[12] These books made the reading public of the eastern United States and England aware for the first time

7

of the extent, diversity, and grandeur of the American West. An indication that
these publications retained their influence through midcentury is that versions
of Lewis and Clark's journals were republished in 1840 and 1842 and carried by
many booksellers.[13]

The army's Topographical Corps followed Lewis and Clark with many exploratory and mapping expeditions, several of which produced published reports
that were listed in the booksellers' catalogs. Immediately following the return
of Lewis and Clark, Zebulon Pike probed the upper Arkansas and Rio Grande
rivers (1806–1807), and his report was published in 1807 before Biddle came out
with his version of the Lewis and Clark journals.[14] Reports of several expeditions
undertaken between the 1820s and the 1840s were available to the goldrushers
in the mid-1840s, including Charles Wilkes's (1838–1842), which included a
description of his exploration of Oregon and California, and Stephen H. Long's
(1819–1820) about his expedition along the Platte River and into Colorado.[15]
William Emory, a lieutenant who traveled with Stephen Kearny on a military
and exploratory expedition on the southern trails to California during the Mexican War wrote a geographic and scientific account of the trip and the territory
through which they passed.[16]

The explorer of the West who was best known to the goldrushers was John
Charles Fremont, who commanded three major expeditions: to Wyoming (1842);
Oregon, the Great Basin, and California (1843–1844); and again to the Great Basin
and California (1846–1847).[17] In addition to the expeditions' reports, its maps
were published and became essential documents for western travelers. Fremont's
1845 report and its associated map, drawn by Charles Preuss, became a bestseller
in that year when the Senate authorized a printing of twenty thousand copies and
the House of Representatives another twenty thousand. Many goldrushers who
went overland carried a copy of Fremont's 1845 book, which was republished
in 1849 as a kind of guidebook. These reports were book-length narratives of
the trips, generally structured as a kind of journal with much botanical and
geographical detail, written in a style that conveyed the majesty of the mountain
West. Fremont's entry for August 10, 1842, as his party began their climb into
the Wind River Mountains is an example:

> Here a view of the utmost magnificence and grandeur burst upon our eyes.
> With nothing between us and their [the mountains'] feet to lessen the effect
> of the whole height, a grand bed of snow-capped mountains rose before us,
> pile upon pile, glowing in the bright light of an August day. Immediately

below them lay the lake, between two ridges, covered with dark pines, which swept down from the main chain to the spot where we stood. Here, where the lake glittered in the open sunlight, its banks of yellow sand and the light foliage of aspen groves contrasted well with the gloomy pines.[18]

The report is filled with such descriptions, and at times goldrushers attempted to mimic this style. The influence of such passages was likely to be that traveling to the West was an adventure that had compensations beyond the lure of gold.

Goldrushers knew about the mountain men. Names such as Jim Coulter, Jedediah Smith, James Clyman, Jim Bridger, Thomas "Pegleg" Fitzpatrick, Joseph Walker, William Sublette, Joe Meek, and Kit Carson were mentioned in their journals; in fact, many of them were still there when the goldrushers traveled to the West.[19] Goldrushers' knowledge of mountain men came primarily from news sources such as the reporting of Jedediah Smith's discovery of an easy crossing of the Rocky Mountains at South Pass and from the publications stemming from the exploring expeditions in which mountain men acted as guides or scouts.[20] Fremont's publications made a national hero of Kit Carson. The image of the mountain man as a solitary, half-savage fur trapper came primarily from novels such as Timothy Flint's *The Shoshonee Valley: A Romance*.[21] These stories of the mountain men were popular, and goldrushers probably read them; the novels may have reinforced the idea that individuals could conquer the wilderness if they had the skill, knowledge, and courage to do so.

A major preoccupation of the goldrushers as they prepared for their trip was Indians, and many of the gold rush companies had very unrealistic ideas about whether and how they would interact with Indians. This confusion was understandable because of the vast differences in how the various books about the West depicted Indians. The Lewis and Clark publications gave generally positive and exotic descriptions of some of the tribes; the Mandans, for example, provided the expedition with protection and a place to stay during its first winter. Lewis and Clark's journal entry for October 12, 1804, somewhat elaborated on by Biddle, probably interested potential goldrushers:

these women [the Arikaras] are handsomer than the Sioux; both of them are, however, disposed to be amorous, and our men found no difficulty in procuring companions for the night. . . . [T]he Sioux had offered us squaws, but we having declined while we remained there, they followed us with offers of females for two days. The Recaras had been equally accommodating.[22]

9

Other tribes, however, were unfriendly, and the expedition had a fight with the Blackfeet the following year. Edwin James's book about the Long expedition related an incident in which the Pawnees stole 126 horses and some meat: "it soon became necessary to protect our baggage by arranging ourselves around it; still, however, in despite of our vigilance, many of our small articles were stolen."[23] The incident was serious in that it stopped the progress of the expedition until more horses could be obtained and it triggered a face-off with the Pawnee war party that was just short of a disaster. Many goldrushers feared the Pawnees greatly at the beginning of their journeys, and they assumed at the outset that they would need to guard themselves from theft by Indians.

Images of Indians came not only from written sources, but also from two published artists, George Catlin and Maximilian, Prince of Wied, whose books of engravings were available in the mid- and late-1840s through bookseller's catalogs.[24] In 1832 Catlin embarked on several western trips that lasted until 1839 in which he painted highly stylized portraits of Indians and kept a careful record of their customs and dress. Back in New York, he established the first gallery of paintings of Indians and published a catalog of his collection and a book of engravings that went through many editions. Maximilian was a German prince with a penchant for comfortable but exotic tourism who did a tour of the United States from 1832 to 1834, including parts of the trans-Mississippi West, with a Swiss artist Karl Bodmer. In general both artists depicted the "noble savage" but with a certain emphasis on the merely savage. For example, one page of Catlin's book showed images of scalps and Indians who had survived scalping.

Catlin's and Wied's books were the primary pictorial representations available to those that contemplated western travel. They must have made an impression because in many emigrant journals goldrushers appeared to have had preexisting expectations about the appearance of Native Americans. The plains Indians seemed to meet their expectations in that they were generally healthy, exotically but not indecently clothed, and fierce looking without actually being a danger. The Indians of the Great Basin, however, who were not painted by either Catlin or Maximilian, were contemptuously described as naked, starving, and dangerous.

The largest trans-Mississippi emigration before the gold rush was to Oregon, and newspaper editors and book writers extolled Oregon as the new frontier.[25] Washington Irving's books on Oregon and the Rocky Mountains were very popular, going through many editions and still for sale in the book catalogs of 1844–1848.[26]

The Oregon emigrations consisted of settlers—good free farmland was the main attraction—and it was frequently compared with the trans-Allegheny emigrations of the eighteenth century.[27] Robert Greenhow asserted the case for overland travel to Oregon, but warned of Indian danger, in a popular book published in 1844.[28] This warning came to life in 1847 when Cayuse Indians attacked Marcus and Narcissa Whitman's mission on the trail to Oregon, killing the Whitmans and twelve others including their children. The news of this "massacre" reached Washington in May 1848 through one of the mountain men, Joe Meek. Although the themes of the frontier literature that encouraged settlement were not likely to have been a great influence on the goldrushers, since very few intended to settle in the West, they would not have ignored the accounts of Indian hostility on the Oregon Trail and in the Oregon Territory. These well-publicized problems of the Oregonians may explain why in their preparations for the trip so many gold rush companies chose a military-like organization and armed themselves heavily.

With one important exception, little was written about the inhabitants of the Mexican province of California. The exception was Richard Henry Dana's *Two Years before the Mast*, published in 1840, republished in Harper's "Family Library" in 1847, and prominent in booksellers' catalogs.[29] The book was a narrative of Dana's life while he worked as a seaman on a merchant ship from 1833 to 1835. Although much of his commentary was meant to protest the hardships and injustices of a sailor's life, the book contained detailed descriptions of parts of California and the Mexican population. Dana described the generosity of a mission friar, a funeral, a cockfight, a horse race, the government, and a wedding, all filtered through his New England sensibilities and his Harvard-trained pen. The general impression of Mexicans in these descriptions was of lazy men, except when they were on horses, and immoral women; to Dana, these were people without Yankee enterprise or self-discipline who led a pleasant but backward existence. California, in this view, appeared ripe for a military, social, cultural, and economic takeover, and, vastly accelerated by the gold rush, that is what happened. These impressions of Mexicans in California, called "Californians" by the goldrushers, were part of the background that they used in assessing information necessary for their trip. Dana's descriptions may also help explain why the goldrushers had little respect for or much to do with the Californians, who were for the most part swept aside, ignored, and repressed during the gold rush.

The impressions of the West formed in part by this early literature provided the background for gold fever and molded opinions about Indians, the environment,

11

the Californians, and the adventure of going to the West. They created the mindset with which hundreds of thousands of people, particularly those from the East and the current Midwest, greeted news of California gold, first with skepticism, then with growing belief, and finally with great enthusiasm. They did not, however, provide the information necessary for the eastern greenhorns to actually make the trip, and most potential goldrushers realized this fact. Thus, their quest for riches began not with steamboats, wagons, and sailing ships but with newspapers and booksellers as they started their task of finding what they hoped would be timely and accurate information about the West, California, and gold.

# CHAPTER ONE

# Newspapers
## *Credibility and Information*

The idea of going to California to mine gold occurred to many in December 1848, and information about the place and how to get there became prime commodities. Led by newspapers, the various print media were the first to make money off the gold rush, and they were quick off the mark. The story of the spread of news of the gold discoveries, which filtered through to eastern newspapers as early as August 1848, has been well told in gold rush histories.[1] What has not been well described is how individual newspapers developed the story and made it credible; whether, and how, newspapers disseminated useful information for prospective goldrushers planning their trip; and whether gold rush news and information differed by type of newspaper or by region of the country. These are the questions addressed in this chapter.

The focus on newspapers as an information source extends the scholarship on information diffusion as well as being part of the larger history of journalism. Richard Brown in *Knowledge Is Power* concludes that by the mid-nineteenth century "it was the task of print, not word of mouth, to impart public information."[2] The increased reliance on print for information attenuated the importance of personal relationships between information providers and receivers that was important to creating credibility in the eighteenth century. Although newspapers were one of the two main printed sources of information (books were the other), newspaper histories do not usually consider information diffusion as a major function of mid-nineteenth-century newspapers.[3] This case study of the gold rush shows that newspapers were a major source of information, but that the relationship between print and personal sources of information was complicated by the changing perception of the credibility of printed information as the goldrushers gained experience with the West.

*Newspapers*

The survey of newspaper coverage of the gold rush is not a scientific sample, but it includes newspapers of different sizes in different locations, and from the religious press. This chapter is organized geographically because not all regions had the same interest in gold rush information. For example, in New York City, the newspaper capital of the country at the time, and in New England and Baltimore, the most obvious way of making the trip was by sea; in the current Midwest, overland travel was indicated. In the South, where it was equally convenient in many places to go by land or sea, the news of California was complicated by slavery and regional political interests. There were also differences in the gold rush coverage among large and small newspapers because small newspapers did not have the resources to find out for themselves what was happening outside their towns. The important religious press of the time also covered the gold rush extensively, led by the desire to condemn those who would leave their homes and families to search for riches and by their motivation to expand their missionary activities to California.

### The East and Mid-Atlantic States
### The *New York Herald*

The gold rush coverage of James Gordon Bennett's *New York Herald* provides a good illustration of how newspapers developed the story of the gold rush and created credibility. Bennett is an example of the progression of an influential editor in the country's largest newspaper market from skeptic to reporter to information provider to promoter of gold fever. Within this progression, one can infer what made the news credible to Bennett and how he attempted transmit this credibility to his readers. The *Herald* will provide a baseline of gold rush coverage in newspapers with which the reporting and provision of information in competing newspapers and those in other markets will be compared.

The *New York Herald*, one of the first successful "penny" newspapers in New York, by 1848 had the largest circulation and was probably the best known newspaper in the country.[4] James Gordon Bennett was the founder, owner, and editor of the *Herald*. Politically, he was an ardent expansionist, a jingoistic supporter of the Mexican War, and, at that time, a proslavery Democrat, although his *Herald* was supposedly nonpartisan.[5] Bennett's journalistic style was sensationalistic. He "fed his readers a steady diet of violence, crime, murder, suicide, seduction, and rape both in news reporting and in gossip. . . . [but] The *Herald* was not merely salacious; Bennett also appealed to the self-interest of his readers. He took a booster attitude toward local developments and reforms."[6]

Bennett organized the most extensive network of reporters and correspondents of any newspaper in the nation and was the first in New York to hear of the California gold strike in 1848 and publish the news. One of Bennett's correspondents was Thomas Larkin, U.S. consul at Monterey, California, who was the first to inform Bennett of the gold discovery. Since 1843, Bennett had been publishing letters from Larkin about California under the name "Paisano," describing Larkin as his California correspondent. In the mid-nineteenth century, correspondents were not paid employees of the newspaper, they were letter writers whom the editor used frequently. Larkin's use of "Paisano" as a pseudonym, meaning countryman or compatriot, seems fairly natural for an American writer in a foreign country. Later, when Larkin was writing about the gold rush, Paisano was identified in the pages of the *Herald* as the U.S. consul at Monterey. Bennett published most or all of Larkin's letters since they shared the view that California was a likely and beneficial place for United States expansion.

Early news reports of California gold were not credible for eastern newspaper editors. Although the *Herald* was the first newspaper in the United States to mention the gold discovery, on August 19, 1848, several newspapers in California and Salt Lake published earlier articles reporting the story. Some of these were sent back to the States, but eastern editors ignored them.[7] Larkin wrote the first enthusiastic account of the gold discovery published in the East in a letter dated July 1, 1848, which was printed by Bennett September 17. In this letter, Larkin began the exaggerated stories that eventually fed the gold fever: "Rivers whose banks and bottoms are filled with pure gold—where a Hingham bucket of dirt, with a half hour's washing in running water, produces a spoonful of black sand containing from seven to ten dollars worth of gold." Although Bennett never minded hyperbole, he was apparently unimpressed. Perhaps he knew only too well the slender core of truth in some of his own sensationalistic journalism to swallow another person's incredible claims whole. This was also the heyday of P. T. Barnum's hoaxes, with which Bennett was very familiar.[8]

On September 21, 1848, Bennett wrote an editorial in which one begins to see elements of what created credibility in his mind. His comment on a *Washington Union* account of gold discoveries reported by Mr. Edward Beale following a fast trip from California indicated that he was still skeptical but wavering:

All Washington is in a ferment with the news of the immense bed of gold, which, it is said has been discovered in California. Now, for our part, we do not know what to think of this gold story. It looks marvelously like a speculation to induce a rapid emigration; but then again, it is certified by the American Alcalde, at Monterey [Walter Colton] and the American Alcalde is a very proper man, having once been a Presbyterian preacher."

Perhaps in this piece Bennett was being sarcastic, but the importance given to the perceived reputation of the source and Colton's connection with officialdom were attributes of credibility that were repeated in many assessments of gold rush news. Bennett was not convinced at this point, however, and, after a short article cribbed from the *Washington Union*, the *Herald* published nothing more about California gold until November 28. The election and the insurrections in Europe dominated the non–New York news printed in the newspaper.

In late November, however, credibility was established by having a more substantial mark of officialdom and physical evidence in the form of a report of the military governor, Col. Richard Mason, along with 230 ounces of gold. Lt. Lucien Loeser carried the report and the gold across the Isthmus of Panama west to east. Mason's report and his pouch of gold were enough to change Bennett's mind:

From the various accounts that have been received from California, from time to time, within the last eight months or one year, we think there is little room to doubt that the newly acquired territory of the United States is rich, to an extraordinary and almost unparalleled degree, in mineral resources. . . . Instead of the accounts first received from there being exaggerations, they were, if the intelligence recently received from that country is to be credited, rather within the truth.[9]

A more general turning point of eastern skepticism came with President Polk's message to the Thirtieth Congress, which Bennett, and almost all other Democratic newspaper editors, printed in full on December 6, 1848.[10] About in the middle of the speech, Polk devoted four long paragraphs to California in which he confirmed the extent of the gold discoveries by referring to the fact that public officials verified the quantity and quality of the gold: "The accounts of the abundance of gold in that territory are of such an extraordinary character as would scarcely command belief were they not corroborated by the authentic reports of officers in the public service who have visited the mineral district." Interestingly, Bennett couldn't dispel all his skepticism because in his editorial the next day, "The President's Message and California," he wrote primarily about the Douglas bill for admitting California as a state and only mentioned the gold in the last sentence: "Meantime, we should like to have some of this gold dust from California assayed and analyzed, to ascertain whether it is mica, or iron pyrites, or gold."

Gold fever, however, was news. In the same issue in which his editorial questioned the quality of the gold, he had two articles on ships making ready for California and a California association being formed in Baltimore to sail as soon as January 1. On December 8, he published in full the long (two entire columns) dispatch from Colonel Mason, the commanding military officer in California, who presented "the fullest descriptions we have seen of the gold 'placers' of that distant region." It included a geography of the territory and an account of the initial gold discovery, a description of gold mining techniques, reports of amounts of gold taken by some miners, and how much merchants like Sam Brannan were making off the miners (thirty-six thousand dollars from the first of May to the tenth of July). From then on, there was at least one article about California gold in almost every issue through March 1849.

Once credibility had been established, the reputation of sources became less important because now unsigned accounts, some of them fantastic and not true, were published side by side with official reports and dispatches. Some of these were taken from issues of San Francisco's newspaper the *Californian* that were filtering to the East and being reprinted in spite of inability to establish the reliability of the articles and letters. Other articles reflected on the effect of the gold on the United States, but the bulk of the articles reported on the growing desire and plans for emigration; "Ho for California" became a common headline in most newspapers in the East.

In addition to knowing about the existence of gold, the most immediate information needed by potential goldrushers concerned how to get to California. By mid-December, Bennett began publishing articles that concentrated on the geography of California and the gold regions and then on the various routes to get there. During December in New York, the only choices seemed to be by sea—either over the Isthmus of Panama or around the Horn. On December 13, the entire first page was devoted to a series of articles entitled "The Discovery of El Dorado—Its Position, and its Advantages to the Commerce of the United States—The Way to get there." One article asserted,

For the information of the many who purpose going to California, we will state that there are but two routes by which it may be reached with any degree of comfort or economy. Persons desirous of saving time should take what is called the land route, or more properly, the Chagres or Isthmus course. . . . The other route we speak of doubles Cape Horn. This is the most acceptable as far as cost and facilities are concerned, but the loss of time balances the difference in price of passage.

These early informational articles, compiled by the *Herald* staff and reprinted by other newspapers, were very detailed, which probably increased their credibility to readers in December 1848. The articles described the rather complicated route across the isthmus, what to take, prices, and distances and times on each stage of the route. One article mentioned that "a new route [would] be opened in a few weeks, through the Isthmus of Tehuantepec in Mexico," and in another there was a table comparing the two routes in terms of price, distance, and time. The articles did not, however, give any hint of the major difficulty of the Panama route—that emigrants could wait a very long time on the Pacific side to get a ship to San Francisco—which became the most serious obstacle to the thousands who left early for California by this route.[11] On December 13, 1848, the front-page coverage ended with a letter from James R. Snowden, treasurer of the U.S. Mint, answering Bennett's question about assaying the gold that had come from California: "Mr. David Carter . . . has deposited with me for coinage 1,804 59/100 ounces of the gold of that region. It is of excellent quality, and the amount will yield about $35,000."

Also during mid-December, advertisements began to appear that provided another type of information to potential goldrushers. These ads were mostly for ships going to California, companies being formed, and items for sale that might be used by emigrants, everything from clothing, food, tents, and India-rubber boats, to one of the most frequently purchased—guns. From mid-December 1848, through March 1849, twenty to thirty ads appeared daily in the *Herald*, usually a full column, featuring California or gold.

One kind of ad, for lectures designed to attract potential emigrants, indicated well the type of information that goldrushers in New York felt they needed at this time and the importance of credentials and titles for information providers. For example, on December 15, 1848, one of the ads was headed,

CALIFORNIA GOLD—PRACTICAL LECTURE at Clinton Hall, this (Friday) evening, explaining the most approved modes of washing Gold, mining. . . . how to distinguish gold from substances of similar appearances—a specimen of

California Gold—by Dr. R. H. COLLYER, Professor of Chemistry, four years assistant to Dr. Turner, University of London.

People trying to form a company to go to California organized this lecture. The all-caps heading was common in ads, but this is the only gold rush ad in the issue that used the word "practical." Most likely the writers of this copy felt that much of the information available to potential goldrushers at the time was not practical—and they were right. The advertisement established credibility for the lecture by proclaiming Collyer's title, "Dr.," and his position, "Professor of Chemistry." The ad did not say where he was professor but felt it necessary to state his prior, somewhat vague, connection with the University of London. Professional titles of various sorts were prominently displayed in printed content concerning the gold rush.

## The *California Herald*

Bennett did not feel that his daily and weekly editions filled the need for information, and he published a special edition he called the *California Herald*. On December 24, 1848, Bennett advertised "To the Emigrants to El Dorado—An Extra California Herald . . . to contain a great deal of valuable information relative to the Gold region and the routes thither, accompanied by a map of the gold and quicksilver region." On December 26, the first of four issues of the extra was published and sold separately from the daily for six cents per copy. The issues were the same size as the daily but with a plainer masthead simply saying "CALIFORNIA HERALD." Bennett invested a great deal of his staff's time, as well as his own, to obtain information for these extras. The content of the *California Herald* provides the best indication of Bennett's transformation from news reporter to information provider and good examples of how the newspaper and its correspondents attempted to create credibility for their information.[12]

The first and most obvious informational innovation in these special editions was that the front page of each issue showed a large map. In the first issue, December 26, 1848, the map was entitled "Gold and Quicksilver District of California" and covered about two-thirds of the front page. Maps became one of the most important types of publications that conveyed information to goldrushers, and this one was the first detailed map of the gold region published in newspapers. Bennett described it as "the latest and most accurate in existence; it was drawn on the spot by an officer of the army, and embraces all the principal points in *El*

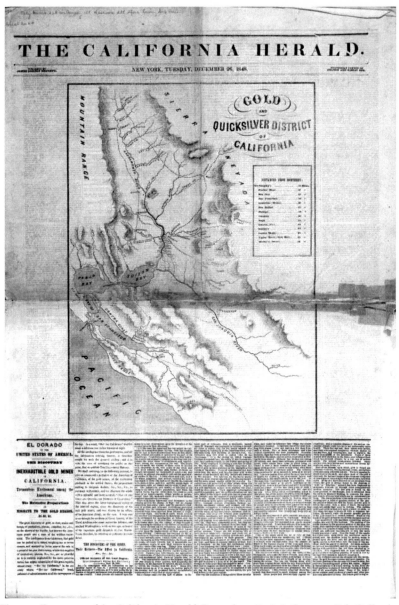

Figure 1. Front page of the *California Herald*, December 26, 1848. Courtesy Yale Collection of Western Americana, Beinecke Rare Book and Manuscript Library.

*Dorado.* Such a map, with the information accompanying it, will be of the greatest value to those who intend to seek a fortune, or something worse, in the rich valleys of the Sacramento." The credibility of the map was proclaimed by the text, which stated, "It was sent to us through the medium of Lieut. Loeser, of the Third Artillery . . . as the bearer of the important gold dispatch of Gov. Mason. It can, therefore, be relied on as authentic in every detail."[13]

The text of the first *California Herald* began with a short introductory article that proclaimed that the central purpose of the special editions was information for potential goldrushers:

> The great discovery of gold, in dust, scales and lumps, of quicksilver, platina, cinnabar, &c. &c., on the shores of the Pacific, has thrown the American people into a state of the wildest excitement. The intelligence from California, that gold can be picked up in lumps, weighing six or seven ounces, and scooped up in tin pans at the rate of a pound of the pure dust a scoop . . . has set the inhabitants of this great republic almost crazy. "Ho! for California," is the cry everywhere. . . . All the intelligence from the gold region, and all the information relating thereto, is therefore sought for with the greatest avidity; and it is with the view of satisfying the public on this point, that we publish THE CALIFORNIA HERALD.

The lead article of this first issue was a good indication of the importance of military information as a credible source and of military titles as markers of this credibility. The article was entitled the "Official Account of the Gold Region" and began with complete transcriptions of two letters (written September 18, 1848, and October 8, 1848) of J. L. Folsom, "Captain and Assistant Quartermaster, to Maj. Gen. Thomas S. Jesup, Quartermaster Gen. U.S. Army." In the first letter, Folsom gave several examples of miners striking it rich, and the location of two producing mines were clearly marked on the map, which showed a trail going right to them—marked "upper mine, and lower mine." To enhance the effect, Folsom wrote, "You will be anxious to know where this is to end. I see no prospect of exhausting the mines." In his second letter, written about three weeks later, he gave examples of prices and wages and the difficulties of living in a place where everyone had gone to the mines. These examples gave the impression that even if one could not find gold, one could earn much more money than in the East, even someone with no particular skills: "The prices of labor here will create surprise in the United States. Kannakas, or Sandwich Islanders, the worst of laborers, are now employed constantly about town in storing and landing merchandise at a dollar an hour each." The implication was clear: even if one were unlucky enough not to find gold, one could work as a common laborer at eight times the average wages in the East. At least for 1848 and 1849, his assertions were probably right (see appendix B).

Not all the information published in the *California Herald* enabled and encouraged potential goldrushers. A cautionary note was published in another letter, signed "Viator," who, the newspaper explained, was Mr. J. G. Bennett, Esq., "a gentleman of this city, who from a lengthened residence at Panama, and frequent journeys across the Isthmus, is fully competent to give a clear and correct idea of the route, and to its difficulties." Viator was probably James Gordon Bennett.

If [a goldrusher] has a passage engaged through to San Francisco, the Isthmus route is decidedly the quickest, and, all things considered, the least weary. But—and here I speak now more particularly to those who have but a limited amount of funds—just sufficient to carry them through to San Francisco without any stoppages—let those travelers beware how they try the Isthmus, if they have only engaged passage as far as Chagres; after their toilsom journey to Panama (if they escape delay and fever at Chagres), they may have to wait weeks for a passage to San Francisco, and when the long wished for opportunity occurs, they will find themselves unable to take it, as their expenses in Panama will have exhausted their means. Thus, situated in a strange unhealthy country, moneyless and friendless, their spirits depressed by their situation, it requires no prophet to predict a heartrending termination to their gold schemes.

The second edition of the *California Herald* came out January 8, 1849, and in addition to the kind of detailed information in the first edition, it added an element of investigative journalism. It also mentioned the overland trails for the first time. A map of the San Francisco Bay Area, including Pablo and Suisun bays, covered about three-quarters of the front page. Page 2 was mostly taken up by reprinted articles and letters from other newspapers but had an introductory article with a warning: "there are speculations on foot, originating from selfish and dishonest motives, offering grand inducements to entrap the uninitiated. . . . [T]here are a large number of vessels of all classes now up at this port for San Francisco, of which one-half, at least, are nearly, if not entirely, unseaworthy." In the reprinted articles, there were twenty-two companies mentioned and described. The list included a company forming to go overland from Fort Smith, Arkansas, and the description gave contacts for those who wished to go that way. One small reprint from the *St. Louis Union* gave a plug for the northern overland route: "The route across the plains offers the stronger inducements [compared with the Chagres-Panama route] to persons of limited means."

In the third edition, January 16, 1849, Bennett became an avid booster of emigration to the gold rush. He wrote on the first page, "Every statement is caught up and swallowed with the greatest avidity. . . . All this indicates the height of the gold excitement. It runs high throughout the Union . . . The correct accounts from California are as rich and as gorgeous as the most ardent gold-hunter need desire." This lead article went on to specify ships (with names, dates, and number of passengers). It gave a table showing thirty-six vessels with a total of 1,682 passengers on board bound for California via Cape Horn (from New York, Boston, Nantucket, Norfolk, Baltimore, Salem, New Bedford, and Philadelphia), and seven vessels bound for Chagres with 530 aboard. These emigrants should have been safe since Bennett stated, "a better class of vessels is now in the market; those that were found to have been wanting in character and capabilities are withdrawn." This was a remarkable improvement in one week; one wonders if his readers found this remark credible.

The fourth and last edition of the extras Bennett produced for goldrushers was published January 31, 1849, and he appeared to be running out of gold rush stories. Three-quarters of the first page was a reprint of the map of the gold rush region printed in the first edition, and most of the fourth page was a reprint of the San Francisco Bay area map in the second issue. On the first page, under the map, was an article with the headline "The Very Latest News from the Gold Region of California," which mainly consisted of a letter from Thomas Larkin, signed "Paisano," dated November 16, 1848. Larkin described the amount of gold many people had found, "Your Paisano can point out many a man who has, for 15 to 20 days in succession, bagged up 5 to 10 ounces of gold a day," and the high wages, "The pay of a member of Congress will be accepted here by those alone who do not know enough to better themselves."

### The *New York Tribune*

The New York newspaper market in 1848–1849 was dominated by a rivalry between James Gordon Bennett and Horace Greeley, part owner and editor of the *New York Tribune*. Although both were penny newspapers, the *Herald* and the *Tribune* differed in their approaches and their politics, and this difference showed in their coverage and provision of information to potential goldrushers. Both newspapers had to establish the credibility of their gold rush coverage, and their different ways of doing this provide a contrast in nineteenth-century journalistic styles.

Bennett and Greeley both began poor in 1830s New York, and both were pioneers in developing the penny press. They quickly grew apart, however, politically and in the way they used their newspapers. Greeley was a crusader, a reformer, and a power in the Whig Party, although, like Bennett, he disavowed a partisan stance for his newspaper.[14] He staunchly fought against the Polk administration's Mexican War, was against the annexation of Oregon and Texas, and was a fervent abolitionist. He is well known for the phrase, "Go West Young Man," which had nothing to do with California or what is now called the West.[15] He was originally against the annexation of California since he was afraid that it might bring in another slave state, and rather than that, he preferred that California should be an independent country; he changed his mind about California statehood after its 1849 constitution disavowed slavery.

Greeley was excited about California gold, and he provided early news and information about the gold discoveries and fever in a way similar to Bennett's. The *Tribune*, however, never reached the level of coverage and informational content of the *Herald*'s. Greeley did not try to compete with Bennett's *California Herald*. He sought to establish credibility for his gold rush information by providing an eyewitness who was known to his readers. Greeley sent one of his paid reporters on a trip to California, not to mine gold, but to mine the income potential of gold rush reporting from the scene. This reporter was Bayard Taylor, who was known more for his literary skills than as a reporter.[16] He left for California in June 1849 by the Panama route and arrived in late August. He traveled through the mines until December 1849 and attended the California constitutional convention in Monterey, where he wrote back that the "clause that prohibited slavery was met by no word of dissent." He frequently sent letters that were published in the *Tribune*. He headed back to New York after only four months, without an ounce of gold but with a fortune in notes from which he published in September 1850 one of the first and best-known travel books of the gold rush, *Eldorado: Adventures in the Path of Empire*.[17]

Paying for Taylor to go to California was a brilliant journalistic idea that succeeded on several levels. First, and most obviously, it provided Greeley with ongoing communications that enlivened his gold rush coverage for almost a year. Second, by choosing a man with literary talents rather than, for instance, a mountain man or government explorer, Greeley ensured the newspaper of lively copy and a book that would sell in the eastern literary markets. In fact, Taylor's book became extremely popular, and although published by Putnam rather than the newspaper, Greeley lost no money in paying for Taylor's trip. Third, and most important from the point of view of this study, Greeley was apparently not content to rely on official sources for credible information; he wanted one of his reporters as an eyewitness, someone who would be a keen observer regardless of title or official position. Bennett had to depend on receiving letters from correspondents like Larkin who had interests other than informing eastern newspapers and who were not known to their readers. Greeley's idea foreshadowed changes in credibility sources for goldrushers.

### The *Boston Evening Transcript*

Newspapers in New England were not as enthusiastic about the gold rush as those in New York and were not as quick off the mark. Unlike the New York newspapers, there were no examples from New England of special California editions or special reporters going on the trip west primarily to send back information to the newspaper. Most of their information came from the exchanges. The exchanges were arrangements among newspapers and the Post Office to exchange newspapers through the mail for free.[18] Even more intensively than in the other big city newspapers, advertisers used the newspapers in this region to milk the gold rush market.

The *Boston Evening Transcript* was representative of big-city newspapers from New England. It was established in 1830 as a Whig paper, one of the first of the penny press newspapers. In 1848–1849 Eppes Sargent, a well-known poet and author of the time, edited the newspaper.[19] As a Whig and an editor with mainly literary interests, Sargent did not take an early interest in the gold rush; unlike the New York newspapers, he did not reprint the stories from the *New Orleans Picayune* or *St. Joseph Gazette* that appeared earlier than Polk's speech of December 5, 1848. After Polk's address, however, articles began appearing daily, usually short news pieces about gold fever or the gold rush companies that were beginning to form in New England and New York. In January 1849 the newspaper's coverage of the gold rush became more frequent and began to be more information oriented. Sargent, however, was not a California booster and published many articles warning enthusiasts about dangers.

Sargent's presentation of California information in the *Boston Evening Transcript* provided more instances of the importance of official information and titles in creating credibility. An article announced, "Government have received accounts which go beyond any that have been published [containing the] latest advices from San Francisco."[20] These advices apparently were a collection of horror stories that Sargent summarized as "there was much distress among all the gold diggers for the want of the common necessaries of life," and added that everything was scarce except gold. He gave no indication of the sources for these stories except the vague, but apparently necessary, reference to "Government." In January 1849 information began to appear about the difficulties of the Panama route. Sargent did not make up a letter concerning the delays in Panama, as did Bennett, nor did he reprint the Viator letter from the *California Herald*. He did, however, describe an article in the *St. Louis New Era*, about a "Dr. Jett of Missouri who [had] arrived in St. Louis . . . direct from California by the way of Panama . . . [where] it [was] impossible to procure any kind of accommodation for less than $4 a day."[21] After mentioning Dr. Jett, the article in the *Transcript* went on to detail the trip from Chagres to Panama City, including the distances, the cost of each part of the trip, and how to get from San Francisco to the diggings. The article emphasized that Jett was a doctor (spelling it out in one instance and referring to him as "the Doctor" in another).

Possibly because of Sargent's literary interests, the *Evening Transcript* printed many more ads for books, guidebooks, and maps, as well as articles announcing new books and maps, than did the *New York Herald*. For example, he referred to the publication of Edwin Bryant's third edition of *What I Saw in California* on the editorial page and reprinted details of the overland route recommended by Bryant.[22] In the same issue, F. S. Saxton, T. Wiley, and Redding and Company, all Boston booksellers, advertised books and maps on California, ads that continued for several days. On January 8, James Weeks and Company joined the competition, and Saxon advertised G. G. Foster's *Emigrants' Guide to the Gold Mines*, one of the first guidebooks available in the East. On January 20, Ticknor and Company began advertisements for Bryant's third edition, and Redding and Company began advertising a new "California Map Worth Having, from actual survey of the Gold, Silver and Quicksilver Regions of Upper California." As in the case of the editors, some of the advertisers felt they had credibility problems and addressed this by stressing that their information came from official sources or was endorsed by public officials. For example, on January, 5, 1849, F. S. Saxton advertised Foster's guidebook with the heading "GOLD, GOLD, GOLD . . . prepared from official documents and other authentic sources." T. Wiley Jr. advertised "a map of the valley of the Sacramento, including the gold region: Map is a copy of Ridwell (Land Surveyor) Map, by Thos O. Larkin, Esq., late Consul of the United States for California." Redding and Company advertised, "NEW WORK ON CALIFORNIA. No Catchpenny but a reliable book—and now ready. CALIFORNIA AND ITS GOLD REGIONS . . . prepared from official and other documents."

### The *Hartford Christian Secretary*

Religious newspapers formed a specialized although important information marketplace in the mid-nineteenth century and, surprisingly, kept their readers informed about the gold rush through articles, letters, and advertisements.[23] The Baptist *Christian Secretary* of Hartford, Connecticut, carried extensive coverage of the gold rush throughout 1849 perhaps because the American Baptist Home Mission Society established a mission to California in 1848. In the December 29, 1848, issue the editor wrote, "the Missionary Society has already sent out its agents to bear to the poor and destitute in that region, the GOLD of heaven. Hundreds of poor beggared souls are lying for want of this." The adventures, trials, and tribulations of their missionary, the Rev. O. C. Wheeler, formed a continuing story for the newspaper through the early gold rush years.

The editor never doubted the reality and the importance of California gold, writing in a three-column spread on December 15, 1848, "California is the richest gold region in the world." On December 29, 1848, he published a short piece from the *New York Journal of Commerce*, whose editors had just examined "specimens of the 40 lbs. Gold dust, or scales, deposited in the Mechanics' Bank of this city, by Lord, Warren, Salter & Co. . . . [and] found [it] to be 21½ carats fine." The newspaper continued printing articles about the gold rush in every issue from December 1848 through March 1849.

The *Christian Secretary* would deplore the moral values of the gold rush at the same time as writing articles that would inflame gold fever. For example, beginning January 12, 1849, the editor reprinted a sermon that was the first "of a short series of discourses on the evils and dangers of being carried away by the excitement for gold," and each week for the next month the editor reprinted parts of sermons with that message. On February 2, 1849, however, under the headline

"EXCITING NEWS FROM CALIFORNIA" the editor reprinted a letter from a Lieutenant Larkin of the New York Volunteers "containing further confirmation of the previous dispatches, public and private, and far outstripping all other news in its exciting character," that gold was "increasing in size and quality daily." Also, on February 26, 1849, a letter from a Commander Jones described how the gold fever in California would make deserters even of "some of the best petty officers and seamen, having but few months to serve, and large balances due them." The article deplored the desertions but gave readers the idea that the rewards of the gold rush must be very great indeed if "the best petty officers and seamen" would leave dishonorably with large balances due them.

### The *Philadelphia Christian Observer*

The *Christian Observer*, a Philadelphia Presbyterian weekly newspaper, which focused on church and religious news and opinion, published a short piece as early as December 2, 1848, on emigration to California, although without mentioning gold. On December 9, the issue that covered the president's speech also contained a remarkable little article, not reprinted from other papers, that reflected the secular excitement about California gold well before the gold fever caught on in the majority of the population:

> It is not gold in the clouds or in the sea, or in the center of a rock ribbed mountain, but in the soil of California, sparking in the sun and glittering in its stream. It lies on the open plain, in the shadows of the deep ravines, and glows on the summits of the mountains, which have lifted for ages their golden coronets to heaven.

Other articles on December 16, 23, and 30 discussed the significance of California gold for the congressional debates on the possible extension of slavery in the territories (which it opposed). The editors accepted the reality and importance of the gold discoveries, and there was no moral crusade by the newspaper against the gold rush.

### The *Baltimore Sun*

The gold rush coverage of the *Baltimore Sun* was more extensive than the *Boston Evening Transcript*'s and can probably best be compared to James Gordon Bennett's *New York Herald*. The *Sun*'s editor and owner, Annuah S. Abell, founded the newspaper in 1837 as Baltimore's first penny newspaper.[24] Like Bennett,

Abell was a Democrat, expansionist, and an ardent supporter of the Mexican War; he did not, however, have Bennett's major interest in the West. The *Sun* concentrated on local and Washington DC, news, and on being the fastest out with the national political news. Baltimore's proximity to Washington and the fact that it was a city with both northern and southern connections affected the newspaper's coverage of most topics, including the gold rush.

The *Sun*'s early articles on the gold rush were primarily copied from the newspaper exchanges, with the New York and Washington newspapers used most intensively. Abell's use of the exchanges allowed him to provide his readers much more information about the gold rush than he would have been able to obtain from only his own correspondents. The *Sun* first reported on California gold on September 20, 1848, by excerpting from the same the *Washington Union* article (announcing the arrival of Beale from his rapid trip across Mexico) that Bennett used September 21. Abell displayed the same pattern as Bennett of skepticism that turned to enthusiasm with President Polk's December 5 speech. The day after the president's speech, Abell wrote, "Here in Baltimore, as elsewhere, hundreds of young men are actually preparing, or waiting an opportunity to embark for the land of wealth. . . . The gold fever runs like the cholera in this city." The *Sun* published articles on California almost every day during December 1848. By the end of the year, before most goldrushers got serious about planning a trip to California, the *Baltimore Sun* printed over forty large articles on the gold rush, many copied from the exchanges but increasingly from its own reporting. This was an even more extensive coverage than in Bennett's *Herald*, for the month of December 1848.

Another type of reporting that Abell obtained mostly through the exchanges was news of gold rush companies being formed in other cities throughout the North. In one article on January 15, 1849, there was news of companies being formed in New York City, Boston, Pittsburgh, Utica, Otsego, Buffalo, and even Platteville, Wisconsin, which gave the correct impression that a major emigration was under way, primarily from the North. Such information would have been useful to readers who were contemplating signing up with the many ships that advertised for passengers in each of the main eastern ports. It is significant that in these articles no mention is made of anyone going from the South in spite of the *Sun*'s southern connections.

The *Sun*'s gold rush coverage can best be compared to that of other large city newspapers in the East through articles not copied from the exchanges.

*Newspapers*

The first such article concerning the gold rush was from a "Correspondence of the Baltimore *Sun*," (the writer's name was not given) on November 28, 1848. This letter gave mildly enthusiastic support to the reality of the gold discoveries because of Colonel Mason's official account to the secretary of war. The author, however, reported that the gold rush story resembled "in more than one respect, the Arabian Nights' entertainment." In the same issue, another unnamed correspondent also expressed belief in the gold discoveries but wrote primarily of the political implications because "adventurers [would] be attracted in great numbers, by the unparalleled richness of the mineral districts."

Another type of non-exchange article was local coverage of gold rush companies. The first "Ho for California" article appeared on December 4, 1848, with the announcement of the formation of the Baltimore California Association, and went on to say, the "expedition is not to be for the hunting of gold . . . in the yellow sands of the rivers of California. They are going out for gold, which they expect to obtain from the furrows of the plow, from the ringing music of the anvil, the rapid glide of the shuttle, and the sharp clicking of the axe." By late December the gold rush from Baltimore was big news, and reports of Baltimore ships bound for California were featured in the *Sun*, not only with announcements about companies being formed, but with information from the emigrants after they started on their trip. For this reporting the *Baltimore Sun* had exclusives from letters sent by passengers from American ports of call during the trip to Chagres or around the Horn. Like Greeley, Abell attempted to establish credibility through accounts of local people traveling west.

Most advertisements about the gold rush were also local and represented distinctive outlooks on gold rush information in newspapers. For example, on December 14, the *Sun* ran an advertisement:

> to Capitalists. . . . A Gentleman, forty years of age of healthy and robust constitution, business habits, temperate and unexceptionable character, not a resident of Baltimore, desires to profit by the recent discoveries in California provided he can raise the funds necessary to place his family and his present business in a condition to leave them.

This advertiser proposed that a "capitalist" advance him $1,500 to $1,800, and he would, after finding gold, return the principle and one-half of all profits. He would also take out a life insurance policy in favor of the lender. This kind of ad was not unique to Baltimore, but it indicated that some potential goldrushers thought of Baltimore as a center of gold rush activity. Other ads in this issue, which were very common in most newspapers, were for ships sailing to Panama and for "A complete outfit of India Rubber for the Gold regions of California."

Throughout the gold rush, contradictory information was common, and Abell made no attempt to avoid or hide this problem. Most of his information came from travelers, correspondents, and the exchanges, and contradictory information was unavoidable. The situation in Panama was an example. In the December 22, 1848, issue of the *Baltimore Sun*, in an article from the *New York Sun*, the route through Chagres and Panama was disparaged with a story about a goldrusher who did not make it: "A Quaker Gentleman who, with five hundred dollars in his pocket, started for the Gold region a short time since, returned yesterday with barely twenty-five cents. He went to Panama, but there was no means of going farther, and he had to return." The same article, however, quoted from the *New York Journal of Commerce*: "I unhesitatingly say that in my opinion the route via Chagres is the one combining the most advantageous, especially if the emigrant has but little money, and wishes to reach the gold region early. . . . The story that 7000 to 8000 persons are at Panama, waiting a passage, is without foundation."

Since Abell obtained so much of his information through secondary sources, the problems of credibility were even more severe than for the New York newspapers that invested heavily to obtain firsthand gold rush information. Sources of credibility and markers of these sources were important in Abell's articles. An indication of these sources and markers from January 27, 1849, is contained in an article that Abell constructed from accounts in other eastern newspapers, beginning with the *New York Tribune*, about people who were in California in 1848 and had returned with substantial amounts of gold:

Mr. Lippet, formerly a teacher in the school of the Brothers Peugnet, in this city and who went out as a captain in the California regiment, has written a letter which, at his request, was read to the scholars of Messrs Peugnet's school, among whom he was always a favorite. He states that he is in excellent health and will return in here in six months, with half a million dollars, in gold. . . . We saw yesterday a half-eagle, coined at the Philadelphia mint, from a late deposit of California gold dust. It had the true ring and luster, and bore, as a distinctive mark, the letters 'Cal' over the head of the eagle. . . . The steamer Falcon has brought several bars of gold from California, consigned to Messrs Bishop & Co., amounting in value to from 6,000 to $7,000. They are brought home by Capt. Baker, who went out in the bark Undine, and were assayed at Valparaiso. The precious metal is twenty-one and a half carats fine. Our informant has seen and handled these bars, and knows that [*sic*] whereof he speaks. So the question is settled—the returns have begun to come round.

In this article officialdom and firsthand accounts were important in establishing credibility, although private-sector officials have joined government officials as credible sources. Mr. Lippet, the fortunate miner who supposedly had the remarkable sum of one-half million dollars of gold, was identified as a former teacher, probably in a religious school, and a captain in the California regiment. These titles were markers of credibility. In addition to the number of examples, the presentation of the details was important. The former captain asked that his letter be read to the students at the Brothers Peugnet's school where he was a favorite, the implication being that he would not have done this if the story were not true. Finally, the eyewitness accounts— the editors saw a half-eagle with "Cal" embossed on it, and their informant saw and handled bars of gold from the bark *Undine*.

The importance of personal attributes and skills indicated by titles or professions was apparent in advertisements in the *Sun* for gold-mining companies soliciting for members. On January 28, 1849, an advertisement in the paper appeared for a Baltimore gold mining venture, "The California Company of Baltimore." They were soliciting "one hundred men, of known integrity, and temperate and industrious habits: Scholars, Merchants, Mechanics and Laborers," each of whom must contribute $250. In order to have some credibility, the advertisement described the organizers as "gentlemen distinguished for scientific knowledge, and skilful as practical merchants and mechanics, [who] have already joined this association, which already numbers thirty-two." The ad was signed by "The Committee" and dated January 22, 1849. From the point of view of implying credible sources, this advertisement had many similarities to the ad for the gold rush lecture of Dr. Professor Collyer that ran in the *New York Herald* December 15, 1848.

### The *Cumberland (Maryland) Alleganian*

Most of the newspapers throughout the country were weeklies from small towns, and they differed in several ways in their gold rush coverage from big-city newspapers. First, their editors received most of their information from the exchanges and had little ability to check the accuracy of what they reported. Second, they were more closely a part of their communities than the larger newspapers. Third, they had less competition than in the big cities since there were seldom more than two newspapers in a small town. Finally, they were much less financially secure than the larger newspapers, and they went in and out of business frequently.

The *Alleganian* was caught by one of the more outlandish frauds of the gold rush when on January 13, 1849, the newspaper ran a column-long advertisement for Signor D'Alvear's goldometer. The advertisement, which read like an article, stated that "the first discovery of Gold in California was made by Don Jose D'Alvear, eminent Spanish Geologist, Chemist and Natural Philosopher." The ad went on to say that D'Alvear arrived in New York with a million dollars of gold and a new machine that he had invented in California, called the "Goldometer." Although the machine should be worth thousands, the generous Don Jose advertised that he could produce it for "less than $20," and would sell it for only three dollars. The advertisement invoked fancy titles to provide credibility. The machine and Don Jose were frauds and were uncovered in New York by the postmaster in early March 1849, who had received numerous complaints that no goldometer was sent after customers had paid their three dollars. Don Jose was actually John T. Houghton, a New York resident, who fled the city after finding out the postmaster was after him. Apparently, neither Mr. Houghton was apprehended nor the money he took in recovered. The *Alleganian* ran the full-column ad for D'Alvear's gold machine only once and on April 14 ran a retraction explaining the hoax.

Small-town editors were more at the mercy of misinformation and fraud than their big city counterparts not only because of their inability to obtain independent checks on information but because some frauds, like D'Alvear's, brought substantial advertising revenue. The *New York Herald*, the *Baltimore Sun*, and the *Boston Evening Transcript* never ran the ads; the largest newspaper in the West, the *Cincinnati Daily Commercial*, ran a short article January 3, 1849, on "Arrival of Don Jose D'Alvear, the First Discoverer of the Gold Mines," but he was not mentioned again, and they never ran the advertisement.

### The South
In most gold rush coverage by southern newspapers, any enthusiasm was tempered by the major questions of whether slavery would be allowed in California

and whether gold mining was suitable for slave labor. When southern editors encouraged southern goldrushers to go to California, their motivation frequently concerned slavery rather than the opportunities for the individuals. For example, one Georgian "suggested that if three to five hundred Georgians emigrated to California, each accompanied by one to five slaves, they would force the admission of California as a slave state."[25] Many prospective slave-owning goldrushers, however, were not convinced in early 1849 that slavery was right for California as indicated in this October, 26, 1849, editorial from the *Jackson Mississippian*. The editor tried to reverse earlier opinions that slaves would not be useful in California:

> The developments which have taken place in California since the discoveries of the gold placers, have materially contributed to change the opinions of our people in regard to the resources of that country for the profitable employment of slave labor. Whatever may have been our opinions at a time when but little information of the topography of California was at our command, and when we were left to judge of its capacities more from the belief that it was a comparatively barren and unproductive country, and unfit for the general culture of our Southern staples, we are now in possession of well authenticated facts that prove conclusively the profitable fruits of slave labor.

More than two thousand African Americans migrated to California by 1852, primarily as free blacks joining white Americans, Mexicans, and other foreign nationals in the gold fields.[26] Runaway slaves who entered California before statehood were considered fugitives and liable to arrest. Even after statehood in 1850, with the state constitution prohibiting slavery, some slavery continued primarily with slaves brought into the state before statehood. These slaves were frequently given the opportunity to purchase their freedom with part of the proceeds of their mining, the rest going to the slave owner.

### The *Charleston Mercury*

To the *Charleston Mercury*, the California story concerned slavery as much as gold. The *Mercury* was one of the best-known newspapers of the South, and in the North, it was the most infamous. The newspaper was predominantly political and sectional and became "the chief organ of the secession press of South Carolina."[27] The newspaper played a role in the nullification crisis of 1831 and staunchly supported Calhoun in his debates with Webster and abolitionists. The masthead stated that it was published and edited in 1848–1849 by John E. Carew, "City Printer" for Charleston, but its editorial compass was actually set by Robert Barnwell Rhett (Sr.) and John C. Calhoun.[28] The *Mercury* had influence well beyond its circulation, and its gold rush coverage demonstrated how regional sectional issues could affect strongly both the news and the dissemination of information concerning the gold rush.

Since the *Mercury*'s overriding interest was sectional politics, it covered the gold rush quite differently than the major northern newspapers. Carew ignored most of the early notifications of the gold discovery and first mentioned it December 2, 1848, saying only, "The California gold mania continues." His next mention of California gold was in his scanty (less than one column) coverage of the president's address to Congress, which scornfully ended by chiding the *Washington Union* for devoting twelve columns to the full address. In this article, one sentence mentioned, "He [Polk] speaks in glowing terms of the acquisition of California and of her mineral riches as developed in the recent discoveries." On December 9, however, the paper published the whole of the speech. Throughout the rest of December, there were several small disapproving articles reporting on the northern mania, with leads such as "The gold fever is raging to an alarming extent in Hartford, New Haven, Springfield, Salem, Boston, etc." Early in January 1849, Carew proclaimed the "Decline of the Gold Fever" and wrote "The New York *Commercial* is satisfied that not half the vessels advertised there for California will sail for that place."[29]

In spite of Carew's (and Calhoun's and Rhett's) evident dislike of the gold rush, the *Mercury* reported southerners going to California. On January 3, 1849, the newspaper published its first "For California" article: "[O]ur enterprising fellow-citizen, R. H. Tucker, Jr . . . ha[s] purchased the ship Othello . . . and [is] fitting her out for the Gold Region. . . . This is the first vessel for California from the South." Also, some ads appeared concerning gold rush ships from New England and New York that were scheduled to land in Charleston and that would accept passengers. Cyprian Cross, of East Florida, placed an ad in the newspaper offering for sale his plantation of three thousand acres to finance his trip to California "to change the 'Plough for the Spade and Rocker.'" In the January 27 issue, Carew reversed his previous editorial on the decline of gold fever and announced, "The Gold Fever Delirious. . . . We have indubitable evidence all around us of a spasmodic increase of the California gold fever the present week."

*Newspapers*

The large majority of articles in the *Mercury* about the gold rush castigated "northern" gold fever and events in California. In the same issue in which Carew reported that Tucker was outfitting a ship to go to California, a headline proclaimed "Rapine and Murder in California." On January 8, Carew printed a small article from the *New York Express* about someone buying up copper to take to California in order to pass it off as gold and another article about a gruesome murder of a claim jumper in California. The January 25 issue had an article from the *New York Sun* about a "young girl" who tried to finance her trip to California by raffling herself to a forming California company and agreeing to marry the person who won the raffle. She apparently refused to follow through but agreed to go along with the company to cook and wash for them. One should note that newspapers throughout the country were fond of these types of unusual human-interest stories, and they were frequently copied through the exchanges. In the case of the *Mercury* writing about the gold rush, however, one gets the feeling that Carew deliberately used these stories to debunk the gold rush since they were not countered by other positive stories as they were in northern newspapers.

The *Mercury* characterized the gold rush as something exotic, foreign, and disagreeable. The newspaper made almost no attempt to provide information that would help prospective goldrushers as did the northern newspapers. The major point concerning California for the *Mercury* was not mineral wealth but that the Missouri Compromise line be extended to the Pacific and that territories be organized only if slavery were allowed south of the line.[30]

### The *Montgomery (Alabama) Tri-Weekly Flag and Advertiser*

The *Charleston Mercury* was an extreme in southern newspaper coverage of the gold rush, and newspapers elsewhere in the south presented a more balanced coverage. Other southern newspapers, however, still emphasized the southern view of slavery in new territories. An example of newspaper coverage in the interior of the south was the *Montgomery (Alabama) Tri-Weekly Flag and Advertiser.* This newspaper, edited by M'Cormick and Brittan, was not dedicated to politics, although its sectional interests were clear, and it did not have a particular interest in either debunking or pushing the gold rush. Early in December 1848, the editors seemed convinced that the gold story was true, and on December 12, 1848, they published a three-column article accepting the reality of the gold discoveries. Unlike the northern newspapers, however, M'Cormick and Brittan, rather than developing the theme of gold and providing information about getting to

36

California, used the lead of gold to give arguments for extending the Missouri Compromise line to the Pacific Ocean. There were no further articles on California until a front-page announcement on January 11, 1849, that Bryant's book *What I Saw in California* was available in Montgomery: "To those who contemplate a trip California ward, [*sic*] this little work must prove interesting and useful." In January and February, about one dozen short articles on California appeared.

The *Flag and Advertiser* published none of the informational material found in the New York, Baltimore, or Boston newspapers. Most articles were about the reported hardships of gold mining and stories of gold successes—including reprinting the article about Mr. Lippet, the teacher from the Brothers Peugnet school.[31] There were no advertisements for companies going from Alabama and only two ads for ships sailing from Mobile that readers might possibly catch. The coverage on the whole was fair but not designed to assist readers who may have been interested in going to California.

### The *New Orleans Picayune*

A few newspapers in the South carried the gold rush stories more enthusiastically and helpfully than the *Mercury* or the *Flag and Advertiser*. These were primarily in Tennessee and, because they were jumping off places for goldrushers, in New Orleans and Fort Smith, Arkansas. The *New Orleans Picayune* took the lead and became one of the most copied newspapers for gold rush stories.[32] The *Picayune* was a New Orleans version of the penny press when it was founded in 1837, although it cost one Spanish "picayon" (hence its name), worth about six and a quarter cents. Its flamboyant and acerbic style, its declaration of non-partisanship, its large reporting and press staff, and its emphasis on local news and personalities fully qualified the newspaper to be in Bennett's class of penny press journalism.

The *Picayune* became well known to eastern readers during the Mexican War when the newspaper became the focal point for war coverage. Wilkins Kendall, one of the founders of and a writer for the newspaper, led a group of six *Picayune* writers to the front lines to get stories and cover the Mexican press.[33] His reports, which were carried by a special pony express from the war zone to the coast, were published by the *Picayune* and then carried to the East in a private express that beat the Post Office by several days.[34] The reports were avidly copied by newspapers around the country.

The *Picayune* continued this innovative and aggressive reporting during the gold rush. Since many returnees went through Panama to New Orleans, the newspaper was well positioned to be the first to publish official and private accounts of the gold rush. It was the first to publish an account of Lieutenant Beale's dispatch on September 12, 1848, even before Beale arrived in New Orleans. This account was taken from a correspondent in Mexico who wrote about Beale's trip and the news he carried. The newspaper also established correspondents in California, although it did not send out its own reporters, as Bayard Taylor was for the *New York Tribune*.

**The West of the Mid-Nineteenth Century**

The West of the 1840s—now the Midwest—was a distinctive region with respect to the gold rush. The newspapers of the West provided information primarily about the overland trail, and the credibility criteria that were used in the introductions and advertisements for this information emphasized the personal experience of men who had been west of the Mississippi. The region had only one large city, Cincinnati, and only a few large towns, for example, St. Louis and Louisville. Compared to the East, a much larger proportion of the population lived in rural areas, and most newspapers were small and integrated into their communities.

One western newspaper, the *Marshall (Michigan) Statesman*, provided an excellent example of how newspaper coverage and information provision could not only convey information in ways the editor thought would be credible but connect the gold rush to a local community. James Pratt, the editor of the *Statesman* in 1848, organized a gold rush company from the area around Marshall that he called the Wolverine Rangers. His idea was to fully participate in the gold rush and to use his newspaper to describe the overland trip and convey information about the progress of the company. This took Greeley's idea of sending Bayard Taylor to report on the gold rush one step further. The company succeeded in getting to California and beginning mining, although none of its members struck it rich. The entire progress of the company was chronicled in letters published by the *Statesman*. These letters not only provided information and a connection of the company to the community but established new credibility criteria for the prospective goldrushers of 1850.

**The *Cincinnati Daily Commercial***

Cincinnati at the time was the largest city in the region and an important way station for goldrushers using the Ohio River to get to the trailhead towns. The *Cincinnati Daily Commercial* advertised on its masthead "Commerce, News, Literature, and the Belles Lettres," and was a large circulation "two-penny" newspaper with a paid subscription of five thousand.[35] The publisher was J. W. S. Browne and Company, and L. G. Curtiss was the editor. This newspaper was an interesting example of the region's gold rush coverage of news and information since the editor was convinced early on that the stories of gold were true, but he also realized as early as January 1849 that gold fever would produce such a crowd of gold seekers that it was unlikely that any one of them would make money after expenses. Curtiss printed this opinion on February 10, 1849: "In the adventure for wealth in California, a few will, doubtless, be fortunate, whilst many will return broken in health and poorer in purse than they were when they left their families and homes." Without moralizing or doubting the reality of the gold, he got it right.

To a much greater extent than the eastern newspapers, the *Daily Commercial* gave credibility to private accounts of the gold rush. Curtiss began publishing news and information about California gold early in December 1848, and in many respects his early coverage was similar to the eastern newspapers, beginning with the early information carried by Beale. He also printed, however, two reports that Bennett, Greeley, and Abel did not: one from St. Joseph, Missouri, on December 9 about a private party from California carrying considerable gold and another December 16 about the Mormon gold finds. Curtiss believed the stories at a time when his big-city eastern counterparts still required the stamp of officialdom to attain credibility. Advertisements for California overland emigrants began to appear as early as December 21 along with notices of the formation of Cincinnati companies. The full prospectuses of two companies were published January 10.

The *Daily Commercial* published two kinds of informational articles that were different from those in the newspapers previously described. One was a reprint of part of Bryant's book *What I Saw in California,* which advertised this book as a source of specific information for those who wished to go overland to California on the northern trails; the second was a letter from Mr. William Gilpin who gave a guidebook-like account of how to outfit and provision and the costs for the overland route through South Pass. He also provided an endorsement for using Independence, Missouri, as a trailhead.[36]

### The *Hamilton (Ohio) Intelligencer*

The *Hamilton (Ohio) Intelligencer* was weekly newspaper in a small town on the National Road from the mid-Atlantic coast to the West, and it took the gold rush very seriously. The newspaper's coverage started December 2, 1848, and there were articles on California gold in every issue through February 1849. Like most small-town newspapers, most of the coverage was copied from the New York, Baltimore, and Washington newspapers. The *Intelligencer*, however, also reprinted an article from *Hunt's Merchant's Magazine*, giving details of California history and geography. This was unusual for a small newspaper because, although the editor received copies of other newspapers postage free in exchange for copies of his own newspaper, he had to pay cash for magazines, both for the subscription and the postage.

The editors of small-town newspapers were freer than the editors of the larger city newspapers in the East to present their personal views of the gold rush. The *Intelligencer* was an example in which the editor disapproved of the gold rush and made this clear in his newspaper. The first major article on California gold in the newspaper was not printed until December 28, 1848, and it was skeptical and disapproving:

> Richer than Pluto's mines is the representation of the gold regions in California. . . . [T]he dreamy fiction of Aladdin's wonderful lamp is realized. . . . Yet we own we are rather incredulous. . . . Suppose, however, it all proves true, will it be a blessing or a curse? . . . Such an abundance of gold will lead to indolence, luxury and enervation.

The *Intelligencer* was a Whig newspaper that was taken over by a Mr. J. P. Charles, of Eaton, Ohio, in late 1848 at the behest and with the financial support of prominent local Whigs. Perhaps Charles disapproved of the gold rush because he felt it was inconsistent with his Whig politics or because of his religious or social views. The major purpose of the paper was Whig politics, but its prospectus stated, "It [the newspaper] will be emphatically a Family Newspaper, containing a variety of useful and entertaining matter—News, Foreign and Domestic, Tales, Miscellany, Poetry, Wit." Neither Whig politics nor strong religious opinions deterred other editors from emphasizing the gold rush in their newspapers as we have seen from Horace Greeley's *Tribune*, and the religious press in Philadelphia and Hartford.

The *Intelligencer* was also taken in by the D'Alvear fraud. Unlike the *Cumberland (Maryland) Alleganian*, however, which printed only the D'Alvear advertisement, Charles published the D'Alvear story as a news article without comment or skepticism. On January 11, 1849, he announced the "arrival [from California] of Don Jose D'Alvear, the first discoverer of the gold mines . . . the celebrated Spanish Geologist, whose famous treatise on the 'Age of the Earth' must be known to many of our readers."[37] The advertisement for the goldometer was also published. By the end of January, the editor didn't believe D'Alvear's story: "We can't imagine how the Signor can afford to sell so valuable an instrument for $3, unless upon the same principle as the Irishman who being asked how he could afford to sell a certain article for less than cost, said 'he couldn't if he didn't sell *so much of it*!'"[38]

## Conclusion

The introduction to this chapter lists three questions concerning newspapers' coverage of the first few months of the gold rush that have not been addressed in gold rush or newspaper historiography. The first is how individual newspapers developed the story and, most important, made it credible; the second is whether and how newspapers disseminated useful information for prospective goldrushers planning their trip; and the third is whether gold rush news and information differed by type of newspaper or by region of the country. This survey of newspaper reporting of the early gold rush provides answers to these questions.

Concerning the first question, the coverage of the *New York Herald*, the *Baltimore Sun*, and the *Boston Evening Transcript* provided examples of how large urban newspapers transformed an incredible "Arabian Nights" fairytale into news sufficiently credible that thousands were willing to act on it. The most important aspect of this transformation was the reputation of the sources, and the most reputable sources were those with governmental and, especially, military credentials. Other markers of reputation were titles that related an information source to an institution, such as ship captain, teacher, church pastor, or professor. Finally, the number of stories and the personal vignettes lent credibility to gold rush articles by showing that the emigration was not an event carried out by a few unusual characters but something that many people similar to the newspapers' readers were doing.

With regard to the second question, the evidence shows that newspapers turned news into useful information for prospective goldrushers. In the New York, Boston, and Baltimore newspapers surveyed in the chapter, articles included news reporting, information provision, and investigative reporting. For example, articles on shipping would include all three of these aspects of journalism. In many newspapers, the heading "Information for Emigrants" became common along with "Ho for California" and "News from California."

*Newspapers*

The third major question is whether there was significant variation in news and information based on the type of newspaper and the region. With respect to type of newspaper, the weeklies in small towns both in the East and the West used the exchanges to obtain most of their gold rush coverage; also, they had fewer resources than the larger newspapers to check out fraudulent stories such as that of D'Alvear's goldometer. Religious newspapers formed another class that covered the gold rush that had particular interests evident in their reporting, such as maintaining their local members and advertising their missionaries.

This review of selected newspapers in the Northeast, the South, and the West shows larger differences in coverage between regions than within regions. For example, there were few differences in the informational content of large urban newspapers in the East (although Bennett's *California Herald* was an exception). There were, however, significant differences between the informational content of newspapers in the East, South, and West. Except for New Orleans and the trailhead area of Arkansas, southern newspapers did not emphasize the gold rush story or provide much practical information to prospective goldrushers as did newspapers in the other regions. In the West, attitudes and interests were different than in the East or the South. The main differences concerned their focus on practical advice for travelers on the overland trail.

The credibility criteria embedded in the newspaper stories of the gold rush substituted for the more personal information assessment of face-to-face communications in earlier periods. One should not, however, take this argument too far. Print, such as political pamphlets, was influential in raising the consciousness of colonists before and during the revolution, and newspapers were crucial to inflaming partisan passions in the early national period.[39] Also, in the gold rush, people talked and wrote to one another about the news from California, and church opinion was communicated more through sermons than through the religious press. What makes the gold rush such an interesting case study in the history of communications and information dispersal is the remoteness of the subject, the speed with which information had to be disbursed, and the consequences of bad information.

# CHAPTER TWO

# The Marketplaces for Information
## *Guidebooks and Maps*

Along with newspapers, books and maps were part of the complex of print information sources that strongly affected whether and when potential goldrushers
decided to go to California and how they tried to get there. Like newspapers,
these publications differed in their usefulness, the ways in which they attempted
to create credibility and expand their market, and their availability in various
parts of the country. This chapter examines various guidebooks and maps with
a view to illustrating the diversity and usefulness of these information sources
to goldrushers at a time when information was scarce and urgently needed. The
chapter also provides more evidence about how information was produced and
assessed and examines the sources and markers of credibility in this competitive
information marketplace.

This case study of information provision and assessment illustrates complex
and interactive relationships among book, map, and newspaper publishers in
the mid-nineteenth century.[1] Newspapers, books and maps both competed with
and supported one another as classes of print. Guidebooks usually contained or
referred to specific maps; some maps that were published individually contained
guidebook-like information or referred to specific guidebooks; newspapers advertised and commented on the usefulness of various guidebooks and maps;
and the guidebooks gave credibility, by their presumed authoritativeness, to
newspaper stories about the gold rush. The competition and interaction among
books, maps, and newspaper publishers resulted in the publication of much
contradictory information. Large regional variations in the availability of books
and maps further complicated the problem of information assessment for the
emigrants as they moved across the country towards the trailheads.

Authors and publishers produced a wide variety of guidebooks and maps
that were marketed to goldrushers in the early months of gold fever. Several au-

thors repackaged earlier books that they had written as histories, geographies, and tales of exploration, and republished them as guidebooks. Map publishers dusted off old maps and adorned them with hand-drawn yellow swatches marked "gold region" and resold them as maps for the gold rush. Writers who had never been west of the Missouri River combed through books and newspapers' files to compile travel information to be put out as guidebooks. And a few people who really knew the road west published or republished their more authoritative travelogues and guidebooks.

This remarkably responsive, unregulated, and competitive publishing marketplace disseminated almost two hundred publications in more than twelve countries about California and the gold rush in the years 1848 to 1851, with more than half being printed in 1848 and 1849. Gary Kurutz of the California State Library has compiled a comprehensive bibliography of publications printed during the early years of the gold rush and books published later pertaining to the gold rush during those years.[2] Appendix C lists and classifies by date, country, and type of publication all the books, maps, sermons, company prospectuses, and other publications listed in Kurutz's bibliography that were printed in 1848 through 1851. The list includes forty-three guidebooks, twenty of them published in the United States.[3] In spite of this plethora of publications, it is not clear how many guidebooks were available to potential goldrushers in the East from December 1848 through March 1849 since the month of publication is seldom known. Also, the distribution of the various guidebooks and maps varied considerably depending on the place of publication and publisher.

Like other studies in the history of reading, communications, and the book, this case study must consider indirectly to what extent the guidebooks and maps were used by goldrushers in early 1849.[4] There is, unfortunately, almost no direct evidence about what information sources goldrushers used to plan their trips. Although goldrushers' diaries frequently mentioned guidebooks and maps that they took on the trip, they seldom mentioned how they were used.[5] Even when detailed records exist about the organization, financing, and articles of incorporation of emigrant companies, there is no information about how they decided whether to go by sea or overland and which route to take or how they planned the trip. One of the few detailed descriptions of the organization of an emigrating company was that of J. Goldsborough Bruff and his Washington City and California Mining Association. He wrote,

Having made duplicate drawings of all of Fremont's Reports, maps, plates, &c. for the two houses of Congress—it revived the Spirit of adventure. . . . At first I mentioned it to a few friends whom I thought might desire to try it also: they told others, and we were nearly resolved on forming a Company.[6]

Clearly Bruff and his colleagues used Frémont's reports and maps, but did they have other sources of information? His letters, notes, and diaries do not say. Bruff and the Washington Company did not, in fact, follow Frémont's route west. Indirectly, however, one can obtain an idea about how potential goldrushers used the information marketplaces by studying the availability of different content and formats of information at various times and in different places.

**A Crowded Market: The Earliest Guidebooks and Maps in New York**
The large New York book industry was the first in the country to respond to the new market created by gold fever, and in the late 1840s, New York dominated the publishing trade.[7] A good indicator of the guidebooks and maps that were rushed to print in December 1848 and early 1849 was the "book trade" advertisements in Horace Greeley's *New York Tribune.* Like Eppes Sargent of the *Boston Evening Transcript*, Greeley prided himself as running a literary newspaper, and the books advertised in this newspaper in December 1848 form a representative sample of the early gold rush guidebooks published and available in New York.[8] The books in these ads included most of the types and varieties of California guidebooks, and they indicated some of the relationships between book and newspaper publishers in that market. It is from these advertisements that people interested in going to California would have looked for publications about California. The title pages of the guidebooks show how authors and publishers presented and advertised their books (see appendix D).

Advertisements in the *Tribune* for new and reissued guidebooks and maps to California began quickly after the newspaper printed President Polk's address on December 8, 1848. On that day Bedford and Company advertised the sale of Emory's *Notes of a Military Reconnaissance* under a "Ho! For California" lead. The next day, Dewitt and Davenport, a publisher and bookseller whose offices were in the Tribune building, announced a forthcoming guide, *The Goldmines of California,* to be written by G. G. Foster, a well-known New York author. The ad claimed that Foster's book was based on information from a New York Volunteer of the Mexican war who had returned from California. Four days later, Joyce and

Company advertised *The Emigrant's Guide to the Gold Mines: Three Weeks in the Gold Mines, or Adventures with the Gold Diggers of California* by Henry I. Simpson, supposedly another one of the New York Volunteers. On December 11, D. Appleton and Company advertised a reissue of the two most popular books about the West published before the gold rush: John C. Frémont's *Narrative of the Exploring Expedition* and Edwin Bryant's *What I Saw in California*, which they had just brought out in October 1848. On December 15, H. Long and Brother advertised a reissue of William Emory's book as "A New Work on California Worth Having," and on the same day, Stringer and Townsend announced that *California in 1849* by Fayette Robinson would soon be issued.[9]

The guidebooks gave different information and recommendations than did the newspapers. These books can be separated into three broad categories: reissues of old travelogues and western narratives (Frémont, Emory, and Bryant); books written by New York authors claiming, at times fraudulently, to report their experiences in the West or that their books were based on letters from gold rush participants (Simpson and Foster); and books of compiled information (Robinson). Although the style, coverage, and information of the three categories of guidebooks differed greatly, several commonalities distinguished them from the information and advice contained in newspapers. The most striking of these differences was that most of the guidebooks discussed in detail the land routes to California, whereas the newspapers at that time concentrated on the sea routes. Each of these guidebooks contained maps, and these maps were frequently central to the content of the book. Another difference was that the guidebook publishers, unlike the newspaper editors, appeared to feel little need in their texts to assess the accuracy or even assert the credibility of the information they provided. Credibility was asserted primarily in the advertisements and the title pages, perhaps because books were one-time purchases.

## Republished Travelogues and Government Reports

The first category of books shows the opportunism of the publishers as they turned older books about the West into gold rush sales. These books were not originally written as guidebooks and generally did not refer to the gold rush, but they were more popular with goldrushers than many of the guidebooks published in late 1848 and early 1849. Observing this market advantage, publishers quickly came out with new editions that contained guidebook-like information for the emigrants or appended such information. The most well known of this type of publication was a reissue in December 1848 of John C. Frémont's 1845 *Narrative of the Exploring Expedition*, which was perhaps the best and certainly the most popular of the books about the West in the mid-1840s (figure 1, appendix D).[10] Frémont had built-in credibility as the "pathfinder." This reputation helped sales of Frémont's 1848 *Geographical Memoir upon Upper California*, first published by the Senate in June 1848 and reprinted by Appleton in September 1848 (figure 2, appendix D). The original purpose of the *Geographical Memoir* was to introduce the map by Charles Preuss, his geographer and mapmaker.[11] The map provided the first detailed overview of many parts of the West. From the point of view of the goldrushers, however, the usefulness of the map and the *Memoir* was limited because Frémont did not travel on the California Trail used by most of the emigrants. In early 1849, Appleton repackaged Frémont's work, along with Emory's, and put them out as *The California Guide Book*.[12]

The republications in various forms of Edwin Bryant's *What I Saw in California* was an example of the marketing strategy to produce a rapid sequence of editions, each providing more information to goldrushers (figure 3, appendix D).[13] Having originally published it in the spring of 1848, Appleton followed with three editions in 1848 and, as had been done with Frémont's *Memoirs*, repackaged it as a guidebook with several more editions in early 1849. The guidebook's text was the same as the original travelogue's except that it included as an appendix a letter Bryant had written to the *Louisville Journal and Courier* December 9, 1848, that provided more specific practical information for the overland traveler. The appendix also included a reprint of Richard Mason's report on the gold discovery. Bryant's book in its various forms became one of the most popular books taken on the trip by goldrushers.[14] The book's popularity continued, and by 1850 it had been republished again in the United States, as well as in England, France, and Sweden.

*What I Saw in California* was an account of Bryant's trip and subsequent adventures in California in 1846 and 1847. Bryant was the editor of the *Louisville (Kentucky) Morning Courier* from 1844 to 1845. He left the newspaper in 1846 to travel to California with the group that included the Donner party, although he left that company before they got into trouble in the Sierras.[15] He returned to Louisville in 1847 and wrote his travelogue.

The popularity with goldrushers of Frémont's government reports and Bryant's travelogue indicated that the reputations of the authors were more important as credibility criteria than the immediate usefulness of the content. Frémont had the "pathfinder" reputation, and the success of Bryant's book established his reputation as a seasoned traveler in the West. Neither Frémont's nor Bryant's books, however, related directly to the gold rush, described the California Trail, nor gave practical advice about how to outfit and provision a wagon train. Also, the two books contained contradictory information about routes. Bryant's letter, appended to the 1849 edition of his book, strongly advocated against taking the route described in the book, including the Hastings Cutoff: "we would most earnestly advise all emigrants to take this trail [the old California Trail], without deviation, if they would avoid the fatal calamities which almost invariably have attended those who have undertaken to explore new routes."[16] This strongly worded advice not only made many of the descriptions in the book invalid for someone planning a route, it ran counter to Frémont's, who described a fairly easy trip across the Great Basin, one of the deviations Bryant warns against.

### The New Guidebooks of Early 1849

George G. Foster's *The Gold Mines of California*, an example of the second category of guidebooks, was aimed directly at potential goldrushers and illustrated a relationship between newspapers and the early guidebooks in New York City (figure 4, appendix D).[17] Foster, a popular New York writer but one without any reputation as an expert on the West, edited the book and asserted similar credibility criteria as newspapers. He wrote that it was based on "such authorities as were already accessible, in addition to [his] own private sources of information, and the official documents which ha[d] recently emanated from the State Department."[18] Advertisements in the *Tribune* proclaimed the book as "containing most interesting details of the Gold Mines, quantity of Gold obtained, method of procuring it . . . from the notes of a returned Volunteer. . . . Accompanied with a map of the country, and particularly of the Gold region."[19]

Foster was born in upstate New York in 1814 and died in New York City in 1859. He was a poet, newspaper reporter, editor of satirical magazines, and author of several remarkably diverse books.[20] He was city editor for Greeley from 1844 to 1847, and he clearly stayed in contact with the famous editor long after leaving the newspaper. Also, it was probably not coincidental that the offices of Foster's publisher, Dewitt and Davenport, were in the Tribune building. In late 1848, he was freelancing and working on his "travelogue" of the disreputable sides of New York City, *New York by Gaslight*, which was published in 1850. Although there is no direct evidence, it seems likely that in December 1848 Dewitt and

Davenport, possibly encouraged by Greeley, asked Foster to drop what he was doing and write a quick book to cash in on gold fever.[21]

Whether or not Greeley or the *Tribune* instigated the publication, the newspaper publisher heavily influenced the text. The preface of the guidebook said it had two main purposes: "first, to present to those bitten with the gold fever, a true and *unexaggerated* statement of the facts in the case as far as they are at present known, and next to turn the attention of the overcrowded sea-board to the magnificent agricultural and mining region . . . recently added to our territories by the treaty of peace with Mexico."[22] The preface continued like a Greeley editorial, extolling emigration to the West as a way of ridding New York of its surplus population. It appeared that Greeley, through Foster, saw a chance to plug his pet idea for the poor of New York City to go west.

In addition to editorializing, Foster wrote both some useful and some misleading information for readers interested in emigrating, which he appeared to have culled from the best-known descriptions of the West.[23] These sources were pre-1848 books published for reasons other than providing practical information for prospective emigrants. Also, the map that came with the book was only a rough sketch of California and had many mistakes, including showing the gold region to be in the central valley of the Sacramento rather than in the foothills of the Sierras. Readers, however, were unlikely to have known of these problems. Dewitt and Davenport promoted Foster's book heavily in the *Tribune* on December 16, when the book was released, and then throughout the remainder of the month. On January 4, 1849, the publisher announced a third edition because of the "unparalleled sale" of Foster's guide.

Fayette Robinson's *California and Its Gold Regions* (figure 5, appendix D) was a compilation that combined useful advice and a confused understanding of trail geography.[24] Robinson, who had previously published *Mexico and Her Military Chieftains* in 1847, was another New York writer with no experience of the West. His guidebook was first advertised January 5, 1849, and by mid-January there were three editions in print. The advertisements gushed, "the third large edition . . . [contains] a large, complete and accurate map of the Geography and topography of every mile of the country . . . together with every sort of information touching ailment, health and sickness, clothing, equipment, and general management. The price is 50 cents—to many it will prove worth $500."[25] The first three chapters were a history and geography of California, but the last quarter of the book was more like an emigrant's guide in that it discussed routes

49

and outfits. The accompanying map, which was folded into the front cover and was printed on durable canvas-like paper, was one of three maps published by J. H. Colton in late 1848 and early 1849 that showed California, Oregon, Texas, and the adjoining territories. Carl Wheat writes that it was taken largely from the Preuss map in Frémont's *Memoir*.[26]

Robinson's suggested route was what he called the "northern route" beginning at Council Grove, Kansas, citing Bryant as authority: "this was the route selected by the far most graphic and intelligent of all the civilians who have yet written of that sun-set land of the United States, Mr. Edwin Bryant, long the Alcalde of San Francisco."[27] Council Grove, Kansas, however, was on the Santa Fe Trail going in a different direction than the route taken by Bryant. Robinson goes on to discuss the trails explored by Kearney and St. George Cooke during the Mexican War, through the current states of New Mexico and Arizona. Any prospective goldrusher who read both Bryant and Robinson could be excused for being very confused.[28]

The publishers appeared to be aiming Robinson's book at both emigrants and those left at home. The one-page preface, signed "Fayette Robinson, *Philadelphia, Dec.* 1848," stated that the author had collected and studied material relating to the West and noted, "while thousands are now on their way to this land of promise, that portion of the public which remains at home is anxious to know what are the prospects and probable fatigues of the more adventurous gold seekers."[29] This self-description sets this book apart from many of the others and shows that the publishers were searching out other market niches for the sale of information about California and its gold.

The heavily advertised *Emigrant's Guide to the Gold Mines*, by Henry Simpson, supposedly of the New York Volunteers, is an example of a fraudulent guidebook (figure 6, appendix D).[30] It was a blend of imagination and information culled from newspaper accounts geared toward the gold fever dreams of easterners and peppered with a few legitimate names in an attempt to secure credibility. The publisher's preface stated the text was a letter from Simpson written from Monterey, California, September 17, 1848, recounting three weeks in the gold mines. It is, however, not clear who actually wrote *The Emigrants' Guide*. The roster of the New York Volunteers did not include a Henry I. Simpson, and the supposed letter dated September 17, 1848, from San Francisco could not possibly have traveled across the country in time for the publication of the book.[31]

50

The book's fanciful letter was pure fiction. Simpson claimed to have found the Mother Lode after just two days prospecting in a stream that "for several yards, apparently ran over a bed of gold."[32] In addition to the letter, the book contained advice, presumably written by the publisher, on how to get to California. This part of the book seems to have been copied from the pages of various newspapers since it was the only guidebook in this sample that featured the sea routes, in particular, the Panama route. The book also mentioned the "Rocky Mountain Trail": "a route which we can by no means recommend."[33] This opinion was buttressed by a sensationalistic account of the Donner tragedy. There was a map enclosed with the book that was primarily of Mexico and was probably drawn for some Mexican War project. Franz Drystra sums up some of the shortcomings of the map: "The Rocky Mountains do not exist at all. The Great Plains are simply described as 'desert'. The Sierra Nevadas appear only in Northern California, vaguely trending east and west. Many of the rivers are pure fabrication."[34] Any goldrusher who tried to follow the advice of this book or its attached map would have been in serious trouble.

Simpson's blend of fiction and factual references is an example of how publishers could take advantage of the information marketplace. There was nothing in the book that was not easily available elsewhere, yet the publisher felt that he could make a profit if he could publish quickly at low price and with effective advertising. Simpson's was the first off the presses of the various gold rush publications in December 1848 and sold for twenty-five cents with the map.[35] The book was apparently sold by mail order, and possibly by subscription and agents, rather than in bookstores.[36] The advertising stressed its informational content:

> Advice to Emigrants, and full instructions upon the best method of going there. . . . This work gives a vivid and life-like description not only of Gold Digging, but of entire California . . . and a map which not only shows the entire country, but *all* the routes which lead to it. In short, this work presents every possible information relating to the Gold Regions, and how to get to there.

Although the author was listed as a member of the New York Volunteers, there was no other attempt to create credibility by referring to government sources or elaborating Simpson's professional background.

This sample of the earliest entries into the guidebook market in New York City shows a chaotic menu of choices and a variety of advice, much of it conflicting.

The most fundamental conflict was about which route to take. Frémont described a route south of Salt Lake through the Hastings Cutoff; Bryant also traveled this route but recommended against it, as did Foster. Fayette Robinson described favorably the southern trail through what is now New Mexico and Arizona but called it the northern route. Both Foster and Simpson also discussed the sea routes, which were the primary recommendations of the newspapers at this time. The different routes required different starting times and different beginning locations, so a choice had to be made at the outset. The books also contained conflicting advice about outfitting and provisioning. Bryant recommended pack mules, unless a family was going on the trip, while the others mostly recommended wagons loaded with no more than 2500 pounds of food, tools, and weapons.

The competition among authors and publishers in the East heated up in the first six months of 1849 as many New York, Boston, and Philadelphia publishers produced competing guidebooks and maps. Publishers in London, Paris, and Berlin also produced gold rush guidebooks.[37] New York map publishers, J. Colton, Ensigns and Thayer, and Robert Creuzbaur, produced additional maps, generally derivative of Frémont-Preuss and Emory, that were sold both separately and as part of other guidebooks. C. Averill, A. J. H. Duganne, S. Mitchell, and D. Walton, published guidebooks in Boston and Philadelphia, and twelve other books were published that asserted they had necessary information for travelers to California, although they did not identify themselves as guidebooks (see appendix C).

### Not All Is Gold that Is Printed:
### Some Failed Eastern Gold Rush Publications

Not everything that was written in the East to cash in on gold fever succeeded in the mainstream book trade, and brief descriptions of two of the failures provide another indication of the working of this information marketplace. A manuscript of a guidebook by Washington P. Gregg was rejected by a mainstream Boston publisher, and a map and guidebook by T. H. Jefferson was published only privately. These publications were no worse than the more successful ones in terms of the usefulness or accuracy of the information they contained; indeed, the map and guidebook by T. H. Jefferson is sometimes extolled by gold rush and western historians as one of the best of the western trail guides.[38] What these authors did not have were the legitimate (or illegitimate as in the case of Simpson) claims to credibility as official sources or well-known names in literary circles. The failure of these guides in the book trade indicates an aspect of the marketplaces for print information that worked to the disadvantage of the goldrushers: information that was disseminated depended on publishers' perceptions of what would sell and such books did not always put the highest priority on information accuracy.

The example of Gregg's manuscript shows that timing as well as content was crucial to getting published. In early 1849, Washington P. Gregg, a lawyer and clerk in the Common Council in Boston, sent his manuscript, entitled *The American Emigrant's Preliminary Guide to the Gold Mines of California*, to W. E. Hutchings, a publisher in Boston.[39] It was not printed, and unfortunately, we do not have the rejection letter. There is no indication of when Gregg originally sent the manuscript to the publisher, but he wrote a note to the publisher dated June 4, 1864, that claimed that it would have "circulated widely as there was nothing of the kind then [mid-1849] to be had in book form." The manuscript's content was similar to but broader than Foster's and Robinson's guidebooks, and nothing similar had been published in Boston. Gregg described both the Panama and overland routes and gave the proper precautions about obtaining passage in advance from Panama to San Francisco (this advice was copied from a referenced article in the *New York Herald*). The manuscript contained no indication of an accompanying map. In this case, the publisher's rejection was probably the right decision; by June 1849, it was too late. By then, one needed new information, and this was supplied by returning goldrushers and letter writers who had made the trip.

A guidebook and accompanying map by T. H. Jefferson is a better indication than Gregg that characteristics of the publication marketplace did not always work to disseminate the best information for travelers on the California Trail. The centerpiece of the Jefferson publication was a strip map showing just the trail with textual explanations printed in the blank spaces on the side of the trail. The guidebook was a small pamphlet that accompanied the map, containing the kind of provisioning and outfitting information that Bryant included in his letter to the *Louisville Courier*.[40] Although its style and some of its content were similar to Frémont's *Narratives*, the Jefferson publication was more detailed and contained original cartography.[41] Even to the uninformed reader it would have been clear that Jefferson had made this trip and had made careful observations. In fact, he was part of the California migration of 1846 and must have started out in the same wagon train as had Bryant, Hastings, and the ill-fated Donner party.[42]

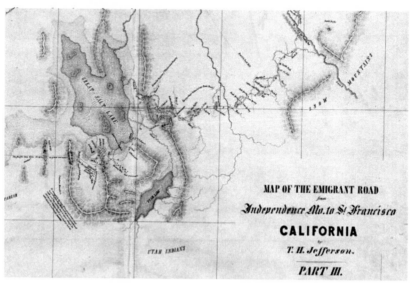

Figure 2. Detail from Map of the Emigrant Road by T. H. Jefferson, Part III. Courtesy Library of Congress Prints and Photographs Division, cat. #G4051 1849P2.

The guidebook-like "Accompaniment to the Map" was published by the author and for sale by Bedford and Co., 2 Astor House (figure 7, appendix D). It must have been available early in the year because it was mentioned by J. Goldsborough Bruff in his journal, and Bruff left Washington DC on April, 18, 1849.[43] Jefferson must have been well-off to have paid for the intricate work necessary to print the fine detail on his map. The advice in the guidebook was also very practical and detailed, even though it was just a pamphlet, and it appeared to be written for an eastern city reader—he assumed little knowledge of the trail. For instance, for packers, he recommended two horses each (not mules, he did not say why) and gave detailed descriptions of the "Tuckapaw saddle-tree—light pad top and bottom, stuffed with deer hair. Saddle cloth of sheep skin, dressed with the wool on—used with the skin part next to the horse's back."[44] Similar details were given for the tents, wagons, provisions, and outfits.

This publication was not commercially successful. The map and guide sold for the very hefty price of three dollars, which probably limited its market since most of the others sold for under a dollar. [45] In spite of the obvious advantages of this map and guidebook in the opinion of later historians and trail buffs, it was not mentioned by subsequent mapmakers and guidebook writers (as were Frémont's and Bryant's, for instance), it was not advertised in newspapers, it did not appear in bookseller catalogs (and thus was not distributed through the mainstream book trade), and there were no subsequent editions.

From the point of view of market constraints to information dissemination, it is significant that one of the most useful publications in the East failed to find a commercial publisher or achieve influence. One possibility as to why the Jefferson map and guidebook did not find a mainstream publisher is that Jefferson could not claim any of the attributes of credibility that we have observed in newspaper articles or books about the gold rush. Jefferson was not known as a writer (as were Foster and Robinson), as a government official or one with claims to official information (as were Frémont and Emory), nor as an explorer (as was Bryant). Historians also do not know the identity of T. H. Jefferson, which has been called "one of the unsolved mysteries of the great westward migration to California in the mid-nineteenth century."[46] Although Jefferson may have been both educated and wealthy, he was apparently not part of the literary establishment of the East, and this may have been one of the reasons for the commercial failure of the map and guidebook.

## A Different Market: The Western Guidebooks

Geography played a role in dissemination of printed information in the gold rush. Guidebooks and maps were published in the West in 1849 and earlier and in several respects were distinct from their counterparts published in the East. First, to a greater extent than those published in the East, they provided better and more practical information for the overland trip.[47] Second, none of these guidebooks were distributed through the eastern book-trade networks, as shown by bookseller and trade sale catalogs; as a result, they were most likely not available in the East. Overland travelers from the East did manage to obtain copies of these guidebooks, however, on their trips to the trailheads. Finally, the western publications introduced a new category of guidebook not available among the early eastern publications, the waybill. The waybill was a detailed trail guide giving brief descriptions of landmarks and possible campsites every fifteen or twenty miles.

The information in these guidebooks, compared with those of the East, is an indication of the changing information available to goldrushers as they traveled west. The three best-known efforts published or republished in the West in the first few months of gold fever were Lansford W. Hastings, *The Emigrants' Guide to Oregon and California* (Cincinnati, 1845, 1847–49); William Clayton, *The*

*Latter-Day Saints' Emigrants' Guide* (St. Louis, 1848, 1849); and Joseph Ware, *The Emigrants' Guide to California* (St. Louis, 1849).

Lansford Hastings's *The Emigrants' Guide to Oregon and California* was in 1849 an example of a republished version of an older book (figure 8, appendix D).[48] Hastings was an early emigrant to California who greatly desired to increase American settlement in that area. His guidebook was originally published in 1845 to boost emigration to California, but by 1849 it had an unsavory reputation because of his connection with the Donner party. In this guidebook Hastings theorized that "the most direct route, for the California emigrants would be . . . southwest to the Salt Lake," although he had not been along this route.[49] In 1846, Hastings decided to travel this route west to east to meet emigrant parties at Fort Bridger before they had to make the choice to go to Oregon or California and to persuade them to come to California using this "shortcut." The cutoff was presumably a selling point for California as a destination for the emigrants, but it wasn't actually shorter and the traveling was much more difficult than on the old route that went north to Fort Hall. Thus, he inaugurated a kind of trail advertising based on persuading travelers to take a particular route for reasons not wholly related to the distance or ease of travel. The group he met at Fort Bridger was the wagon train that had started for Oregon carrying Edwin Bryant, T. H. Jefferson, and the Donner party.

Hastings's *Emigrants' Guide* was one of the first practical and useful guides, primarily because of the concluding chapter on provisioning. This chapter became a model for subsequent western guidebooks that provided advice to overland travelers, but such a chapter did not appear in the compiled guidebooks published in the East. The chapter described—in addition to the lists of foods to take and whether to rely on buffalo hunting—such practical details as what kinds of cooking utensils and beds to take. His advice on wagons, horses or mules, wagon covers and tents, forming corrals, and hunting buffalo and elk was widely copied. It was this kind of very practical advice for the novice traveler, much more detailed than advice in Bryant's letter or T. H. Jefferson's pamphlet, that differentiated many western guidebooks from their eastern competitors. Hastings's original edition was the first publication of this kind, and even in 1849, his last chapter was one of the better articles for emigrants who knew little about how to prepare for the overland trip. Thomas Andrews, who has written extensively about Hastings's *Guide*, concludes: "When published in 1845, the practical instructions offered by Hastings comprised one of the earliest accurate and full appraisals of the emigrant's needs. During the next two years, guidebooks . . . [were] expanded and refined but did not significantly revise the type of information found in the final chapter of the Hastings guidebook."[50]

William Clayton's *Latter-Day Saints Emigrants' Guide* was the earliest and probably the best example of a waybill, an annotated "Table of Distances," which he calculated using a "roadometer" to accurately record daily mileage (figure 9, appendix D).[51] His *Guide* was based on his observations during the 1847 Mormon exodus from Winter Quarters to Salt Lake on which he was clerk of the camp and assigned to write a journal of the expedition. No map, however, was ever published to go along with the trail descriptions. Despite the absence of a map, this would have been a comforting publication for someone worried about getting lost on the way.

Clayton returned to Winter Quarters in October 1847 and attempted with varying success to exploit the potential commercial value of his waybill. With the approval of the church hierarchy, and with the church possibly paying for the printing, a St. Louis printer, Chambers and Knapp, printed five thousand copies, which sold quickly among the Saints in 1848. Regarding Clayton's waybill, a Utah settler wrote in October 1849, "If you could have learned the great demand there has been for the Guide. . . . Five dollars is what they have been sold for, but twenty-five dollars has been offered for them, and they could not be had."[52] In spite of this success among the Mormon emigrants, and although several editions were published in St. Louis, the last in 1852, it was, like Hastings's guide, never printed in the East and never appeared in bookseller or library catalogs, or in the trade sale catalogs.

Clayton's waybill had several disadvantages from the point of view of the non-Mormon goldrushers. First, it was known as the Mormon Guide and showed the Mormon Trail along the north side of the Platte River; many goldrushers would have nothing to do with the Mormons.[53] Second, it emphasized the trail markings and had little information on outfitting and provisioning; and third, the waybill ended at Salt Lake, about two-thirds of the way to California, leaving out the most difficult and dangerous part.

Joseph Ware's *The Emigrants' Guide to California*, like Foster's and Robinson's in New York, was an example of a guidebook compiled from locally available sources.[54] This guide was the best and most frequently mentioned guidebook in journals kept by overland travelers (figure 10, appendix D).[55] Ware was a journalist in St. Louis who had not previously traveled to the West.[56] His book was probably instigated by a newspaper, the *St. Louis Union,* and it was printed by the *Union.* Ware had access to better sources than his eastern competitors, and in addition to using Frémont, Bryant, and Hastings, he used Clayton extensively as well as interviews with western explorers such as Solomon Sublette.[57] Ware also published a strip map with his guidebook, much of it derived from Frémont-Preuss, which traced the complete route along the California Trail (not showing the Hastings Cutoff going south of Salt Lake, which was the route shown in Frémont, Hastings, Clayton, and Bryant). The book is mentioned in several trail diaries, frequently for two mistakes that got several emigrant parties in trouble.[58] In addition to trail descriptions, Ware provided outfitting and provisioning advice and included a somewhat silly appendix on mining gold, something about which he could obtain little information in St. Louis at that time, and on the Panama route, which he cribbed from the Bennett's *California Herald.*[59]

Ware attempted to instill credibility in the preface by citing authorities and official sources:

> In the following pages the author has aimed at one thing only—accuracy.
> . . . We have had means within our reach, that could not be obtained by any
> of those [guidebook writers] preceding us, having the aid of government
> data, maps, profiles, &c. . . . Our distances are based upon actual survey,
> made by the talented Fremont. . . . We acknowledge our obligations to Mr.
> S. Sublette.[60]

Thus Ware invoked the most-used journalistic credibility markers: government, famous people, and eyewitnesses. He tried to differentiate his book from his eastern competitors by stating he had the same official information that they did, and he had in St. Louis more access to western explorers such as Sublette. It is ironic that one of the errors in the guide concerned the Sublette Cutoff, which he presumably described from interviews with Solomon Sublette.

Did potential goldrushers in the East have access to the superior guidebooks from the West? Although the direct evidence is not conclusive, it is likely that these western guidebooks were not commonly available in the major eastern book markets, if at all. Part of the evidence comes from the work on American book distribution, which unfortunately is a relatively neglected subfield in the history of the book, particularly for the nineteenth century.[61] Overall descriptions of the book trade in this period emphasize the dominance of New York by the mid-1840s, and most histories of individual publishers from this period concern those in the East. There is considerable evidence that books from eastern publishers found their way to the West and to a lesser extent to the South, but there is little evidence of trade in the other direction.[62] Although Cincinnati was a center of publishing and book distribution in the West, Walter Sutton shows that in the 1840s it was a western distribution center for its own publishers and publishers in the East, and that the major market for Cincinnati publishers was primarily in its own region.[63]

Trade sales, traveling agents, and subscription were mechanisms to distribute books over wide areas, but there were no major distribution channels for books moving west to east in 1849. Trade sales were elaborate, large scale book auctions that publishers from throughout the country used to sell to booksellers. They were organized by major auction houses primarily in New York, Philadelphia and Boston.[64] They were, however, held only irregularly until 1855 when they were reorganized by the newly formed New York Publishers' Association. Distribution through traveling book agents, also called colportage, and subscription publishing, began in the 1840s but grew sharply after the Civil War. They were primarily a means to distribute eastern books to markets in the current Midwest.[65]

Direct evidence for tracing the distribution of particular books can be obtained from newspaper and other advertisements, as well as from catalogs of booksellers, trade sales, publishers, and libraries of the time. There were no advertisements for Ware, Hastings, or Clayton in the sample of eastern newspapers reviewed in chapter 1.[66] A sample of booksellers and library catalogs from the American Antiquarian Society (AAS) and the Newberry Library contained many listings for Frémont, Bryant, and Emory, but no listings of Robinson, Ware, Clayton, or Hastings.[67] Eastern library catalogs for these years show no guidebooks, although they do contain books about the West and California such as those of Frémont (1845), Irving, Wilkes, and Emory. The dominance of eastern publishers is evident even the in the large and well-funded St. Louis Mercantile Library, as shown in the letters and minutes of the 1849 to 1852 purchasing trips to the East. The 1850 catalog of this library contains Bryant and Frémont, as well as several other books published about western explorations, but none of the guidebooks published in the West.[68]

## Conclusion

Geographical and institutional constraints of the publishing industry in the mid-nineteenth century strongly affected the quality and availability of various kinds of information relevant to the gold rush. Market pressures in the East demanded that guidebooks, if they were to be profitable, had to be produced quickly and advertised aggressively. There was an incentive to publish books with inadequate or simply made-up information as long as they were marketed using credibility criteria that convinced their customer base—potential goldrushers. Known writers in New York City were hired to compile these guidebooks, even though they had no experience of the western trails or California. In the West, the publishing centers of Cincinnati and St. Louis marketed a more useful type of guidebook, particularly for the overland traveler. The eastern writers such as Foster and Robinson, however, either had no access to these books or chose not to use them, because in their compiled books they did not include the kind of advice that was in print from Hastings's and Clayton's books. Also, the western guidebooks did not appear to be marketed directly in the East because they were not included in the eastern trade sales or bookseller catalogs.

These geographical and institutional constraints in the information marketplaces, combined with the lack of assessment mechanisms and lack of information about information providers, made it difficult for goldrushers to plan sensibly for their trip. For overland travelers, bad planning sometimes resulted in disasters or even fatalities. The informational problem must have become apparent to many goldrushers as they traveled west, first to the trailheads, where they became aware of guidebooks that they considered superior. The next two chapters show that this led to emigrants seeking and creating novel forms of communication and information dispersal and new credibility criteria.

# CHAPTER THREE

# To the Trailheads
## *From Advertisements to Rumors*

Once potential goldrushers decided to go to California and made their choice
of land or sea routes, their informational problems had just begun. If going by
sea, they had to choose a company and/or a ship, decide what to take, and make
arrangements for families and friends for while they were gone. Those deciding
to go overland had more choices and needed more information. They had to
select a company or go on their own and decide on a route, when to begin, which
trailhead to head for, and what and where to outfit and provision. These were
complicated and interrelated decisions, and, as described in chapters 1 and 2,
the information they had in the East was frequently contradictory and difficult
to assess. Also, they faced problems not mentioned in the eastern newspapers
and guidebooks, such as cholera and where to cross the Missouri River. As they
started toward the trailheads, new information became available as they read
newspapers in towns along the way, new guidebooks and other print sources that
were not available in their hometowns, and advertisements. They also received
new information as they talked to agents from the competing trailhead towns and
to other goldrushers also going to California. These new sources of information
further complicated their assessment problems and caused them to reconsider
not only the specific information that they had used to plan their trips but the
credibility criteria with which they assessed that information.

The new assessment problems stemmed in part from the variety of sources of
new information. In addition to the western guidebooks described in chapter
2, goldrushers read many articles and editorials from newspapers in the various trailhead towns, which read like boosterism. They essentially were town
advertisements, both positive and negative, and they were probably viewed that
way by the emigrant readers. This interpretation of the newspaper articles and
editorials did not detract from their importance to the goldrushers as sources

of information; advertisement was information. These articles and ads created, however, a new assessment problem because eastern goldrushers had no way of deciding what was real and important and what was false and self-serving. This chapter examines the material that the towns used in competing for the gold rush business both from the point of view of the towns, for which the gold rush business was crucial, and from the point of view of the goldrushers on their way west. What reads at first glance as simple boosterism becomes complicated when credibility criteria, rhetoric, methods of communication, and information combined to influence important decisions of the travelers.

The stories of this chapter follow several groups making their way from different parts of the country to the various towns from which they began the California Trail over the South Pass.[1] These stories illustrate how the various and changing information sources affected the way goldrushers assessed information and how new information influenced their decisions. Several groups of goldrushers drastically changed their plans on the basis of new information, sometimes at a considerable expense in money and time. As these gold rush companies traveled farther from what was familiar, the information they used to plan their trips appeared less relevant because of new problems that their information sources had not mentioned and less accurate because some of their recommendations appeared to be ill-advised.

### The Trailhead Towns

The geography and history of western Missouri and the rivalry of the four major trailhead towns are the context for understanding how new information affected decisions of the goldrushers. The context is important because it determined how the towns attempted to influence the goldrushers and the credibility of these attempts.

Goldrushers reacted variously to the trailhead towns of Independence, Westport and Westport Landing, and St. Joseph in Missouri and Kanesville in Iowa. For many goldrushers from the East and the current Midwest, these towns were their first encounter with large numbers of others heading for California and with people familiar with the trail. Frequently, they did not like the Missourians they met, and their impressions of the trailhead towns ranged from indifference, to surprise at how developed they were, to indignation at their vice and the price gouging of their merchants.[2] William Swain, a teacher and farmer from Niagara

County, New York, arrived at Independence May 3, 1849, and found himself in familiar surroundings:

> [It is] a business town, presenting the most business-like appearance of any town we have seen since we left St. Louis. Here are many fine build-ings, stores, taverns, and dwellings. In fact, it presents the appearance of a northern village of some 1,500 to 2,000 inhabitants, situated in a good place for mercantile pursuits.[3]

Dr. Charles Ross Parke, from Como, Illinois, who got to St. Joseph the same day, "found St. Joe in an uproar. Men of all grades, classes and conditions striving to get away. . . . all sorts of rascals in town and as a matter of course carrying on a high game."[4] J. Goldsborough Bruff, from Washington DC, reached St. Joseph on April, 27, 1849, a week ahead of Swain and Parke and was not impressed enough to describe it in his extensive diary or in letters back home.

Trailhead town advertisements usually emphasized their geographic advantages relevant to the trail. The most important geographic feature was the Missouri River, on which most goldrushers arrived at the trailheads. Going upriver, it cuts roughly east-west across Missouri from its confluence with the Mississippi near St. Louis, and then makes a sharp turn to the north on the western border of the state (see map 1). Many of the emigrants who wrote about this part of their trip appeared to have a good knowledge of western Missouri because there were several good maps of Missouri published in the East.[5]

The Missouri River's turn to the north, called the "big bend," played a crucial role in the sites chosen for the various towns. The Santa Fe Trail ran southwest from the big bend; the Oregon-California Trail ran northwest towards the south bank of the Platte River. The Platte flows into the Missouri River just north of Missouri's border with Iowa. For emigrants going to California and Oregon, trails led from the various trailhead towns north and west to intersect the Platte at Fort Kearny in the current state of Nebraska about 250 miles from the confluence of the Platte with the Missouri.[6] The Mormon Trail paralleled the north bank of the Platte and was used intensively by the Mormons in their migrations to Salt Lake. The two trails merged east of Fort Laramie in what is now eastern Wyoming.

The relative advantage of each town as a trailhead for the various western trails depended in large part on its location on the Missouri River.[7] Independence was several miles south of the river near the bend. This allowed the large commercial trains going to the Santa Fe Trail to avoid crossing the river, and Independence

63

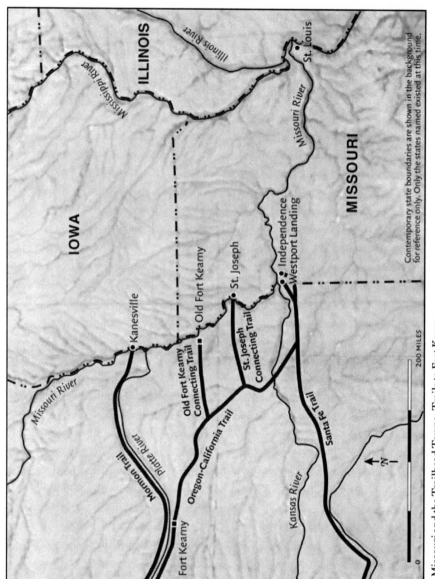

1. Missouri and the Trailhead Towns: Trails to Fort Kearny

Contemporary state boundaries are shown in the background for reference only. Only the states named existed at this time.

became the primary starting point of that trail as early as the 1820s. Westport, also on the south side of the river, had this advantage for the Santa Fe Trail but was on the river, allowing easier access for supplies when in the 1830s regularly scheduled steamboat traffic developed on the Missouri as far as the big bend. A better river landing site, called Westport Landing, began to be used just north of Westport because it was at the confluence of the Kansas and Missouri rivers. This landing was used for warehouses and stores and, as it grew, merged with Westport and became Kansas City at about midcentury.

Farther north, on the east side of the river, in 1826 Joseph Robidoux established a trading post that grew into the town of St. Joseph. By 1846, St. Joseph was a popular trailhead for the Oregon Trail. Finally, Kanesville, Iowa (which became Council Bluffs), was near the gathering place for Mormons preparing to move west and was the best location for quickly and safely reaching the Mormon Trail.

Each of the trailhead towns had a history of catering to western traders and knew the economic advantages of attracting goldrushers. They used their respective histories of servicing western travelers as selling points in their advertising. These towns, each having somewhere between fifteen hundred and three thousand residents in 1849, were located in a rich agricultural hinterland that had developed a substantial surplus of farm products over the previous ten years. Important for the gold rush, these surpluses were not only in crops but in the expanding cattle industry.[8] Before the gold rush, these products were generally sold to the Santa Fe caravans, the fur trade companies, the army, and emigrants to Oregon or shipped to St. Louis on the growing steamboat service on the Missouri River.[9] Independence, for example, as the terminus for the Santa Fe Trail had developed as early as the 1820s a substantial outfitting industry, including livestock, mules, and wagons.[10] By the mid-1830s Westport was thriving and had challenged Independence as the main outfitting, merchandising, and warehousing center for the western Missouri region. In addition to the commercial activities related to the fur and Indian trades, Westport, Westport Landing, and Kansas City developed manufacturing establishments related to trail business, such as making harnesses, saddles, tents, wagon covers, yokes, and bows.[11]

The two trailheads to the north became major competitors for the Oregon and early California emigrants. By 1849, St. Joseph had a population of more than fifteen hundred and contained "eighteen stores, two pork-packing establishments, two steam sawmills, two flour mills, two mechanic shops, three churches, two newspapers, several saloons, a courthouse, and a triweekly stage."[12] The most northerly trailhead, Kanesville, Iowa, had a substantial advantage for emigrants using the Mormon Trail. In 1849, however, the town had existed only for two years and lacked the infrastructure and developed agricultural hinterland of the Missouri trailheads. Also, Kanesville and the Mormon Trail were full of Mormons, which was a problem for many goldrushers from the East and current Midwest because of prejudice and the fear that Mormons would retaliate against the persecution they had suffered over the previous several years in Missouri and Illinois.[13] Only about nine hundred goldrushers departed from Kanesville in 1849, although it became much more popular in the rush of 1850.[14]

Newspapers were the primary means of disseminating printed information and propaganda to goldrushers coming from the East. Except for Westport, each of these towns had an active press in 1849, and articles from the *St. Joseph Gazette*, the *Independence Western Expositor*, and the *Kanesville Frontier Guardian*, advertised their towns and disparaged the others.[15] Also, the nearby town of Lexington (an agricultural and marketing center in western Missouri) published the *Democratic Journal* and the *Express*, both of which covered the gold rush intensively.[16] St. Louis newspapers, the largest and most influential of which was the *Missouri Republican*, played a special role in this rivalry. St. Louis merchants and suppliers competing for the gold rush business realized they had to attract the goldrushers before they moved on, and they advertised heavily in the *Republican*. The St. Louis newspaper was frequently copied by eastern newspapers through the exchanges. The editor felt a special responsibility to report conditions on the trailheads and provide information not only to its own readers but to readers in the East.[17]

The *St. Louis Republican* hired a correspondent who wrote under the name "California" to report from March through May 1849 on conditions at the trailheads. He also provided information on prices and availability of outfits and provisions while remaining evenhanded with respect to the trailhead town rivalries.[18] A good example is an article first published April 2, 1849, by the *Republican* and reprinted in the *New York Herald* April 19. In this report, the *Herald* described California, as "a correspondence of the St. Louis *Republican*." It began,

> The immense emigration to California by this route has given an impetus to business in the towns of Independence, Westport, Weston, and St. Joseph. . . . Which of these points afford the greatest advantages for this purpose [supplying their outfits] is a bone of much contention between the good

66

people and business men of these several places, and especially between those of Independence and St. Joseph. It is not my intention, in corresponding with you from this portion of our State, to express any partiality in regard to this matter, but simply to give a true and accurate report.

He then compared prices of mules and oxen at Independence and St. Joseph, giving the edge to Independence. He gave his home city a plug by saying that there were many more accommodations for goldrushers in St. Louis than in any of the trailhead towns for those who were not prepared to camp outdoors until early May when the grass would be sufficient to begin their trek across the prairie.

Merchants and farmers around the trailheads realized that to sell their merchandise they had to sell their town, and to do that they had to at least appear to be providing credible information. They attempted to get the information out primarily through their local newspapers and to establish credibility by getting endorsements from well-known western explorers and officials. The example of Independence illustrated this strategy well. By 1849 Independence was losing out to Westport and St. Joseph as the most popular trailhead because its primary geographic advantage was its access to the Santa Fe Trail, but the Mexican trade had been stopped by the war. Although merchants in Independence expected, rightly, that the Santa Fe trade would pick up with the end of the war, they saw the advantage of competing aggressively for the gold rush business. Three prominent citizens of Independence and its hinterland took the initiative. They were Smallwood Nolan, a farmer and owner of the largest hotel in the state outside of St. Louis; Samuel D. Lucas, clerk of the circuit court and owner of a store in the town square; and Samuel Ralston, a farmer and the only one who had traveled to the West.[19] They wrote to Col. William Gilpin January 1, 1849, asking him "to prepare a circular for publication under [his] own signature" that would provide answers to letters they had "received from various parts of the United States, making enquiry relative to the best date [to begin] from Missouri to Oregon and California, and the facilities . . . for furnishing outfits to persons going to either place."[20] Gilpin was a good choice for a celebrity plug. He was an army officer who had served in the Seminole War in 1835 and traveled with Frémont and Kit Carson in the 1843-1844 expedition. In the Mexican War he received considerable acclaim as a member of Stephen Kearny's "Army of the West" and in Alexander Doniphan's expedition in Chihuahua.[21] He was a very prominent citizen of Independence and was sure to give readers "information" favorable to the town.

Gilpin obliged with a letter printed in the *Independence Expositor* on January 8 and reprinted in the *St. Louis Republican,* January 25, the *Cincinnati Daily Commercial* February 6, and the *Louisville Examiner,* March 3, 1849.[22] It was everything the merchants wanted.

> Independence, now, for twenty years, the emporium of the commerce of the Prairies possesses indisputable and peculiar advantages over all other places, as the point of rendezvous and final embarkation for emigrants and travelers going to the Pacific. . . . [I]t recommends itself from the unlimited abundance of supplies to be had at all times, their excellent quality and adaptation for the journey to the plains and mountains.

The pitch is clever and designed first to establish credibility for the town on the basis of its history. The phrase, "commerce of the Prairies" is a reflection of the title of what was then a well-known book by Josiah Gregg, *Commerce of the Prairies,* first published in 1844 about Gregg's trading expeditions to Santa Fe.[23] Gregg's book was also in most bookseller catalogs and many library catalogs.

Gilpin next related the main geographic advantage of Independence: "It is upon the bank of the Missouri River, but *beyond* [italics in the original] that river . . . the great river here deflecting to the North, makes it the extreme available landing for steamers towards the west." This may have confused some goldrushers who had one of several good maps of Missouri available in the East, and the maps showed, correctly, that traveling farther north on the river would get them closer to the California Trail. But Gilpin quickly goes on to the main point for the merchants:

> Apart from the decided excellence of Independence as a geographical point, it recommends itself from the unlimited abundance of supplies to be had at all times; their excellent quality and adaption [*sic*] to the journey of the Plains and mountains . . . a body of skillful mechanics, and all kinds of complete manufacturing establishments in every department of the trades, combined with stores, filled with supplies for all wants and tastes. . . . [I]n short, flour mills, rope mills, wagon manufactories, tinners, leather manufactories, saddle and harness makers, hatters, farriers, clothing establishments, a sorted [*sic*] goods for the Indian trade . . . are all here established on a permanent and ample scale and furnish articles of a substantial and durable character—calculated to carry the traveler safely beyond the wilderness.

68

Gilpin goes on to discuss the route—that it must go through South Pass and Salt Lake, but he doesn't mention Hastings's infamous cutoff—and then prices. He ends with a dig at the competitors: "Other points higher up the Missouri, as Weston, St. Joseph and the Mormon settlement near Council Bluffs have occasionally been selected by emigrating parties. These places have all the disadvantages of being on the eastern bank of the Missouri, and as yet are far behind Independence in the abundance, adaptation and cheapness of supplies." Thus Gilpin covered the main informational points that the goldrushers would have been least secure about in their hometowns in the East: locational advantage and the availability and prices of supplies.

St. Joseph fought back primarily through the pages of the *St. Joseph Gazette* and also sought endorsements during the winter of 1848-1849 from well-known travelers. The newspaper published accolades from Commodore Robert Stockton and Gen. Stephen Kearny, military officers well known for their exploits in the West, and mountain men Moses Harris, Miles Goodyear and Joseph Meek.[24] The *Gazette* continued its campaign by printing excerpts of letters from "ordinary" travelers who had gone west the previous year; these letters praised St. Joseph merchants, citing cheap and abundant supplies.[25] An editorial in that issue countered Gilpin's claim that Independence was better located for California travelers than St. Joseph, because one would not have to cross the river to get to the prairie trails. The *Gazette* editor pointed out that there were good ferries crossing at and near St. Joseph, and that if starting from Independence, the wagons would have to cross the Kansas River, which was frequently flooded and had no ferries. Most important, St. Joseph was about eighty miles, or about six days travel, closer than Independence to the trail on the Platte River. On March 9, 1849, the *Gazette* asserted, "the universal testimony of all emigrants is that the route from St. Joseph is decidedly the shortest and best."

In April and May, the campaigns became more fierce, and St. Joseph, in particular, complained about misinformation fostered by the rival town, particularly with regard to availability of supplies and accommodations and the difficulty of crossing the river. For example, the *Independence Expositor* asserted on April 21 that because of slow ferry crossings, "emigrants waiting to leave from St. Joseph might still be stranded there as late as July 1"; the editor of the *St. Joseph Gazette* responded, "this was one of the many thousand lies you have told about St. Joseph and its facilities to accommodate the emigrants."[26] In fact, the river crossing at St. Joseph was a serious issue for the goldrushers. Daniel Robinson from Bloomington, Illinois, described the problem in a letter written to his sister on May 3: "there were three or four hundred teams waiting to cross the river." They would have to wait two or three days, something they could not do since they had no feed for their cattle and "to buy corn in St. Joseph . . . [was] out of the question."[27] J. Goldsborough Bruff from Washington DC described the scene at the St. Joseph crossing two days later:

> The crowd at the ferry is a dense mass—fighting for precedence to cross. 2 teamsters kill'd each other on one of these occasions, with pistols, at the head of their wagons. 2 crazy scows very insufficient for the occasion, as soon as a wagon enters the boat, the next moves close down to the edge of the bank, and the long mass of wagons in rear close down, while companies are falling in the rear, and this goes on from earliest dawn till midnight day after day.[28]

Later in May, the situation became worse: one emigrant, writing as "Old Boone," from St. Joseph to the *Missouri Statesman*, May 25, 1849, complained, "The ferry is overrun and some four or five days behind in crossing wagons, and unluckily one of our company is caught on this side waiting for its shipments, and we will likely have to leave it."

The saving grace for St. Joseph was that there were many ferries between St. Joseph and Kanesville; a company could outfit and provision in St. Joseph and then go north to a less-busy crossing point. The *Gazette* was quick to point this out: "Up to Thursday near three hundred wagons had crossed the Missouri river at Duncan's Ferry, four miles above town, while more than double that number had crossed at the different ferries between this place and the Bluffs."[29] Robinson never told his sister where his company crossed the river, but Bruff, after his observations on May 5, and likely hearing more rumors around town, decided to take his company ninety miles north on the east side of the river and cross at the old Fort Kearny.[30]

The prevalence of cholera in the various towns was another major aspect in the negative advertising and, by late April and May, was probably the most serious issue for many eastern emigrants on their way to the trailheads. The terrors of cholera were well known, and the majority of the 1849 goldrushers going on the California Trail passed through St. Louis just as the epidemic, traveling up the Mississippi River from New Orleans, reached the city.[31] The correspondent California reflected the emigrants' fears in early April but with some doubt as to their veracity. He reported from Independence, "considerable fear is manifested by many in consequence of reports of deaths from cholera in this vicinity. The reports cannot be reliably traced, and are, no doubt, exaggerated."[32] By early May, however, California was less sanguine, particularly about Independence, when he reported, "a few cases of sickness here within the past week supposed to be cholera." Four days later, he wrote that cholera was "still prevalent at Kansas and Independence and both places were nearly deserted."[33] This was clearly an exaggeration, but the effect on the emigrants was real. J. Goldsborough Bruff, a careful observer and recorder of his trip, did not mention the disease until after leaving St. Louis on April 18; six days later, on the steamer *Meteor*, he wrote, "Heard of much Cholera on the river."[34] Alonzo Delano had a closer encounter with the disease when, on his second day on the steamer *Embassy* from St. Louis to St. Joseph, one of the passengers died of cholera. He described the reaction of the passengers (and presumably himself): "amid the gaieties of our motley crowd, a voice was heard, which at once checked the sound of mirth, and struck with alarm the stoutest heart—'the cholera is on board!' For a moment all voices were hushed—each looked in another's face in mute inquiry, expecting, perhaps to see a victim in his neighbor."[35]

The town rivalries were not confined to the newspapers, and again Independence took the initiative. First, merchants began printing handbills that were distributed in St. Louis.[36] Then they became more aggressive, sending agents to towns farther east that most emigrants would pass through to convince the travelers to use their towns as the trailhead. Again, the St. Joseph competitors complained, as shown by a letter from a "Hoosier Emigrant" printed in the *Gazette*:

> Emigrants are told at many points along the Mississippi and Missouri rivers, that St. Joseph is the last place to start from for California and Oregon. . . . I feel that I can claim, with a clear conscience, to be totally impartial in advising emigrants in future, to disregard all the idle tales of agents, runners and interested persons tending to disparage the advantages of this point [St. Joseph]—to make this town their place of rendezvous, where they will find plenty of such articles as they may wish, and at fairer prices than other more assuming *cities* on the line of march from an eastern home to the western plains.[37]

In spite of this Indiana emigrant's claim of impartiality, it was most likely clear to readers of this letter that it was another shot in the trailhead rivalry. And, in spite of the *Gazette*'s complaints, the use of agents was not unknown in trail advertising. As described in chapter 2, Lansford Hastings in 1846 was an agent who attempted to convince Oregon-bound travelers to come to California. The tactic was probably used because merchants in Independence felt that a personal appeal would be more effective than print advertisements.

The towns' rivalries, which were wars of words carried on mostly through the newspapers, were extremely important to the goldrushers because they provided the emigrants with new information they needed. First, the prices and availabilities of wagons, mules, and supplies were of crucial importance to the travelers, and information directly from the trailheads seemed more reliable than prices and availabilities of supplies printed in the East months previously. Second, the eastern emigrants knew the general lay of the land and the relative positions of the towns from eastern maps, but details such as the trade-off between a longer trip from Independence and the necessity of crossing the Missouri River at St. Joseph were not discussed in eastern print sources. They had to rely on the new information from trailhead town newspapers. Third, these newspapers provided information on the state of the prairie grass and when the trains could start on the trail and provided guidebook-like advice on packing wagons, breaking mules, and dealing with Indians.[38] Finally, as discussed in chapter 2, the western guidebooks, such as Joseph Ware's and William Clayton's, were generally better than guidebooks that goldrushers had from the East, and these were advertised in the western newspapers.[39] The importance of the newspapers, as well as of the new guidebooks, showed that print was still the primary means of disseminating information, but that the most credible sources in that print had changed.

The goldrushers' information assessment problems were greatly complicated by this barrage of new information. They had to combine new information with what they had from eastern sources and decide whether or not to change plans if the new information conflicted with the old. For most decisions this was probably not too difficult, and usually new information won out since it was more current. The travelers also had to sort out conflicting new information, and this was much more difficult. One problem was that the old credibility criteria of looking for official, and particularly military, sources could not be used consistently, if at all. Reputation in the West was based more on perceived trail expertise and knowledge of the land than official titles. To gain more understanding of how different groups of goldrushers coped with these problems, the next section will track to the trailheads several gold rush companies which traveled overland.

## The Trek Begins

The gold rush companies described below form a diverse group for the purposes of illustrating the problems of obtaining and assessing information essential for their trip. They were from diverse parts of the country, began with different degrees of planning, took various routes to the trailheads, and reacted to their informational problems in different ways. Even those companies that had prepared elaborately for the trip based on the information they could obtain in the East changed their planned actions on the basis of new information. From the point of view of this study, what is important about these stories is that the goldrushers frequently had to assess and adjust to new, mostly local information. The fact that most of these companies adjusted their original plans, some several times, indicates that they considered the new information more credible than what they thought they knew.

### The Washington City and California Gold Mining Association

J. Goldsborough Bruff caught gold fever in January 1849 reading the *Washington (DC) National Intelligencer*, reading the advertisements for gold rush merchandise and guidebooks, and hearing of the formation of early gold rush companies.[40] He organized the Washington City and California Gold Mining Association in January 1849. This company was an example of a goldrusher group that, in spite of meticulous planning and obtaining information in the East, changed plans unwisely on the basis of new, unverified information.

Bruff certainly felt qualified to go. He was a successful draftsman for the Bureau of Topographical Engineers in Washington DC and in 1845 drew the first official map of the state of Florida. By 1848 he was married with several children and reasonably secure financially, but he caught gold fever. He decided early on to go to California overland via the South Pass and to publish a journal and sketches that would be "a perfect guide in every respect to all future travelers on that route." Describing his preparations, he said, "I take with me all the Maps and works on the country, mineralogical works, tests, & etc."[41] Unfortunately, in spite of his copious notes and detailed journal, he did not list the sources he used in planning the trip. From subsequent journal entries, however, we know he carried copies of Frémont, Bryant, T. H. Jefferson, and Ware, although he does not say when and where he obtained each of these guidebooks and maps.

Bruff's Washington DC company left for the trailheads on April 2, 1849, going first to Baltimore and then by the newly opened *Great Western Mail* train to

Pittsburgh. At Pittsburgh, they met up with members of a committee from the company who had traveled ahead to purchase wagons and equipment, which they loaded on the steamer *Robert Fulton* for shipment to St. Louis.[42] They reached St. Louis April 15 and aboard two other steamers reached Independence on April 25, where another advance committee had been sent to buy mules. In spite of the articles castigating St. Joseph in the *Independence Expositor*, Bruff kept with his original plans and proceeded to St. Joseph, where the company disembarked and camped on April 27. Here Bruff became worried about the problems of the river crossing at St. Joseph, which he thought would take the "14 Company and 2 private wagons . . . about a fortnight" and about cholera in the "immense crowd on the other side," the west side of the river.

At this point Bruff apparently sought local advice and probably was influenced by articles in the *St. Joseph Gazette* about alternate river crossings to the north. He called a meeting of the company and "represented the delay and disadvantages of attempting to cross [at St. Joseph] and the advantages on the other hand of proceeding 90 ms. Up the river, to Fort Kearney."[43] He did not say where he got the information about crossing at old Fort Kearney or how long he thought it would take to move the company overland, but he apparently hired a guide to take them north on the east side of the river. It took them almost one month to get to the crossing, where they found that ferry service had been discontinued because of high water.[44] On the advice of a local who had ferried several groups across, they repaired a scow and made it across by June 3, several weeks later than if they had waited in line at St. Joseph. They started west for Grand Island on the Platte River June 5. For Bruff, it appeared that new information was more credible than old, but not better. This was the first, and not the last, time that Bruff believed new information and changed established plans to the detriment of his company.

### The Charlestown Company

Not far west of Washington DC, in Charlestown, Virginia (now West Virginia), on January 22, 1949, Benjamin F. Washington and a small group of men held a public meeting to organize a gold rush company to travel to California to mine gold. They had already done considerable homework and had decided to travel overland beginning at St. Joseph. They organized the company on both military and business lines and encouraged former soldiers to join. The constitution of the company, the original finances, and the planned pooling of resources and sharing of profits were similar to many other companies.[45] Two veterans of the Mexican War, Vincent Geiger and Wakeman Bryarly, signed up, and most of what is known about the Charlestown Company comes from their journals. Like Bruff's Washington DC company, the Charlestown Company seemed to plan in more detail than most. For instance, at an early meeting on February 10, "it created a committee to consult with a certain metallurgist of Frederick County on the techniques of mining; it authorized the purchase of thirty rifles and forty double-barrelled [*sic*] shot guns; and it named a committee to procure supplies." In addition to the purchase of rifles and shotguns, they also required every man to have a pair of pistols, and they purchased and took a small cannon.

One may only conjecture what sources they used in setting these priorities since they did not record them. The fact that they consulted with a local metallurgist suggested that they did not read, or had little faith in what they read, about mining or the "wonderful machines" that were advertised to find gold. Also, their emphasis on a military organization and the priority they gave to purchasing weapons, which was somewhat extreme for a gold rush company, indicated an unusually great fear of Indians.[46] Although Geiger and Bryarly refer to Frémont, Bryant, Ware, and Clayton several times in various journal entries, these sources would not have generated that fear, but Simpson and some newspaper reports would. The journals did not indicate when or where the company obtained the various guidebooks. It is likely that they had Frémont and Bryant, and probably Simpson, before they left Charlestown but that they bought Clayton and Ware in Missouri.

The Charlestown Company sent a committee ahead to buy outfits, animals, and provisions, but sent them to St. Joseph rather than Pittsburgh, where Bruff's Washington City Company purchased their outfits. Their journals did not say on what basis they chose St. Joseph. The company originally planned to use riding animals and only one wagon per fifteen men but changed their mind, possibly after reading Ware's *Emigrant's Guide*.[47] The main body of the company left Charlestown March 27 and took the same train that Bruff's company took from Baltimore a week later. But the Charlestown Company got off at Cumberland and took stages across the Alleghenies to the Ohio River, and then went by boat to Cincinnati and St. Louis, and then to St. Joseph, which they reached April 19, still one week ahead of Bruff. At St. Joseph, they hired a guide, Frank Smith, who had been over the Oregon Trail but not to California. The outfits and wagons joined their camp, and they were undeterred by the crowds crossing the river;

they crossed by May 10, spending their time taming their mules, a daunting task for the eastern greenhorns. This allowed them to be on the trail by May 14, some three weeks ahead of Bruff.

## The East Tennessee Gold Mining Company

South of Charlestown, in Knoxville, Tennessee, Gen. Alexander Outlaw Anderson organized the East Tennessee Gold Mining Company.[48] Like Bruff and Washington, Anderson was a prominent local person and seemed to have prepared diligently for the trip, including obtaining letters of introduction to Gen. Persifor Smith, the military governor of California, from the governor of Tennessee, Neill Brown.[49] The company got off to a poor start, however, because they outfitted fully in Knoxville and began a difficult overland journey through the mountains of east Tennessee and Kentucky toward Louisville. Also, they were overloaded (a common error in 1849), used horses instead of the recommended mules or oxen, and started very late, on May 3, 1849. David Deaderrick recalled, "The travel across our own E. Tene. Mountains to Kentucky was much the worst part of our road; and with our wagons much too heavily loaded, were exceedingly trying to our horses."[50] They reached Louisville May 26.

In Louisville, Anderson and the company apparently received new information and reassessed their situation. They stopped for a week, sold their horses and bought mules, and shipped their outfits to St. Louis by steamer. They also learned of the major new problem of cholera and the implications of being so late. Wilberforce Ramsey, a member of the company, had a letter from his family that warned of cholera on the trail and included an article from the Knoxville newspaper saying that thirty thousand emigrants had passed in front of them and all the grass would have been eaten up. He wrote back to reassure them, presumably on the basis of discussions within the company. First, he told his family that there was "little of that fell destroyer of the human race [cholera] in that city [Louisville]."[51] With regard to all the emigrants ahead of them and the late date, he replied, "From all the information we could get about Louisville there will be but 5,000 [emigrants] in all. That number cannot consume all the grass on the plains—so the chances for reaching the gold diggings in safety is, we consider, very good still." They were not yet ready to change their plans.

Between Louisville and St. Louis, they heard more about cholera, which by that time was raging in St. Louis and on the Missouri River steamboats. General Anderson cancelled plans to go by river and drove his teams from St. Louis towards Independence, further delaying them.[52] Then, hearing that cholera was prevalent in Independence, they drove their teams to St. Joseph, spending an unplanned week in Fort Leavenworth (about half way between Independence and St. Joseph) and were not ready to leave St. Joseph until August 6, some two to three months later than they should have left. By this time it was much too late to take the South Pass route, and they decided to go the southern route to Santa Fe, where they passed the winter. After several other bad decisions and the defection of more than half the company, they finally reached Los Angeles April 12, 1850, and the gold fields May 16.

In a long letter written to his father July 16 from Fort Leavenworth, Missouri, Ramsey wrote of the effect of new information on their plans:

> Ever since we left Louisville we have been reading in the public print of the disasters that were anticipated on the South Pass rout [*sic*]. Such has been the immense number of emigrants that way and such is the scarcity of grass in some places that it becomes impassable for more than one tenth of them to reach California in safety. About 200 miles from the Mormon settlement the narrow mountain passes commence. There the whole emigration will have to follow almost in single file—and hence it is said the rich prairie grass ceased and nothing can be found but very short tough mountain grasses. In the best of seasons it is said there is not enough to supply 5,000 head of stock. Think then of the fearful disaster that will accrue when 30,000 emigrants with eighty thousand head of stock will be crowded in these passes.[53]

This letter must have seemed ironic to his family, who had warned them two months earlier of the trail crowding. Ramsey did not mention the family's earlier letter nor where he heard about the "single file mountain passes." Although they had been getting information from "the public print," it appeared from this letter that General Anderson and Ramsey paid more and more attention to rumors and casual information as they approached Missouri. After they comprehended the mistakes of their original planning and gained an understanding of the rapidly changing situation, the most current local information perhaps seemed more credible than their old information in spite of the fact that it could not be verified.

### The Boston-Newton Company
Back east, in Massachusetts, although the large majority of goldrushers went by sea, several groups prepared for an overland trip, among them the Boston-

Newton Company.[54] The company's actions again illustrate that initial plans that had been made on the basis of eastern guidebooks changed considerably when emigrants obtained new information that they considered more credible than the old. This company, however, did not get into the kind of trouble experienced by the East Tennessee Company

Good records of the Boston-Newton Company's trip were made by Charles Gould and David Staples, both of whom were journeymen at the Petee Iron Works in Newton, Massachusetts.[55] Both had been recently married in 1848, and like so many other goldrushers, neither had any experience of the West. The company was organized in Newton-Upper Falls and recruited from the local area. Albion Sweetzer, a contractor, was one of the directors of the company. He had just lost four thousand dollars in a building speculation and was going to California more to try contracting and merchandizing than to mine gold. His letters from Sacramento to his suppliers in New England form a valuable record of the difficult communication problems of merchants in California during the gold rush.

The company's organization followed lines similar to the others described here, and they decided in the beginning to take the South Pass route and leave from St. Joseph. Their initial plan was to use pack mules instead of wagons, perhaps following Bryant's advice.[56] They purchased considerable supplies, which they thought they could transport easily to Missouri by train and boat. What they thought they would need of mining and other equipment, they sent around the Horn by ship to San Francisco.[57]

The Boston-Newton Company left Boston April 16 and traveled to Albany on a "special emigrant train that had been put into service to take care of the increased traffic westward." From Albany, they procured a private rail car on the condition that they "allowed 10 other emigrants to go with [them], and . . . were very fortunate in having good company."[58] As they moved west towards the trailheads, particularly on the lake and river steamships, goldrushers from different parts of the country traveled together, undoubtedly sharing rumors, information, and misinformation. They went by train to Buffalo and steamship across Lake Erie to Sandusky, Ohio, which they reached April 21. The company then traveled by rail to Cincinnati, where they changed their plans to use pack mules and bought two wagons.[59] They reached St. Louis April 27, where they purchased provisions because, they were informed " they could purchase provisions cheap and a general outfit for a good deal less money than at Independence."[60] Although they bought steamship tickets for St. Joseph, and had shipped goods to that town, they decided to get off at Independence because, as J. G. Hannon speculates, of the April 21 editorial in the *Independence Expositor* about the crowed conditions at the ferry crossings at St. Joseph[61] They landed at Independence May 3 and took ten days to buy the rest of their outfits and animals and organize for the trip. By the time they left for Grand Island, the company had grown to seven wagons and forty-two mules.

## The Wolverine Rangers

In upstate New York, William Swain prepared very much less elaborately than had Bruff, Washington, and Anderson. He was a newly married farmer from around Youngstown, near Buffalo, living on the family farm with his wife, infant daughter, and elder brother, George.[62] The family owned a copy of Frémont's 1845 *Report*, which J. S. Holliday states was important, along with newspaper reports, in Swain's decision to go west. His story began very differently than those of the gold rush companies described so far because he neither organized nor joined a company, and he made few advance purchases. Seemingly without much advance planning, he left for the Missouri frontier with three companions April 11, 1849, on a steamer from Buffalo.

The apparent lack of advance planning did not delay their trip to the trailhead. The Swain party reached Sandusky, Ohio, April 13, about one week before the Boston-Newton Company, then went north to Detroit and then by lake steamer up the length of Lake Huron and back down Lake Michigan to Chicago. Swain stated that this route was the cheapest and would take no longer than a combination of railways and stages.[63] The four companions then took a combination of canal and river boats to the Mississippi and arrived in St. Louis April 25, just two days before the Boston-Newton group. In St. Louis Swain and his friends did some investigation as to where and how to outfit and provision, and he concluded in a letter to his brother George: " the emigration has not kept pace with the supplies sent to the Missouri frontier, and the markets here [Missouri] are abundantly supplied. . . . [W]e have therefore concluded to purchase our outfit at Independence."[64] It seems likely that California's favorable reports in the *St. Louis Republican* about supplies in Independence influenced their decision. Although he apparently wandered about St. Louis, where the cholera epidemic was just beginning, in this letter, he made only one mention of cholera: "I have not heard of a case of cholera, nor have I heard a word spoken of it since we came here." This statement is strange because just three days after Swain's letter to

79

his brother, Charles Gould of the Boston-Newton Company wrote, "Here [St. Louis] they . . . hurried on, on account of the report that the cholera being quite prevalent."[65] Swain must have had some concern about the disease, however, since in the same letter he wrote, "I drink no water, unless necessity drives me to it. This morning I drank a quarter of a cup of coffee at breakfast and two swallows of water at dinner." They left the next morning on the steamer *Amelia* and reached Independence May 2, 1849.

The *Amelia* also carried a gold rush company from Marshall, Michigan, that called itself the Wolverine Rangers. This company was organized by James Pratt, the editor of the *Marshall Statesman*, who thought the trip to California would be an opportunity for the newspaper to report on the emigration as well as providing him a chance to get rich in the gold fields.[66] Pratt went ahead of the main group to Independence to purchase an outfit, animals, and provisions. He wrote back to his newspaper about his activities and to prepare his party for what they would find at the trailhead. It is one of the few detailed accounts of an advance party, and he seemed very well organized. He stopped in Chicago where he purchased wagons to be shipped by boat to Independence. He reached St. Louis March 17 and left March 20 for Independence. Pratt talked with Colonel Gilpin in Independence, who gave him advice about dealing with Indians along the route.[67] While there Pratt compared prices and availabilities with what he observed in St. Louis, and he "ordered all . . . supplies except oxen and bacon to be bought in St. Louis" and brought to Independence by another of the advance party. He scoured the country for oxen and gloated, "[by] picking them up of farmers, I have been enabled to buy 20 yoke at an average of 40 dollars, which is acknowledged by all to be five dollars per yoke cheaper than any one else has purchased this spring."[68]

The main body of the Rangers left Marshall April 18 and took the *Amelia* from St. Louis April 26. Swain mentioned a sermon preached by one of the Rangers on April 29. They landed at Independence May 2; three days later Swain and his friends decided to join the Rangers and were accepted with a payment of one hundred dollars each and plus providing their own wagon and teams. Swain's diary in the intervening days mentioned his now increased concern about cholera and "getting information, pricing mules, wagons and oxen."[69] Swain's decision to join the Rangers stemmed from a meeting he had with Pratt aboard the *Amelia*, during which both men got on well together. Swain was pleased with his decision as he felt, "we have the best outfit I have seen since we arrived here. We have eighteen wagons, fifty-four yoke of oxen, sixteen cows, and nine months' provisions. . . . [W]e have nine messes [eating groups] in all, each with seven men."[70] They had planned to leave by May 12, but their doctor, a Dr. Palmer, got sick and died of cholera May 14, and on May 15 another of their party, a Mr. Nichols, also died of the disease; after the burials, they moved out May 16. In spite of the deaths, Swain was in good spirits:

> We are very comfortably rigged and look forward to the journey with pleasure, believing that we shall have lots of fun. We will pass through Independence in the morning, when I shall get a number of little articles for my comfort, after which I shall have from $120 to $125 in gold to take with me, which will leave me in better circumstances than I expected.[71]

Swain, Pratt, and the Rangers were a confident group that stuck to their original plans in spite of the cholera, and they got off to a good start. As they got farther from familiar territory, however, particularly in the far-western part of their trip, they too were enticed by bad new information to take actions that were detrimental to their company.

### Other Companies

In addition to the above companies, there are four others we will be following as they make their way across the plains, deserts, and mountains toward California. The additional gold rush companies in the sample are well documented in terms of their trail experiences but wrote little of their trip planning or their journey to the trailheads.

Alonzo Delano of the Dayton, Illinois, Company left April 5 from his home, hoping the trip would improve his health as well as his fortune. He joined his team at English Grove, about sixty-five miles north of St. Joseph to cross the Missouri River at a new ferry called Harney's Landing.[72] They left for the West May 3, 1849. Charles Glass Gray joined the Newark Overland Company, organized February 19, 1849, by Gen. John Darcy, and left the New York area for Independence March 1.[73] They purchased their wagons, oxen, and other supplies in Pittsburgh and shipped them by boat to St. Louis. They and their outfits arrived in Independence March 29 and started onto the prairie early, on May 1. In Athens County, Ohio, Elza Armstrong and John Banks joined the Buckeye Rovers, who started for the trailheads in early April.[74] They outfitted in Lexington, Missouri, on their way to St. Joseph, which they reached May 2. Not wishing to wait in line for the ferries at

Table 1: Gold Rush Companies at the Trailheads

| Journal Writer | Name of Company | Trailhead | Start Date |
|---|---|---|---|
| Charles Gray | Newark Overland Company | Independence | 1 May |
| Alonzo Delano | Dayton Company | Harney's Landing | 3 May |
| Vincent Geiger<br>Wakeman Bryarly | Charlestown Company | St. Joseph | 10 May |
| Charles Gould<br>David Staples | Boston-Newton Company | Independence | 15 May |
| John Banks<br>Elza Armstrong | Buckeye Rovers | Savannah MO | 15 May |
| William Swain | Wolverine Rangers | Independence | 16 May |
| Charles Parke | Como Pioneer Company | Old Fort Kearny | 18 May |
| Goldsborough Bruff | Washington City Company | Old Fort Kearny | 5 June |

St. Joseph, they drove their outfits north about twenty miles to Savanna Landing and were on the trail by mid-May. Finally, Dr. Charles Parke, in Como, Illinois, in the northwest corner of the state, organized the Como Pioneer Company and left for the trailheads April 7.[75] Like Anderson's East Tennessee Company, the Como Company outfitted at home and drove their teams and wagons to the trailhead at St. Joseph; unlike Anderson's company, they left a month earlier and had a much shorter and easier drive. They arrived in St. Joseph May 5 and then headed north toward old Fort Kearny, which they reached May 16, about two weeks ahead of Bruff, and crossed there without trouble.

The information various groups received on the trail, and the types of communications they had with other groups, depended in part on their place in the line of wagon trains that by July stretched one thousand miles along the Great Platte River Road. Where they were in the line depended, in turn, on when and where they started. To help keep our groups straight, table 1 above summarizes that information for the companies we will be following across the country to California.[76]

One must keep in mind that it took about two weeks longer to get to the Platte River from Independence than from St. Joseph or points even farther north. Thus, both Delano's Dayton Company, and Geiger and Bryarly's Charlestown Company traveled a few days ahead of Gray's Newark Overland Company although Gray started earlier. In terms of the bulk of the emigration, the Dayton, Charlestown, and Newark companies were near the front of the pack, the Boston-Newton, Buckeye Rovers, and the Como companies were about in the middle, and the Wolverine Rangers and the Washington City companies brought up the rear.

## Conclusion

The stories of the nine gold rush companies' trips to the trailheads illustrate several aspects of the informational problems of the goldrushers as they began their trip. These include some of the ways that they coped with information assessment problems and how they reacted to new information. All the groups described in the chapter attempted to plan thoroughly and obtain information available in the East. Except for Swain, the companies made early decisions about where to outfit and provision and which trailhead to use. These plans were generally in accordance with recommendations in newspaper articles and eastern guidebooks. Even very early in the trip, however, plans changed as new information became available, which indicates that the new information was considered more credible than the old when there was a contradiction. In the cases of the Charlestown and the Boston-Newton companies, for example, early plans to use pack mules, in accordance with Bryant's advice, were changed to accord with the commonly recommended practice in the West to go with wagons.

As the companies moved toward the trailheads, problems developed that were not mentioned in eastern guidebooks and newspaper articles, which indicated that their early information was inadequate and that, possibly, their initial plans were flawed. The most important problems about which they knew nothing in the beginning were the prevalence of cholera on the steamboats and in the trailhead towns and the crowding to cross the Missouri River. As they heard about these problems, as in the case of the East Tennessee Company with regard to cholera, or as they observed them, as in the case of Bruff with regard to crowded river crossings, they sought out and obtained new information. In addition to still important print sources, mainly newspapers and guidebooks, goldrushers sought face-to-face contact with newly found experts such as Gilpin. Also, to a greater extent than before, they believed rumors from other goldrushers. Possibly because previously accepted credibility criteria were breaking down, the groups assessed and reacted differently to the new information: the Wolverine Rangers, for example, stuck to their original plans even when they experienced the cholera directly, and others, like Bruff and Anderson, changed their plans several times and made a difficult situation worse.

83

Why did the goldrushers consider new information more credible than old and on what basis did they change their plans? The clearest generalization is that as they got closer to the trailheads and farther from what was familiar, new information began to trump old beliefs even when the new information would seem to be suspect on the basis of old credibility criteria. The old credibility criteria of government sources providing advice in print must have seemed less relevant when new problems arose that the old information sources did not address. New information trumped old information simply because it dealt with these problems. Eastern goldrushers, however, still had the problem of how to assess and compare the various sources of new information when they were contradictory. The vacillation of some groups, such as Anderson's East Tennessee Company and Bruff's Washington Company indicates that they could not settle on new credibility criteria. In both of these cases, it appeared that the apparent expertise of the information sources became more important than official position, titles, or being in print. They were not able, however, at this time to assess the various claims of expertise. It would take the goldrushers some time on the trail to gain enough experience to develop new commonly held credibility criteria and believe new sources.

# CHAPTER FOUR

# On the Trail

## *From Printed Guidebooks to Mountain Man Experts*

As the goldrushers moved onto the plains in May and early June 1849, their communications with home and other goldrushers changed drastically as did their
information sources. They could no longer get information from local newspapers, there were no new guidebooks or maps to consult, receiving letters from
home was not possible, and unless they had hired a guide, there were no local
experts such as William Gilpin to call upon. They were not alone, however; with
twenty to thirty thousand emigrants all crowding on the same trails leading to
the Platte River and then west to South Pass, the first half of the trip resembled a
one-thousand-mile traffic jam of wagons, oxen, mules, horses, and people. The
lonely wagon train image of some Hollywood depictions of western migrations
was completely off the mark in the early summer of 1849.

Goldrushers frequently communicated among themselves and employed many
mechanisms for obtaining information. Information concerning the trail ahead
was the most important for the travelers, which they obtained from eastbound
goldrushers who had given up and army units traveling east. These failed goldrushers, or "go-backers," and the army also provided a way for emigrants to
send letters home from the trail. The westbound travelers used communications techniques pioneered by fur traders and trappers and previous Oregon
and California emigrants, such as writing notes on animal bones (the bones
express), as well as by signs and notes along the trail. Some mechanisms, such
as trail "post offices," which ranged from a barrel to an abandoned shack, were
elaborated upon and expanded. As the travelers reached roughly the halfway
point, in current Wyoming, they began to encounter Mormons who had settled
for the past year or two and were in business of running ferries and selling
information in the form of handwritten guidebooks. Some of these people had
been to California and provided information about the gold fields and the most

difficult part of the trip, the deserts of the current state of Nevada and the Sierra Nevada Mountains.

Credibility and information assessment for the goldrushers became a different and even more important exercise on the trail than they had been in the planning stages. The credibility criteria for printed information were relatively accepted. How could one assess, however, the credibility of a note scratched on a buffalo skull or a scrap of paper along the trail that asserted that a particular cutoff was the way to go or that the stretch ahead was fifty miles without water rather than the twenty miles stated by the printed guidebooks? How could one balance the advice of a handwritten Mormon guidebook purchased from someone unknown to any fellow travelers against the printed guidebooks or the opinions of other goldrushers who claimed to have better sources of information from others to whom they talked? Unlike on the trip to the trailhead towns, on the trail personal experience to some extent could now provide an avenue for assessment and reassessment of the information sources that predominated before the trip. A major reassessment occurred early on for many goldrushers, for example, in the type and amount of equipment they should carry; the trail was strewn with discarded stoves, gold-mining machines, excess food and household items, and guns. Experience helped little, however, when the unknowns on the trail ahead were of a very different character than those on the road behind.

The route followed by the goldrushers consisted of two distinct parts: the relatively easy half in the east (roughly to South Pass—the Continental Divide—in the western part of the current state of Wyoming) and the harder part in the west. One problem that had bothered many goldrushers before the trip, that of getting lost, was not a worry in the east. The Great Platte River Road, across what is now central and western Nebraska and eastern Wyoming, was well established by 1848, and the massive emigration made it as prominent as Interstate 80, which roughly follows the path much of the way.[1] This part of the journey was also the best-documented and mapped in the guidebooks carried by most of the emigrants. When the travelers reached the western half of the trip, however, there were many alternative routes presented as various "cutoffs"; these thinned out the wagon trains as different groups made different choices.[2]

This chapter follows the gold rush companies described in the previous chapter along the trails to California. The diaries and letters of goldrushers in these companies are used to describe their information sources, their use of new and informal communications, and, where possible, the way they used the information to make decisions.[3] The last section of the chapter is a detailed study of the Lassen Cutoff. This route was taken by several thousand emigrants in 1849 and was a disastrous choice. Many died and wagon trains were decimated on the harsh deserts on the east side of the Sierra Nevada and in the California forests on the west. The history of the cutoff provides a dramatic example of how information spread among the goldrushers as they made their way along the Humboldt River. Also, the story is interesting because the scope of the information concerning the cutoff stretches from the files of the Army Topographical Engineers, to the pages of an 1848 issue of the *Oregon Spectator*, to the signs left along the parched reaches of the Humboldt River.

In the stories of these diverse gold rush companies, there is a common theme of the loss of credibility of the goldrushers' printed information, whether guide-books or maps. As they traveled farther from what was familiar in terms of land-scape and weather, even small discrepancies were magnified between the West of their imagination, formed mostly by their printed information sources, and their actual experiences of the trail. This, in turn, caused a growing distrust of their guidebooks and maps and a shift in trust toward any hint of local expertise. The result was, toward the end of their trip—when the terrain was most alien and their physical and emotional resources most strained—they followed rumors and trails about which they had little or no information.

### From the Trailheads to Fort Kearny: The First Stretch

These were the trails where the goldrushers began their seasoning. Map 1 (p.64) shows the various trails from the trailheads to Fort Kearny on the Platte River.[4] Although the routes were not difficult compared to what they would face in the coming months, they had a lot to learn. Since most of the goldrushers were not physically prepared to endure a two-thousand-mile-mile walk and ride, they also had to get in shape. Swain, for instance, complained in his journal on May 29, "I find that I have worked too hard, as I am very stiff this evening and pains in my breast and side."[5] For the Charlestown Company of Bryarly and Geiger, on leaving from St. Joseph May 10, one of the first problems was the need to tame and brand their mules. Geiger called their camp on May 12 the "Branding Spring": "the next day we branded our mules . . . from the last camp several of our men took flights of[f] ground and lofty tumblings of[f] mules' backs."[6] Other problems included fixing axles that had broken as wagons were hoisted in and out of streams.[7] Many goldrushers encountered Indians for the first time, and they learned that on this part of the trail the tribes were not threatening; indeed, they were friendly and useful to the goldrushers. For example, the Wolverine Rangers purchased some additional supplies from a Shawnee named John Root who ran a grocery on the trail about five days out of Independence.[8]

The most serious difficulty on the trail was the continuing scourge of cholera, which they would not leave behind until well past Fort Laramie. J. S. Holliday estimates from the number of graves mentioned by diarists that cholera killed at least fifteen hundred on the trails east of Fort Laramie.[9] The Wolverine Rangers, who lost two of their party in Independence, lost another, a Mr. Ives, three days out (May 19), and a Mr. Lyon succumbed May 28; a day later two more came down with the disease but recovered.[10] Swain came down with dysentery May 31, and not surprisingly, his journal entries for the next several days concentrated on his health. The graves of emigrants, most of whom died of cholera, were a major distraction for the goldrushers. Geiger commented May 19, "Every day we have passed fresh made graves containing the remains of poor emigrants who have died with the cholera on their way to the golden land."[11] Another member of the Charlestown Company, Edward McIlhany, wrote in his *Recollections*, "Nearly every day we saw graves on the road. At each place there was a path running out diagonally from the trail. It was made by people going out to see who was buried there, and then another diagonal path came out to the road farther on."[12] The large majority of emigrants, however, survived this seasoning and arrived at Fort Kearny (about twenty-three days from Independence and eighteen days from St. Joseph) more fit and feeling better than when they began the trip.[13]

The early difficulties caused some groups, the go-backers, to give up and return to Missouri. Along with traders and military units going east, they formed a countertraffic that was a source of information, a way to send letters home from the trail, and a kind of market in that they would sell, relatively cheaply, wagons, tents, draft animals, and provisions they no longer needed. Any information they conveyed had to be carefully assessed since they would frequently exaggerate the difficulties ahead in order to justify their decision to return. Frontier newspaper editors also cautioned readers, "returnee rumors should be taken with several grains of allowance."[14] Some goldrushers, however, had sympathy for the go-backers and found them useful. For instance, Horace Ladd of the Wolverine Rangers wrote of the backtrackers, "[they] have seen the tail of the Elephant and can't bear to look any farther . . . [and] see worse times coming back than they did going for the emigrants plague and pester and interrogate them . . . [they] are very useful to the emigrants as they supply the place of a mail service and can always tell how far ahead to wood and water."[15] The go-backers would frequently charge for their services, but their reliability as mail carriers was seriously in doubt. Delano, for instance, on June 28, described a sign labeled "Post-Office" near the road with a notice that one of the company was "leaving for the States and would carry letters, &c., &c.,—price 'half a dollar.'": "Many a half dollar was left, but those letters which our company left for the friends never reached them, and it was only a pleasant ruse to gull travelers, and 'raise the wind.'"[16] Other travelers had different experiences. While on the trail between Independence and Fort Kearny, Swain sent two letters home to his wife Sabrina, two to his brother George, and one to his Mother. All reached their destinations.

The crowds on the trail provided an opportunity for communication and comradeship, and for conflict. The crowding of wagons was most evident at the river and creek crossings where, for instance, Charles Gray of the Newark Overland Company was caught in a line of eighty wagons at the Kansas River crossing, about one week out of Independence, and the crossing at the ferry took a full day.[17] The extent of the emigration was clearest where the Independence and St. Joseph trails came together. William Johnson described this rather nicely in his diary May 9:

> In looking behind over the road just traveled, or back over the St. Joseph road, or forward over that to be taken, for an indefinite number of miles there seemed to be an unending stream of emigrant trains; whilst in the still farther distance along these lines clouds of dust, indicating that yet others of these immense caravans were on the move. It was a sight which, once seen, can never be forgotten; it seemed as if the whole family of man had set its face westward.[18]

The closely packed groups frequently got along well as shown by Swain's description of the evening of May 21 when the Wolverine's bugler played for all nearby to hear and a New York company reciprocated with "the Canadian Boat Song, sung in well-cultivated voices carrying the four parts": "Then they gave three cheers for our company, which was returned by our boys for them."[19] But the long lines of wagons had elements of a race, and particularly at bottlenecks, teams competed for position. Charles Tinker of Columbus, Ohio, wrote in his journal June 11 that his company offered fifty dollars to use some boats of a Missouri wagon train to cross the Platte River. They were refused and told the boats were going to be destroyed to prevent others from following.[20] It did not take a river crossing to excite this competition. James W. Evans wrote, "The whole emigration is wild and frantic with a desire to be pressing forward. . . . Whenever a wagon unluckily gets stuck in the mud in crossing some little rut, the other trains behind make a universal rush to try to pass that wagon . . . all this occasioned by a delay of perhaps two minutes and a half."[21]

The crowding of wagon trains fostered communication, and emigrants visited neighboring companies to exchange information, experiences, tall tales, and rumors, frequently about Indians. Bruff described a meeting on June 11, with a Mr. Hughes, camped about a mile away, who said that two days previously, "he was attacked by a party of 500 Cheyennes who robbed him of all his provisions . . . after which they threw down some bead-work, moccasins, sashes, &c as payment for what they took."[22] Bruff's Washington Company sold Hughes some flour, bacon, and sugar but apparently took no notice of any danger. Companies and military trains were also fond of placing signs along the trail, as described by Edwin Banks of the Buckeye Rovers on May 23: "the frequency with which we see scraps of paper or a small board left telling who is ahead is amusing. One: 'The Infantry Company F passed here; all well and in good spirits; plenty of game and good whiskey.'"[23] At this stage of the trip, with few deadly problems except cholera, these types of communications were part of the adventure, and the lack of believability did not matter. Later they would take on a more significant role in the decisions of the emigrants.

### Fort Kearny to South Pass: Seasoned Travelers

Fort Kearny was the first real milestone for the travelers. The fort was not pre-possessing as a military outpost, and Delano derided it as "nothing but a cluster of adobe, low one-story buildings," but most companies camped there for at least a day.[24] The *Missouri Republican* stationed a correspondent at the fort who wrote under the name "Pawnee," and described the scene in a letter to the newspaper:

> The ice is at last broken, and the inundation of gold diggers is upon us.
> . . . Up to this morning four hundred and seventy-six wagons have gone past
> this point; and this is but the advance guard . . . this is an excellent point
> from which to see all that is desirable to be seen, as all the roads unite before
> reaching here. . . . Every state, and I presume almost every town and county

in the United States is now represented in this part of the world. Wagons of all patterns, sizes and descriptions, drawn by bulls, cows, oxen, jackasses, mules and horses, are daily seen rolling along towards the Pacific, guarded by walking arsenals.[25]

Pawnee stayed on his post until the end of June and he was counting; by June 23 he recorded 5,516 wagons with about 20,000 people. If one then adds the number of packers and those who took the Mormon Trail, the emigration past this point in 1849 was at least 22,500 and probably more.[26]

Fort Kearny was for the emigrants a place to reassess, shop, and trade, and to exchange information as well. The major reassessment concerned what they should carry. Goldrushers threw away or sold what they felt they no longer needed, and they purchased or traded for items they lacked. Pawnee wrote May 26, "The result of such want of experience was that almost every wagon that left the frontiers was overloaded. . . . Sawmills, pick axes, shovels, anvils, blacksmith's tools, feather beds, rocking chairs . . . now overboard goes everything."[27] The Charlestown Company "abandoned a great deal of plunder": "picks, hobbles &c and every article calculated to retard our march. The allowance now is about 100 lbs flour & 50 lbs bacon to a man."[28] Bruff's Washington DC company also rid itself of excess baggage: "Held a meeting of the Company, and equalized the private baggage—disgarding [discarding] a great deal of superfluous weight—Sold a wagon to the Sutler for $30—and the Ambulance to the Officers for $50 . . . Forge, Anvil, bellows, some lead & iron, we sold to a Mormon family here for $32."[29] Sutlers were civilian merchants who had licenses from the army to keep a store on military posts. At Fort Kearny the sutler's store had "a good stock of notions—cigars, sardines and some extras for officers' use . . . if he had on hand all the articles Californians inquired for, he could [have made] more money than by going to the gold region itself."[30]

The travelers used the camping grounds at the fort for visiting other goldrushers to exchange information and rumors. They also received new information from soldiers at the fort. One army officer who visited Fort Kearny in May wrote in his diary, "men come in at every moment . . . making thousands of inquiries on every conceivable subject and asking for every sort of assistance."[31] This was the first and probably the most important location for intercompany communication and to obtain new information that they could assess on the basis of actual experience on the trail.

Fort Kearny had another important function for the goldrushers—it provided the first consistent mail service along the trail. Mail was sent officially by a U.S. mail agent stationed at Fort Kearny, a Mr. Bennet, who made trips between the fort and Missouri twice a month.[32] Many goldrushers sent letters from the fort. In addition to Mr. Bennet, there were also private mail carriers: for example, a Mr. P. C. Tiffany collected mail at the fort and along the trail to take to St. Joseph for fifty cents per letter. As the emigration traveled farther from areas served by the Post Office, and in California where goldrushers found the official mail service frustratingly inadequate, private carriers assumed greater importance.

The route from Fort Kearny was the Great Platte River Road.[33] The easiest part of the trip was between Fort Kearny and Fort Laramie. On this stretch all the trails from the trailheads merged, except for the Mormon Trail on the north side of the river, and all goldrushers traveled the same road. There were no choices of alternative routes, and maps and guidebooks were unnecessary. The road paralleled the south bank of the Platte River until a few miles past the fork between the south and north branches of the river. They crossed the South Platte in a variety of easy fords, and headed for Ash Hollow on the North Platte, which they followed past the well-known landmarks of Courthouse Rock, Chimney Rock, and Scotts Bluff to Fort Laramie (see map 2).

Beyond Fort Laramie the trail became more difficult as it roughly followed the river through the Black Hills and around the Laramie Mountains. The wagon trains made a difficult crossing to the north side of the river using either ferries or fords near the current town of Casper, Wyoming, and left the Platte River there to cross some fifty miles of alkaline desert to the Sweetwater River. They then followed the Sweetwater up into the Rockies where they reached the continental divide at South Pass.

Communication mechanisms that were novel during the first phase of the trip became commonplace and more developed after Fort Kearny. This was especially true with notes placed along the trail and sent from train to train, sometimes referred to as the "roadside telegraph."[34] Charles Gray wrote in his diary for May 26, two days out of Fort Kearny, that his Newark Overland Company, led by Gen. John Stevens Darcy, received a letter via another train from New Jersey, from Dr. Ed Darcy, that their company had lost two to cholera. Bruff seemed to know many people in other trains on the trail and frequently left his Washington Company to go visit.[35] After being away from the company for several days, he "found a note in a cleft stick, on the side of the road, from [his] Company."

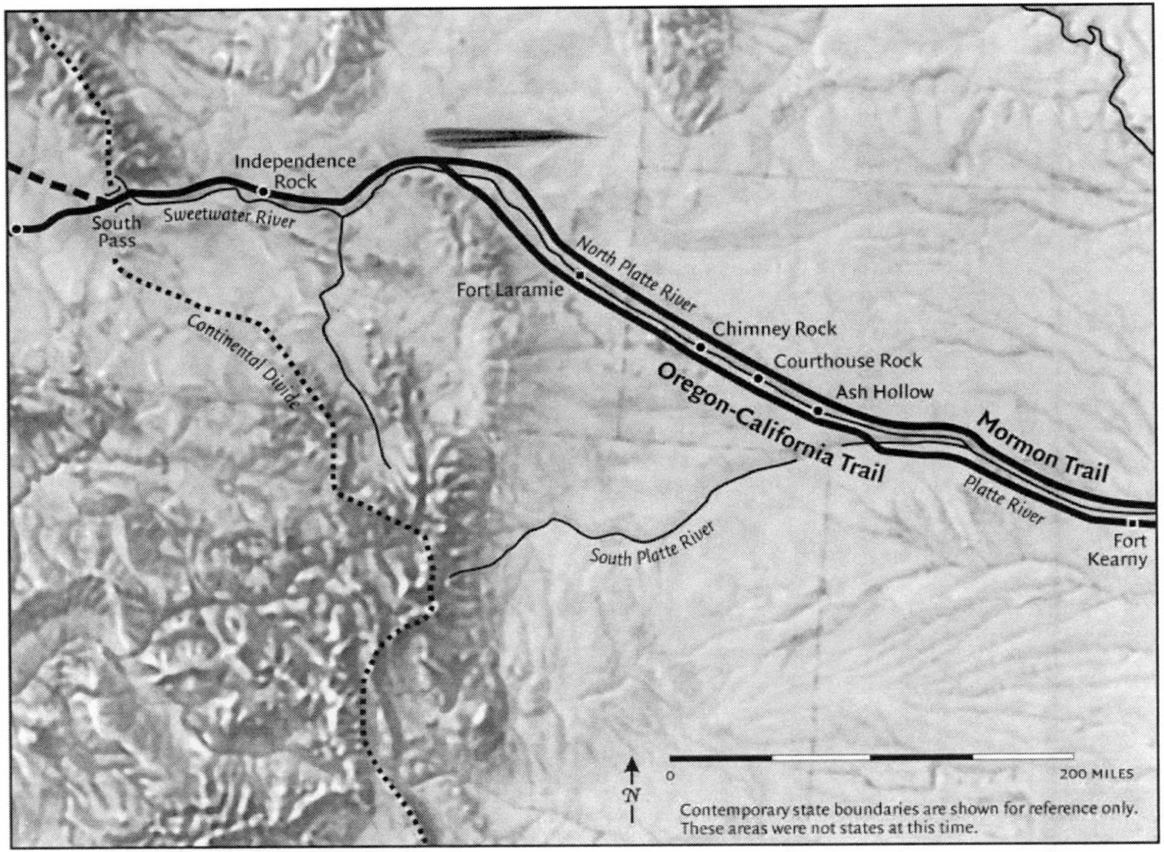
Independence Rock
South Pass
Sweetwater River
Continental Divide
Fort Laramie
North Platte River
Chimney Rock
Courthouse Rock
Ash Hollow
Oregon-California Trail
Mormon Trail
Platte River
South Platte River
Fort Kearny
N
0
200 MILES
Contemporary state boundaries are shown for reference only.
These areas were not states at this time.

2. The Oregon-California Trail: Fort Kearny to the South Pass

The note "was from [his] second in command, stating that they had crossed well and getting along finely; to hurry up & join them soon."[36] Bruff's company was not sure that the note along the trail would reach its recipient because later that day a go-backer wagon handed him another note from the company with the same message: hurry up.[37] Some notes, however, implied that travelers had great faith in the roadside telegraph. Edwin Banks of the Buckeye Rovers wrote that he "saw a notice offering two hundred dollars reward for five horses and the thieves that stold [*sic*] them."[38] The writer must have felt that communication along the trail was sufficiently good for someone to read the note, act upon it, and then find the writer to return the horses and collect the reward. Notes were not only confined to paper; there was also the "bones express."[39] Delano noted, "the usual mode of giving intelligence to friend behind, is to write on a bleached buffalo skull, or shoulder-blade. Thousands of these novel communications lay upon the plain and we frequently got intelligence in this way from acquaintances who preceded us."[40]

Written communications among the travelers had developed to the point where they were a commonplace of trail life and were a useful source of information. In the section from the Platte River to the Sweetwater, oxen trains had difficulty because the alkaline water of many ponds, springs, and streams on that part of the trail were poisonous to oxen and cattle. Delano probably saved some of his cattle when he observed a notice on the road side saying, "The water here is poison, and we have lost six of our cattle. Do not let your cattle drink on this bottom."[41] At other times the notes described where good water could be found. Bryarly, of the Charlestown Company, along this same dreary stretch, was "attracted by a placard, which on reading, described a delightful spring up a very pretty valley to the left": "Some of our company went to it and found it was what it represented."[42]

The possibilities for sending letters back home diminished after Fort Kearny because there were fewer go-backers, but there were still opportunities. Swain, who was always looking for ways to send letters to his wife, Sabrina, and brother, sent one back to Sabrina June 29 from around Scotts Bluff via a "trading wagon," which Pratt called "a government express" from Fort Laramie.[43] Bruff apparently met the same group July 1 at Ash Hollow.[44] Even farther west, Swain found on the Sweetwater west of the Black Hills "a Yankee [who] turned his wagon around to carry letters back to the States": "The price for transmission of a letter was 50 cents, and the Yankee must have realized a large fortune in a few weeks."[45] Letters,

94

usually notes to friends on other trains behind, were cached at various places with signs labeled "post office." Delano describes one at Courthouse Rock, "a ledge called the Post-office. . . . It was full of water-worn fissures and in one cavity we saw a number of letters deposited, for individuals who were behind."[46]

There was a post office at Fort Laramie. Gray found it when he "step'd into a door near the entrance & found it to be the *Post Office*, put in [his] letter for home & amused [him]self for a few minutes in walking around the inside of the fort."[47] Delano, however, described it as similar to that of the various agents along the trail who collected letters for a fee: "a deposit for letters to be sent to the States, and thousands left letters for the friends, to be deposited by a messenger in some post-office beyond the Missouri, on which the writers paid twenty-five cents."[48] There were certainly problems with using the fort as a post office. When Bruff passed Fort Laramie July 9, the superintendent of the fur trading post informed him that there was a letter waiting for him that had been given to an officer at the fort who was acting as postmaster. Unfortunately, "a man belonging to a Company from Tennessee or Kentucky, had enquired for and obtained it!"[49] But Swain, who never missed a chance to send a letter, wrote to Sabrina July 4 and sent the letter from Fort Laramie; it was eventually delivered. For most of the goldrushers, Fort Laramie was the last chance to send letters.

Fort Laramie was another landmark for the emigrants and, like Fort Kearny, a place to trade, try to sell unwanted supplies, and obtain information. It was more developed than Fort Kearny as it had been purchased from the American Fur Company, which had used it as a trading post since 1834.[50] Delano described it, "simply a trading post, standing about a mile above the ford . . . its neat, white-washed walls presented a welcome sight to us, after being so long from anything like a civilized building."[51] The fort was an opportunity to obtain some kinds of information. Gray, for instance, after he had posted his letters, found some copies of New York City papers and read the names of the "voyageurs" on the walls, some of whom he recognized.[52] The market opportunities were more limited than at Fort Kearny since by now most travelers had enough experience to know what they needed and everyone wanted to sell or to purchase the same things. Geiger of the Charlestown Company commented June 14, "They [the traders at Fort Laramie] were destitute of all articles of trade except jerked buffalo meat," and Swain noted, "tried to buy a horse at the fort, but the prices asked were so extravagant—ranging from $100 to $200—that I gave up the idea." Bruff managed to buy a "small seine" (fishing net) for ten dollars, which he found very useful during the following week.[53]

As a stopping place, the fort had many uses, including as a dumping ground for unwanted equipment and supplies. It was also a workshop for repairs and a place to shorten wagons. Isaac Foster wrote in his diary June 16 (the same day that the Charlestown Company was at the fort), "wagons are left here and many burned . . . trunks, clothes, boots, and shoes, lead by the hundred, spades, picks, and all other fixings for a California trip."[54] Parke's Como Company did not apparently even try to trade at the fort but used the opportunity to shorten their wagons, as did the Charlestown Company. Many companies were encouraged to stop and make repairs because of the presence of a blacksmith and all the spare wagon parts lying around. A common repair requiring a blacksmith was tightening the metal tires that ringed the wooden wagon wheels, which had shrunk with hard use and the dry air.[55]

Although notes and letters were major forms of information dispersal along the trail, rumors and stories that spread among the travelers were probably the single most important type of communication. At times the stories that circulated may have played a role in relaying news, for example rumors of crimes. Elza Armstrong, of the Buckeye Rovers, wrote July 2 along the Sweetwater River, "Yesterday we heard that there had been murder committed by a man by the name of Everette. He had formerly lived in Athens, Ohio. He murdered his partner and threw him in Platte River. We heard he was to be hanged."[56] Armstrong's friend John Banks of the same company elaborated the story in his journal entry for the same day, writing,

> They were traveling with pack mules. Some who had seen them on the road asked him of his friend. He answered he saw him drown in the Platte. They immediately took the rascal prisoner, previously having found the deceased pierced by a bullet. An Illinois train has charge of the prisoner. One report says he will be hung tomorrow at the Pacific Springs [just over South Pass], some thirty-one miles west.[57]

Charles Parke of the Como Company was also on the Sweetwater July 1 and 2 and heard the same story, but as with most of the trail stories, the details differed: "There is a man to be tried for murder tomorrow. Of course 'Judge Lynch' holds the Court out here. I do not know the particulars. The murdered man's name was Read"[58] The incident was big news on this part of the trail as variations of the story were mentioned in several other diaries.[59]

This particular story not only relates how oral communication spreads news,

96

it also provides a way of estimating the geographical reach of oral communications along the trail. The fact that the murder was such big news implies that most diarists who heard about it would have written about it. Bryarly, Geiger, and Delano, however, who were about three days ahead of the Buckeye Rangers and the Como Company, did not mention the story. Neither did Swain, who was three days east of Fort Laramie on July 2, some two weeks behind the Buckeye Rangers, nor Bruff, who was even farther back near Chimney Rock on the Platte on July 2. If one assumes that the murder took place on the Platte River, as the stories indicated, we can conjecture from this example that the reach of the trail communications in this area was in the order of two to three days going forward on the trail (where Bryarly, Geiger, and Delano were when Armstrong and Banks wrote about it) and probably longer going back due to go-backers, but not as long as two weeks.

Crossing South Pass was a major event on the trip, although it was a disappointing landmark. It was about the halfway point, but more important to the travelers was the fact that they had crossed the continental divide. Swain remarked, "we have looked forward to this pass with anxiety for weeks, as the spot where half our toils would be over," but Delano was disappointed in the scenery: "the ascent is so gradual that the culminating point is a matter of doubt." Banks wrote, "A short time after we left we heard men cheering; we were through the pass! Until now the waters on which we camp and those that pass my home mingle in one common flood as they roll toward the Atlantic; here they seek the Pacific's tide."[60] The first water that they came to after crossing the pass was named the Pacific Spring. The various companies we have been following reached the pass at very different times, and their order would become important as they received information about the alternatives ahead. Leading the pack of our travelers was Bryarly and Geiger's Charlestown Company and Delano's Dayton Company, both of which reached the pass June 29 (although neither mentions the other). Not too far behind were Parke's Como Company (July 3) and Banks and Armstrong's Buckeye Rovers (July 6). Due to their late starts, Swain's Wolverine Rangers and Bruff's Washington Company did not reach the pass until August 1.

## West of South Pass: Making Choices
On the western half of the trip the difficulties and dangers multiplied, and there were many decisions to be made concerning alternate routes. To make matters worse, the travelers had less information about the routes in the west than they did

about the east, and the information carried by the emigrants became less useful. Also, the difficulties of the trip changed as well as increasing substantially, so their trail experience was a less useful guide in assessing new information when it became available. For the first time, the emigrants could get lost, starve, and be seriously harassed by Indians. These difficulties led to increased intercompany communications and information sharing. Every fork in the trails, places where alternative routes recombined, and the one city they could pass through (Salt Lake) became communications and information nodes of an informal network spread over thousands of miles.

The geography of the western half of the trip, as the goldrushers knew it, played an important role in how they obtained and assessed information concerning the trail. None of the guidebooks included all of the alternative trails in the West, and some of the most popular, for example—those of Robinson, Foster, Clayton, and Frémont, 1845—did not show even one route all the way to California. Hastings, Bryant, and T. H. Jefferson, who did describe a complete path to California, included only the discredited Hastings Cutoff among the alternatives. Only Ware described the full California Trail, including one of the major cutoffs in use in 1849 (the Sublette Cutoff). Four of the most popular cutoffs were only opened for wagons in 1848 or 1849 and could not have been included in the guidebooks or the published maps available to the goldrushers.[61] The best map available to the goldrushers in 1849 was Frémont-Preuss, 1848, and it showed none of these cutoffs; the part of this map that showed the relevant areas of the trail is shown in figure 3.[62] The emigrants' routes in the West can be followed better on maps 3 and 4, which are drawn from modern United States Geographical Survey topographical maps and which trace the various routes and cutoffs.

The first major choice had to be made soon after South Pass; this was whether or not to go to Salt Lake City (via the South Pass to Salt Lake Trail) or to take the first major cutoff, which they called the Sublette Cutoff (see map 3). The information most emigrants had about the Salt Lake route, through Weber Canyon, was from Hastings and Bryant in 1846, and both described it as very difficult. But by 1849 the Mormons had revised the Hastings route and greatly improved the road, which was described in Clayton. If they went to Salt Lake, the emigrants could recuperate in a town and get more immediate information about the rest of the trip. From Salt Lake there were three main routes: the now-infamous Hastings Cutoff south of the lake, which few goldrushers took; the Fort Hall road, which rejoined the Oregon Trail; and a new cutoff, called the Salt Lake Cutoff, which

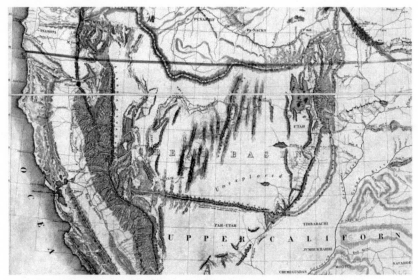

Figure 3. Detail from Frémont's Map of Oregon and Upper California, 1848. Courtesy Library of Congress Prints and Photographs Division, cat. #G4210 1848. F74.

crossed north of the lake and which was taken by most travelers (see map 3). If one chose the Sublette Cutoff, the trail went west from South Pass to the Bear River, where it joined the old Oregon Trail to Fort Hall. A few miles north from where these trails met, emigrants had to decide whether to go on to Fort Hall, seemingly farther north than necessary, or take another new cutoff, about which goldrushers had no information, called the Hudspeth Cutoff. All of the routes except for the Hastings Cutoff joined on the way to the Humboldt River near what was, and is, known as the City of Rocks, and then intersected the Humboldt near the present-day town of Wells, Nevada.

Difficulties compounded along the Humboldt River, over the desert, and over the Sierras. Almost all the goldrushers knew that the desert and the mountains were the most difficult parts of their journey and knew what had happened to the Donner party just three years previously. All the guidebooks in 1849 told of an easy trip along the river but a terrible route across forty miles of desert from the Humboldt Sink to the Truckee River (near present-day Reno, Nevada) and then over the Donner Pass (see map 4). New information goldrushers obtained along the Humboldt, however, complicated their decisions: first, that the Carson Pass to the south (see map 4) had been traveled by Mormons in 1848 with wagons, and then that there was a route to the north that used part of an alternative trail to Oregon and then hooked south through California to the gold fields by way of

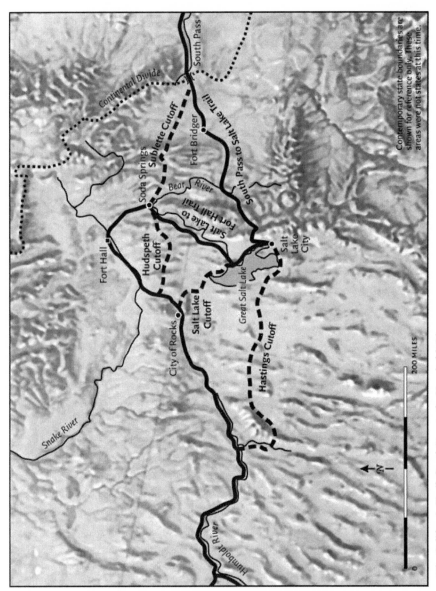

3. The California Trail: South Pass to the Humboldt River

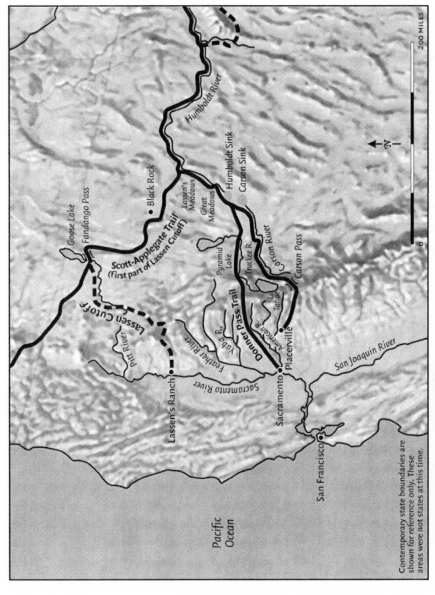

Pacific
Ocean

San Francisco

Sacramento
Placerville

Lassen's Ranch

Pitt River

Feather River

Sacramento River

Yuba R.

American R.

San Joaquin River

Goose Lake
Fandango Pass

Black Rock

Scott-Applegate Trail
(first part of Lassen Cutoff)

Lassen Cutoff

Lassen's
Meadows

Great
Meadows

Pyramid
Lake

Truckee R.

Tahoe

Donner Pass Trail

Humboldt River

Humboldt Sink
Carson Sink

Carson River

Carson Pass

N

0        200 MILES

Contemporary state boundaries are
shown for reference only. These
areas were not states at this time.

4. The California Trail: Humboldt River to the Pacific Ocean

Peter Lassen's ranch on the Sacramento River (Lassen Cutoff, map 4). In fact, the Carson Pass was easier and about the same length as the Donner Pass, although still extremely difficult, and the Lassen Cutoff was about 150 miles longer and more difficult than either of the Sierra passes.

The following subsections describe in more detail the various cutoffs, the choices made by the companies we have been following, and the information available to them to help them make these choices.

## The Sublette Cutoff

Their first major decision point was whether to take the Sublette Cutoff or continue on the old California Trail, either to Fort Hall or to Salt Lake City. This was the easiest of their decisions because most goldrushers carried information that they considered reliable on each of the alternatives. The cutoff had been known for several years, and Ware described it as an alternative route on the California Trail.[63] Clayton described very well the route to Salt Lake City. Many of the travelers seemed to have made up their minds which way to go based on which guidebook they were following. Staples, of the Boston-Newton Company, clearly following Clayton, went to Salt Lake and did not even mention the Sublette in his diary; Parke, on the other hand, who mentioned Ware in his diary, took the cutoff without a mention of the possibility of going to Salt Lake.[64] Not everyone, however, was so sure of himself. Charles Gray of the Newark Overland Company spent the night of July 1 on the Pacific side of the pass spreading "out [his] blankets & on them studied for about 2 hours several large maps of [their] route & destination." They decided to go to Salt Lake and found "but little travel by this route, probably 7 out of 10 going via 'Sublette's cut off' . . . which . . . they will regret."[65] Gray was double checking using the printed information he carried with him, and probably many others did the same. Up to this point, the guidebooks and maps proved reasonably complete and accurate.

The Sublette Cutoff, however, held a surprise that may have started many goldrushers questioning their printed information sources in a way they had not done before. The cutoff began with a waterless thirty-five-mile stretch between the Big Sandy River and the Green River. Ware wrote, "By starting from the Sandy at the cool of the day, you can get across easily by morning."[66] Some groups, like the Buckeye Rovers, who got to the Big Sandy July 8 and took Ware's advice, recruited their cattle and left for the desert in the evening. Armstrong, who recorded the trip of the Rovers, barely mentioned the crossing in his diary, although he did note the distance was forty miles.[67] Others, however, like Parke's Como Company, who crossed the same day as Armstrong, had a difficult time and measured the distance as fifty miles. He said Ware had made "a grand mistake"; the distance mattered.

> The first 25 miles were of the prettiest kind . . . the western 25 miles made up in vileness. . . . We saw quantities of dead cattle strewn along the road-side, caused no doubt from the excessive dust and fatigue. No wonder, just think of the poor dumb beast dragging these heavy wagons all night and nearly all the following day 50 miles without a particle of food or water through alkaline dust that took all the skin off my lips.[68]

Delano, who was even earlier, July 1, measured the distance as fifty miles, and also had a hard crossing.[69] It is interesting that Ware got this distance wrong since in compiling his guidebook he consulted with Solomon Sublette, William Sublette's brother, who was the mountain man and fur trader for whom the cutoff was named. This was, indeed, one of the points that Ware advertised in selling his guidebook. James Davis speculates that the printer transposed the numbers (35 for 53).[70]

When Swain and Bruff came to the cutoff (a month later, both on August 4), they found many signs at the forks on "a stick driven in the ground with a board nailed on it, plastered with notices." The signs did not help, however, because they were mainly notices that particular companies took one route or another; they did not mention the mileage since the companies would not have known it at the beginning of the cutoff.[71] At this stage of the journey, there were few or no go-backers, so news did not travel as far backwards along this part of the trail as it did along the Platte River.

### The Salt Lake Cutoff and the Carson Pass

The complex stories of the Salt Lake Cutoff and the Carson Pass illustrate well the ways that various cutoffs were created; they also provide descriptions of how handwritten and oral information about these cutoffs was produced and circulated among the goldrushers.

Those who did not take the Sublette Cutoff went to Salt Lake, generally following Clayton's guide. The attraction of the route was that in Salt Lake City one could rest (perhaps in a bed); get decent food; trade, sell, or purchase needed items; and generally regroup before heading onto what everyone knew would be the most difficult part of the journey. These advantages were aggressively advertised by Mormons who ran ferries or trading posts and by signs on the trail. Some of the goldrushers, indeed, thought that the Saints followed "an established policy of luring as many travelers as possible through the valley."[72] Of our groups, Gray and the Como Company turned south from the Big Sandy River on July 1, and considerably later, on July 28, Staples and the Boston-Newton Company turned toward Salt Lake.[73] They were both using Clayton's guide as is evident from the place names and the mileages in their journals, and they avoided the nearly impossible Weber Canyon Trail that Bryant wrote about. In a wonderful understatement Clayton describes the new route: "Pratt's Pass, to avoid the Kanyon [*sic*]: The Kanyon is a few miles below, where the river runs between high mountains of rock. Some emigrants have passed through, but it is dangerous."[74]

The problem for the Salt Lake travelers was that before they got to the city they had little information they could trust on the route west of Salt Lake. The Hastings route was well described by Frémont, Hastings, Bryant, and Jefferson but was discredited for good reasons by the Donner story. A new route existed, on a trail blazed the previous year by a pack mule party going from Salt Lake City to California led by Maj. Samuel J. Hensley. The Hensley party went north of the Salt Lake and then cut west to the City of Rocks, where they intersected the California Trail coming south from Fort Hall. This route became the Salt Lake Cutoff. Continuing to California along the Humboldt, they met a wagon train led by Samuel Thompson, composed of members of the disbanded Mormon Battalion that was at that time coming east to Salt Lake from California. Hensley gave Thompson a way bill of the trail they had just taken from Salt Lake. He told Thompson that it would save eight to ten days.[75] Two days later the Thompson party met another group traveling west, led by Joseph Chiles, and gave them a copy of the waybill. The Thompson party took the Hensley route, which they found acceptable for wagons.[76] Ira J. Willis, an enterprising member of the Thompson party, wrote by hand a waybill of the route all the way to California, including the Salt Lake Cutoff. Irene Paden speculates that copying the guide became a sort of cottage industry in Salt Lake as the Mormons realized its value to the large number of emigrants passing through the city.[77] Handwritten copies of the guidebook were sold to goldrushers along the trail and in the city, and became, along with word of mouth, the primary source of information about the cutoff.

There are still unanswered questions concerning how information about the cutoff circulated among the goldrushers. As many as ten thousand goldrushers detoured through Salt Lake City, so it seems unlikely that they would not have had some idea that they found credible about the route west from the city; it is not clear, however, what their sources of information were. No journal that I am aware of mentions the Ira J. Willis guidebook east of Salt Lake City, although there are many references to the guidebook on the trail to the west both by emigrants who took the cutoff and some who did not.[78]

There may have been several handwritten guidebooks sold by the Mormons. David Staples, of the Boston-Newton Company, who went through Salt Lake and took the cutoff, mentioned mileage on the cutoff "according to our guide book," and then goes on to write, "The distance from the City is stated to be 75 miles by some of the guide books, others at 80." It is not clear where Staples obtained these "guidebooks." Perhaps they were sold by the Mormons whom the emigrants encountered at the ferries and trading posts who advertised the advantages of going through Salt Lake. Just before reaching Fort Bridger, Staples mentions meeting a "Mormon Express going back to the states," which informed them "that considerable of the *gold* from *Cal* had arrived at the settlement [Salt Lake]." They were told they "could get vegetables etc. at the Salt Lake."[79] He may also have obtained guidebooks or other route information from them, although he does not mention it in his diary. When Staples and others from the Boston-Newton Company reached Salt Lake City, they "looked about the city for information respecting the wisest way to finish [their] trip."[80] They certainly went to the right place because that evening (August 8): they had dinner with "*Mr. Ira J. Willis*, one of the Mormon battalion who was in *Cal* on the discovery of gold." Gray and the Como Company spent four days in Salt Lake City, resting and repairing their wagons; they must have also obtained information about the cutoff because they also took it and reached the intersection with the Fort Hall road in nine days.

The Thompson wagon train of the Mormon Battalion in 1848, the Chiles wagon train, and the Willis guidebook, played another important role in the information production and dissemination for the gold rush. This concerned the Carson Pass over the Sierras. When Thompson, Bigler, and Willis decided to leave the "Mormon Bar," they decided to "pioneer out a route across the Sierra Nevada and if possible find a nearer way than to go the truckey [*sic*] route [Donner Pass]."[81] They blazed a wagon trail over the Carson Pass (see map 4).

When they met the Chiles party going west, they told them about the new route over the Sierras. Chiles decided to take the new pass over the mountains but also look for another cutoff that would shorten the route from the Humboldt River to the Carson River. Chiles's group succeeded in this, and it became part of the Carson Pass trail over the Sierras. Chiles, however, did not write a guidebook or map that anyone mentions, and the Willis guide is the only written description in 1849, poor as it is, of the Carson Pass. Since Willis did not know the Chiles Cutoff, it was not described in his guidebook. The information concerning the Chiles Cutoff, which became the primary route for those taking the Carson Pass over the Sierras in 1849, must have spread primarily through word of mouth.

### The Hudspeth Cutoff

Far to the east, on the Big Sandy River, most of the emigrants took the Sublette Cutoff and did not have to deal with the uncertain information about the Salt Lake Cutoff. After they crossed Sublette's, however, and regained the old Oregon-California Trail, they had their own decision to make with no written information. This was whether or not to take the Hudspeth Cutoff. This trail was blazed beginning July 19, 1849, by a gold rush company from Jackson County, Missouri, led by Benoni Hudspeth and John J. Myers. These were two experienced mountain men, who decided they could save some fifty miles by not going up to Fort Hall on the old Oregon Trail; they would go southwest from Soda Springs (roughly where the cutoff began, see map 3). If one looks at the Frémont 1848 map (figure 3), it is clear what they were thinking. This area, however, was unexplored at that time, and there is no evidence that either of the mountain men had been on that route before. They simply relied on their mountain skills to get their large (seventy wagons) train through.[82]

Most of the goldrushers who did not go to Salt Lake, and who got to Soda Springs after July 19, took the cutoff although it meant striking out into the unknown. Parke's Como Company reached Soda Springs, the same time as did Myers and Hudspeth, and they followed them, with only this comment: "We left the main road at the bend of the river and bore off to the S.W. following Myers and Hudspeth. The former was a mountain guide, the latter captain of the company—Missouri company. Both have been through to California before."[83] Niles Searls wrote upon taking the cutoff August 2, 1849, "The road having been opened this season, no written mark describes it and no one has returned to tell of its peculiarities."[84] Within a few weeks there was handwritten commentary on the cutoff; E. D. Perkins wrote, "there were at the forks innumerable notes and cards stuck up for the benefit of the various companies behind. Several . . . stated that 'by this cut-off it is only 100 miles to the Humboldt River.'"[85] Like so many of these signs, that was a severe understatement. Bruff's Washington Company voted to take the cutoff because of "reliable information, that it was a good road, and much shorter & better than by the way of Fort Hall." Bruff, however, decided he would go to Fort Hall "to see the mountaineers there for information about the travel after crossing the pass in the Sierra Nevada," and would catch up with his company near the Humboldt. He did not in fact believe the cutoff saved much time, and when he rejoined his company, he compared his mileage to that of his wagons—132 for the cutoff and 134 for the Fort Hall route.[86]

The behavior of the emigrants at the Hudspeth Cutoff was another indication that the travelers were reassessing their printed information and that the way they considered information sources had changed. Although the major guide-books and maps had been reasonably good guides so far, with the exception of Ware's description of the desert beginning the Sublette Cutoff, they were willing to leave the trails of the guidebooks and follow signs and rumors into the unknown. Similar signs and rumors in the eastern half of the trip, for instance stories of Indian depredations, had been received with a great deal of skepticism. The cutoff, however, appeared to make sense if one checked it out on the Frémont map, as Staples did on the Sublette Cutoff, so perhaps there was still some reliance on the printed information. Still, there was a change in how they assessed the information. They were willing to believe from word of mouth that the men who led the first wagon train that took the cutoff had local experience and expertise. The goldrushers were lucky on the Hudspeth Cutoff; Myers and Hudspeth had found a relatively safe route through mountains and came out at least not worse off than if they had followed the old trail. They would not be so lucky on their next major choice, the Lassen Cutoff, where many followed the same two mountain men on a disastrous journey taking about a month longer than the old trails.

### The Humboldt

The trail along the Humboldt River was hard but the descriptions in the travelers' guidebooks indicated that it would be easy.[87] Bryant, writing about his trip in 1846 when, as compared to 1849, there was more rain and a small fraction of travelers along the river, described "proceeding down the river about two miles

. . . in a handsome bottom of green nutritious grass, which the mules cropped with an apparent high relish."[88] Ware, taking his cue from Bryant, wrote of the Humboldt, "its own valley is rich and beautifully clothed with blue grass, herds grass, clover, and other nutritious grasses."[89] Many goldrushers, however, found little grass. Charles Gould, for instance, on September 9 along the Humboldt, "had the misfortune to find none but the poor grass for [their] animals," and again on the next day "had the bad luck to find a poor camping ground, the grass for miles being eaten closely to the ground."[90] Some emigrants blamed Ware explicitly, such as Bennett Clark: "We all began to be greatly disappointed in our calculation of finding good grass on the Humboldt as Mr. Ware had prepared us to expect," while others wrote of "the elegant & imaginative Mr. Bryant," and all the "scribbling asses" who told of "Nutricious grasses." Some of the emigrants renamed the river, the Hellboldt, and others the Humbug.[91]

Although many travelers felt they had reason to mistrust their guidebooks about the river, they were all sure of the terrors of the sink and the desert beyond. Bryant describes the trip through the sink:

> our mules waded through these hills, on heaps of dry and ashy earth, rather than walked over them, sinking in many places nearly to the bellies . . . the plain is utterly destitute of vegetation . . . the sable and utterly sterile mountains, the barren and arid plain, incapable of sustaining either insect or animal, present a dreariness of scenery that would be almost overpowering.[92]

The goldrushers who traveled the Humboldt in the second half of August met a wagon train of Mormons going west to east returning to Salt Lake City from the gold fields.[93] They had three messages for the westbound travelers: one, that the desert past the sink was terrible and should be traveled in one stretch as much at night as possible, but that there was a good camping ground, the "Great Meadow," before the sink in which to prepare;[94] two, that there was a terrible journey over forty miles of desert whether one took the Carson or the Truckee routes; and three, above all, that they should stick to the beaten path and not take the "northern cutoff" (the Lassen Cutoff). For those who did not take the Lassen route, the Great Meadow was not only a place of recruitment and preparation for the desert crossing, it was a place for exchanging information, particularly about preparing for the desert and the mountains, learning about the new Carson River route, and deciding which way to go. Bryarly described it well:

We corralled on a beautiful smooth spot with grass six or eight inches . . .
two hundred yards in front the water from the marsh around collected in
a stream & several feet into a pool . . . the grass between our corall [*sic*] &
this [pool] was knee high & the ground dry, & our animals were in view
the whole time. . . . This marsh for three miles is certainly the liveliest place
that one could witness in a lifetime. There is some two hundred and fifty
wagons here all the time. Trains going out & others coming in & taking
their places is the constant order of the day.[95]

Whether they took the Truckee or the Carson route, the traveling was hard,
but most of the emigrants appeared to know what to expect and described the
desert much as Bryant had.[96] The word must have spread, probably at Great
Meadow, that the Chiles Cutoff to the Carson was the way to go because, in spite
of the Willis guide, that was the road chosen by all those who took the Carson
route. In spite of the hardships and a great loss of stock, there were few deaths
of travelers on either the Truckee or the Carson passes; the trip took about two
to three weeks.

### The Lassen Cutoff: Seeing the Elephant

On August 10, 1849, Alonzo Delano's Dayton Company was about ninety miles
north and east of the Great Meadows when "reports began to reach [them] of
hard roads ahead; that there was no grass at the Sink . . . and that from that place a
desert of sand, with water but once in forty-five miles had to be crossed."[97] Those
reports included "an indefinite tale . . . that a new road had been discovered, by
which the Sacramento might be reached in a shorter distance, avoiding altogether
the dreaded desert, and that there was plenty of grass and water on the route"[98]
A few days later, Delano and a Mr. Fredenburgh, also of the Dayton Company,
visited a "Lieutenant Thompson, of the Navy, who had been in California, and
who had once made a trip overland to the States": "As it was an object to avoid the
desert spoken of, we thought it worth while to gain all the intelligence possible on
the matter." The lieutenant, although he could not have known, confirmed "that
there was a good road leading into the upper part of the valley somewhere; that
the desert would be avoided, and that grass and water were plenty."[99] Rumors
kept flying, and it was clearly a major topic of discussion within and among the
companies. They were fairly sure that at least one train, said to be led by a Mr.
McGee who had lived in California left on the new route August 11. Four days later,

Delano and the Dayton Company also left on that route without even taking on extra water and feed: "we had been assured that there was grass and water on the way." Within a few days of the Dayton Company leaving on the cutoff, the large Missouri train led by Myers and Hudspeth, also turned off on the cutoff.[100]

As many as nine thousand emigrants followed Myers and Hudspeth west and then north into what was, from the point of view of their guidebooks and maps, unknown territory. Myers, in particular, had a reputation as a knowledgeable mountain man who had been there before and knew the route. These two had just led most of the emigration over the Hudspeth Cutoff, another journey into the unknown that had come out all right; also, there was a growing distrust of the guidebooks because of what they felt was the misleading information concerning the Humboldt River. At least one person, apparently, went to see for himself because Delano reported on August 16, "A man on horseback reported that he had rode thirty miles out on the route; that in ten miles there was grass, in twelve grass and water, and in twenty, grass and water in abundance."[101] On August 18, the Newark Company "rec'd some information that [they] were only about 150 miles from 'the diggings'—if [they] took a certain cut off to 'the North.'" The next day, the day before Myers and Hudspeth are estimated to have turned off on the cutoff, Charles Gray of the Newark Company held "a council of War" to decide whether they should follow "the 'cut off' to the North." On August 21, they headed out on a "great drive of *about 70 miles over a desert, without grass or water.*"[102] Soon after the Newark Company took the cutoff, Armstrong and Banks of the Buckeye Rovers would "hear of a cutoff leading to Feather River, a distance of one hundred forty-six miles. Many wagons gone, some seven hundred. Hedgepath [*sic*] first opened it," adding, "No grass for the first sixty miles, a very serious difficulty . . . saw the road to the right, determined not to take it."[103] Three weeks later, Swain put a name to the cutoff and wrote about it in more detail than the earlier travelers: "The captain decided to take Lawson's pass through the mountains, which leads us into the upper part of the Sacramento valley by a gradual ascent like the South Pass. The valley is less than two hundred miles from here . . . but there is seventy miles of road without feed."[104] Bruff and his Washington Company, still the laggards of our groups, took the cutoff a few days after Swain, on September 19. Bruff is a special case among our goldrushers because he knew of the trail before leaving Washington DC and discussed the cutoff with his company almost two weeks earlier.[105]

The cutoff existed on no map nor is it mentioned in any guidebook of the time, but the goldrushers had informal written information in the form of signs and notes at the fork in the trail. The earliest travelers on the route, Delano and Gray, both just days behind Myers and Hudspeth, did not mention notes at the forks, but several days later, Elisha Perkins wrote, "At 4 this afternoon we made the cutoff to Feather River where were put up innumerable notices & letters speaking pro & con of the right hand or left hand roads while reading or trying to read half of them the Pioneers came up to discuss future action."[106] By August 25, when the Buckeye Rovers passed the fork, they noted, "A host of notes left here for friends; lines on cards and boards, all open for general inspection. Matter? Why, taking this or that road, state of health, condition of cattle, and company."[107] One note at the forks said "only 110 miles to the diggings."[108] By September 19, Bruff got to the fork:

> A broad and perfectly level semi-circular area, very dusty, sweeps around the bend—and the two trails, or roads, are broad and as well beaten as any traveled thoroughfare can be. On the right, about a hundred yds. from the Bend, the Desert route branches off, and in the forks of the road, I observed a red painted barrel standing—I rode up, to examine it—It was a nice new barrel, about the size of a whisky-barrel, iron hoops, and a square hole cut in the head; and neatly painted in black block letters, upon it, 'POST OFFICE.' On looking in, I found it half-full of letters, notes, notices, &c.—Near this was a stick and bill-board, also filled with notices. . . . I inscribed a card and left, here, *for the benefit of all whom it might concern.*[109]

Much of the information about the new cutoff concerned the distance and the location of water and grass, probably the two most important concerns of the travelers. The major thrusts of the rumors and notes were that the Feather River, the Sacramento Valley, or the diggings, were about 150 miles away and that, after a desert of 35 to 70 miles, grass and water were good. Swain apparently heard another report, although he does not say from where, of "a middle pass" that would take them over the mountains in a week.[110] On September 22, about three days from the forks, when Swain observed they were traveling north, instead of west as he expected, he wrote, "We found no left-hand [middle] route, although we were twenty-five miles past the point where we expected to find one."[111] Were there other rumors of another pass, which would have actually cut off many miles to the Feather River and the gold fields? Such a pass did exist, but was not opened for three more years.[112] Another possibility is that Swain was looking at Frémont's 1848 map (figure 3) and decided that if the Feather River and the gold fields were only 100-150 miles away, there had to be a route striking west from the middle of the desert.

Although the cutoff was a blank part of the Frémont map, the scale of the map showed that, without the "middle route," the cutoff would have to be at least 150 miles northwest and then another 200 miles back south and west in California. Gray, always double checking, noticed on August 18 the discrepancy between his map and the rumors and notes when they "rec'd some information" that the diggings were only 150 miles from the fork: "I however, who had studied the maps well, didn't believe it & and would be glad to get off at 350."[113] The distance from the fork to the gold fields over the Donner or Carson passes, as one could estimate from the guidebooks and maps they carried, was about 200 miles.[114] A major indicator that goldrushers had lost faith in their printed information is that Gray and the Newark Company took the Lassen route anyway.

The reality was very different than the rumors and notes at the fork. The actual distance was about 180 miles from the fork to Goose Lake in California, where the trail turned south towards the gold fields, and then another 230 miles to Lassen's Ranch (see map 4). The first part of the trail, going northwest to what is now the northeast corner of California, should have been known to people who had been there before like McGee, Myers, and Hudspeth. The half of the Lassen Cutoff on the eastern side of the Sierras, had been open for several years. Levi Scott and Jesse Applegate in 1846 explored this part of the trail while trying to find an alternative route to Oregon that bypassed the Cascades. The Scott-Applegate party was going north to south (coming from Oregon) and almost did not make it due to starvation, sickness, and Indian harassment.[115]

The trail was publicized by Applegate in 1847, the year Scott led a company of between forty-five to eighty wagons over the new route to Oregon. Applegate published a waybill in the April 6, 1848, *Oregon Spectator* that described the route from Fort Hall all the way to the Willamette Valley in Oregon, including the difficult part from the Humboldt River to Goose Lake. The waybill showed the distance from the fork to the summit of the pass of the Sierras to be 150 miles. In addition to good geographic directions, his waybill gave good advice, such as "emigrants should send a party 2 to 3 days in advance to dig out large reservoirs for the water at the springs [Rabbit Hole springs, about 35 miles from the fork] by which means water may be had for their animals."[116] The failure to follow this advice, either because they never heard it or read it or because rumors and notes indicated it was unnecessary, caused great problems for many goldrushers. The waybill also described other difficult passages including the Black Rock Desert and High Rock Canyon. An indication of harshness of this terrain is that even in the twenty-first century there are no paved roads in this area of northwestern Nevada, and trail organizations will not mount expeditions on this part of the trail except in caravans of four-wheel drive vehicles.[117]

Goldrushers suffered on the Scott-Applegate Trail, which, although rugged, was probably not that much worse than some of the territory they had traversed. The problem came from the misinformation about the distance, water, and grass. Far from taking Applegate's good advice, had they known it, Delano's Dayton Company "did not think it necessary to provide against these contingencies [not finding grass or water] any further than filling a small vinegar keg with water."[118] Well ahead of the pack, they got to Rabbit Hole Springs August 16 but "found the promised springs to be only three or four wells sunk in the ground, into which the water percolated in a volume about size of a straw." More than a month later (September 22), when the Wolverine Rangers reached the springs, the scene was worse: "To add to the natural horrors of the scene, about the wells were scattered the bodies of cattle, horses, and mules, which had died here from overwork, hunger, and thirst."[119] Bruff elaborated: "in one [spring] was a dead ox—swelled up so as to fill the hole closely—his hind-legs and tail only above ground."[120] The next water was a set of hot springs twenty miles farther across an alkaline plane, the Black Rock Desert, which "look[ed] like a vast field of ice . . . cover'd with a smooth white encrustation."[121] On the desert, Swain found "wagons and carts were scattered on all sides, and the stench of dead and decaying cattle actually rendered the air sickening."[122] The desert's name was taken from a volcanic monolith at the base of which were several hot springs, which the travelers called the "Great Boiling Springs." The water was fine after being cooled, and most companies recruited there. Another two days travel, about forty miles, brought them to High Rock Canyon, a gorge where "the sides, which rose perpendicular to the height of five hundred feet, stood in massive towers between which openings ran up to the back hills."[123] The rest of the way to the pass was long but not extraordinarily difficult. The pass (now called Fandango Pass) was easy compared to the Donner or Carson passes. Most of the goldrushers had been on the cutoff for over two weeks and felt they had truly seen the elephant; they also thought their trip was almost over.

The travelers were finally in California, but their problems got worse. Although this trail was not more difficult than many they had traversed, it was a long 230-mile trek south and west through a great deal of mountainous forested terrain, and there was little food for people or grass for stock. It was getting late in the year, October for most of the travelers. Snow was beginning to fall, provisions were running out, and, at the end of the 2,000-mile trip, so was endurance. Those who went through early, like Delano and Gray, were better off because they did not have to deal with snow. They had to deal with dying stock, however, because of the lack of grass and cattle being taken by Indians, therefore causing them to have to continue on foot. Even the early goldrushers ran out of provisions. About 20 miles from Lassen's Ranch, on October 1, Gray said, "[I] saw many travelers on foot today to 3 of whom I gave dinner, and they were entirely destitute—no money—no meat—no bread—no nothing. God only knows what will become of many such."[124] A month later, when Swain and Bruff reached the California side of the cutoff, the situation was truly desperate for most of the travelers, as described by Joseph Middleton in late October: "Many emigrants killed their own teams as a last and only resort to avoid a visit from that lank, lean, old monster, Starvation. . . . Many emigrants were afflicted with scurvy—swelled, blotched legs and ankles, and stiff joints."[125] If it were not for government relief expeditions, it is likely that hundreds of emigrants would have starved.[126]

Bruff's Washington Company reached Goose Lake October 4, and found "on [a] bank of [the] stream stood an oak tree, on which was nailed a board, with a neatly written card on it, for the information of the emigrants," a waybill with locations and mileages to "Lassin's house" and then on to Sutter's Fort and to "Sn Francisco." The distance to Lassen's Ranch was written as 228 miles. It was signed by Lt. R. S. Williamson, who was with a U.S. Army team that had been scouting other routes over the Sierras to California.[127] Like most of the other goldrushers, the Washington Company fell short of provisions and lost animals; on October 17, they had about six days' rations, which they divided among themselves, and by October 21 only 37 miles from Lassen's Ranch, only two wagons were operable.[128] At this point the company decided to pack to Lassen's Ranch. Bruff volunteered to camp guarding the company's wagons and common property, and the others promised to return to his camp with fresh animals. They did not return mid-October and Bruff was getting worried; he wrote in his diary, "I cannot abandon my notes and drawings, instruments &c . . . and have no means of getting them in, unless I can procure some animals from the Settlements."[129] He passed up several opportunities to go to Lassen's without his wagons until the weather, his health, and his general situation deteriorated, and he could not get out. He transferred to a cabin in early January and finally walked out in April 1850.

The Wolverine Rangers were at this time almost two weeks behind Bruff and did not mount Fandango Pass until October 13. There they found the government relief team and were told that the distance to Lassen's was "219 miles over considerable bad roads and one desert of forty miles."[130] They decided to dissolve the company and divide the common property. Some packed and some, including Swain, continued with their wagons. By November 3, when they were still about 50 miles from Lassen's, the weather turned worse and after a hard night, "daylight dawned on the lifeless carcasses of sixteen of [their] oxen . . . fallen by the chilling blasts of the merciless storm."[131] They had to break up the wagons and pack; by November 6, they trudged through ten inches of snow. They reached Lassen's on November 8.

Unlike the Scott-Applegate Trail (the Nevada side of the Lassen Cutoff), there was nothing published about the California side of the cutoff. Various routes through northern California had been known for years, however, and had a rather colorful history. In 1843, Joseph B. Chiles, of the Chiles Cutoff to the Carson Pass, led a group on horseback from Fort Hall on a roundabout route to Goose Lake in California. The group included Samuel J. Hensley, John J. Myers, and Milton McGee.[132] From Goose Lake south they traversed territory unknown by European Americans until then; it was essentially what became the Lassen route on the California side. About the time Chiles was coming down the Sacramento River, a Danish immigrant to Mexican California, Peter Lassen, applied for a grant of land along the Sacramento at Deer Creek (see map 4).[133] In December, 1844, he became a Mexican citizen and received the land, where he established a ranch and built a blacksmith shop and a sawmill. In 1846 John Frémont stayed at Lassen's Ranch before exploring a route north to Oregon. Frémont reached Klamath Lake in Oregon when he was overtaken by a Lieutenant Gillespie who summoned him back to California.[134] Lassen probably went with Gillespie, and thus had direct knowledge of the northern California trails. He returned to Missouri in 1847 in a party with Myers and Chiles, and with at least one local Indian, in order to lead a wagon train the following year over the Scott-Applegate and Lassen routes.[135]

In the spring of 1848, Lassen led a train of ten wagons west from Missouri over the Scott-Applegate Trail and down into the mountains of northern California, where he got lost. Lassen missed Chiles's trail, which was by now five years old, and by October they were in desperate straits. Meanwhile, Peter Burnett, later governor of California, was leading a large wagon train south on the Oregon part of the Scott-Applegate Trail to the gold fields through territory that had never been traversed by wagons.[136] South of Goose Lake they came across Lassen's wagon tracks and followed them, overtaking Lassen's wandering train on October 21. Burnett described the Lassen party as on its last legs: "One half of the party became so incensed against Lassen that his life was in great danger. . . . They were, indeed objects of pity. I never saw people so worn down and so emaciated as these poor immigrants."[137] The Burnett party, with the Lassen party, worked their way to the Lassen's Ranch, improving the trail as they went.[138] Once back at his ranch, Lassen apparently wrote a "report" of the expedition that endorsed him as a guide and sent it east to advertise his route.[139]

There are many unanswered questions concerning the Lassen Cutoff. With the publicizing of the Scott-Applegate route and the flurry of activity in 1848 on the California side of the cutoff, why did the goldrushers have such misleading information about the route? Did any of the emigrants know of Lassen's "report?" How did such precise mileage figures get onto the signs and notes posted at the fork of the trail along the Humboldt? Was there another guidebook, or at least some written information, about the route other than the signs and notes? What was Swain's "middle route?" There are no clear answers to these questions, but there are some tantalizing hints from which one can make some reasonable guesses.

The balance of the evidence is that there was information additional to the signs and notes but that it was not written nor uniformly disbursed. This information could not have been assessed in any informed manner by the emigrants. John Unruh asserts that Lassen hired agents to plant signposts and advertise the route but gives no evidence.[140] This seems unlikely, however, because Lassen's name is not connected with the cutoff until quite late, in September. More likely Myers, and probably Hudspeth and McGee, were the sources of the wrong information.

There is evidence that Myers, at least, had a special interest in "selling" the Lassen Cutoff. Before leaving Washington, Bruff found and copied a letter from John Myers to the adjutant general's office in Washington, a sort of job application, in which Myers asserted

> that by the Head of the Sacramento is by far the best Rout through the Mountain [the Sierras] and can be passed in any Season. that leaving Marys

116

River [the Humbolt] about one hundred miles above its sink whare the Suthern road to Oregon now leaves it travel on that road to the Head of the Sacramento which is not over one hundred and fifty miles from the main Valley."[141]

The letter is important not because of what it told Bruff, who was at the back of the pack and could not have informed most of the travelers; it indicates, rather, what Myers thought and probably told others on the trail. It is likely to have been the source of the rumor that it was 150 miles to "the head of the Sacramento" and that was interpreted as being near the gold fields. Myers, and perhaps Hudspeth and Mcgee may also have written some of the notes, or at least provided some information to the emigrants about the history of the trail, in particular about the Chiles excursion in 1843, since they were all together on that pack train. This speculation is supported by the diary of Israel Hale, who got to the fork at the Humboldt August 20, the same day Myers and Hudspeth are supposed to have left on the cutoff. Hale wrote, "the route [the cutoff] discovered by a Mr. Childs was taken by the emigrants. . . . Having had a history of the route before and hearing that Myers and Hudspeth . . . had taken it, we concluded . . . to take it. . . . [T]he route is described in the back part of this book as having been taken from the New York *Herald*."[142] Hale's "history" of the route was Applegate's waybill, which he wrote out at the back of his journal. He did not, however, write where he got it—certainly not from the *New York Herald*. Perhaps his knowledge of "Childs" (presumably Chiles) connection with the route came from Myers.

## Conclusion

These stories of the overland trails describe a process of goldrushers changing, as they traveled west, not only the information they found credible but the sources from which they sought information and the credibility criteria with which they assessed these sources. At the trailheads they found that in some respects their eastern printed sources were inadequate and inaccurate, and they sought new printed information from newspapers and western guidebooks. This new printed information was credible at the beginning of their trip from Missouri. Information obtained through rumors and oral communications such as the stories of Indian depredations or the tales of the go-backers were viewed with skepticism. When their printed information turned out to be dangerously wrong, such as Ware's mileage of the desert part of the Sublette Cutoff and the condition of the grass on the Humboldt River, or out of date, such as Bryant's description of the trail through Weber Canyon, it was the print that was viewed with skepticism.

The experts were alternative information sources. They transmitted information through oral communications, such as Myer's and Hudspeth's advice on the Hudspeth Cutoff, and handwritten documents such as the Willis guide. Goldrushers needed, however, new credibility criteria with which to assess these new sources. Various descriptions from the diaries as to why they took the Hudspeth or the Salt Lake cutoffs indicate that claims of trail expertise were what convinced the travelers. For example, at the Hudspeth turnoff, although Park knew that Myers and Hudspeth had not previously traveled off the main trail at this place, he was willing to follow them because Myers was a mountain guide and Hudspeth the captain of a Missouri gold rush company. At Salt Lake the story is more complicated because of the likelihood of multiple handwritten guides. It is likely that the connection of these guides with members of the Mormon Battalion, who had traveled from Iowa to California through the southwestern deserts and then blazed a new trail over the Sierras, increased confidence in the expertise of the authors. The fact that they were handwritten may have also made them seem more authentic.

The tragedy of the Lassen Cutoff was the culmination of the change in credibility criteria and the assessment of new sources. Much information circulated about the cutoff in rumors and stories along the trail. This included that the cutoff had been traveled before and thus was passable, that it was 150 miles to the California gold fields, and that there was plenty of grass and water. Most of this information was wrong, and none of it existed in writing. Goldrushers could not assess it except on the basis that experts (McGee, Myers and Hudspeth) said it was so. Perhaps most telling is that Gray, and probably others, noted that it was inconsistent with the maps they had and the advice of their printed and handwritten guidebooks to stay on the main trail. In spite of this, thousands followed the "indefinite tale" onto the cutoff.

At the beginning of the Lassen Cutoff, claims of local expertise trumped both printed and handwritten advice, and oral communications became the main information dispersal mechanism. By the end of the Lassen Cutoff, claimed expertise became discredited as a source of credibility, and goldrushers, now turned miners, required recent experience for information to be credible.

# CHAPTER FIVE

# Information and Communications in California
## *Maps, Mail, and Express*

When the goldrushers reached California, their needs for information and their means of communications changed from those on the trail. Although interrelated, the markets for information and communications from 1849 to 1851 developed in different ways and with varying degrees of success, so this chapter will discuss the two in separate sections. With respect to information, the goldrushers' difficulties on the trail resulted in distrust of printed and official information and claims of expertise. A new credibility criterion, that of personal experience, became the way goldrushers assessed new information sources. With respect to communications, institutional constraints hindered the development of the Post Office Department within California, and the slack was taken up by a remarkable growth of private express companies. After 1851 the markets for communications and information began to resemble more the situation in the East, with the widespread growth of newspapers, the printing of more credible maps, and the Post Office finally adapting to the conditions in the West.

When the goldrushers first arrived, they wanted information quickly. Foremost on their minds was the location of the gold fields and how to get there, but there were other urgent questions, such as what to do with the equipment and animals that survived the trip, whether they should continue with the companies formed in the East, and where and how to obtain provisions and equipment so they could begin mining. Frequently one or more persons would be assigned to go to Sacramento to sell equipment held in common and then distribute the proceeds or purchase supplies. Some of the companies, Charlestown, and Boston-Newton in our group, had supplies coming by sea to San Francisco and had to make arrangements to collect and distribute them or sell them and distribute the proceeds. Also, since mining in 1849 was done most effectively in small groups, most of the companies wanted to dissolve soon after reaching California if they had not done so on the trail.

Solving these problems required a knowledge of the geography of California and the ability to communicate and travel within the region. California newspapers, established in San Francisco only for three years, and in Sacramento just a few months, supplied some information. Most goldrushers seemed to have at least a basic knowledge of California geography, probably from descriptions that were available in the East in 1848 and early 1849 along with maps published before the gold rush. More detailed views, including the gold fields, may have been available from local hand-drawn maps that showed reasonably accurately the relative positions of the towns, larger ranches, roads, and gold fields active at the time. The area was large: the gold fields stretched about four hundred miles along the foothills of the Sierras from below Stockton in the south to the upper Feather River in the north.

In addition to needing information and effective communications within the state, the emigrants were starved for letters and news from home. Outside of San Francisco, however, the Post Office was just getting organized in the fall of 1849. To receive or send letters in October 1849, goldrushers generally had to travel to San Francisco, some 150 miles from Coloma or Johnson's ranch, and 250 miles from Lassen's Ranch, in the opposite direction of the mines.[1] Some of the companies appointed a person to go to San Francisco to collect mail for everyone as well as to collect commonly held property. Most goldrushers complained bitterly about the Post Office for good reason; it was completely overwhelmed in the fall of 1849. The first and newly appointed postmaster in San Francisco, Jacob Bailey Moore, had one delivery in the fall of 1849 of "countless newspapers and 45,000 letters" that was so large he had to close the post office for three days to sort it.[2]

Once goldrushers found some gold, which almost all of them did in 1849, they wanted to send a little home, both because without their earnings the need for money at home was great and they wanted to show that they were at least partially successful. The problem was how to send it safely. They would not trust the Post Office to deliver letters much less their hard-earned gold. One of the remarkable stories in the early years of the gold rush was that delivery services for letters, packages, and gold were provided primarily by the rapid development of the express companies, from one person carrying letters and packages on a mule to national corporations that provided sophisticated transportation, communications, and banking services that were trusted by the miners.

120

Before examining the goldrushers' search for credible sources of information, new credibility criteria, and the development of new means of communications, let us see what happened to the goldrushers and their companies that we have been following across the West.

## Our Gold Rush Companies

All of the gold rush companies in our sample broke up quickly after reaching California and had to deal with the problems mentioned above. The earliest companies to arrive were the ones that took the Donner or the Carson passes. The Charlestown Company of Vincent Geiger and Wakeman Bryarly was the first to reach California, arriving at Johnson's ranch from Donner Pass, September 1, 1849. They rested and recruited their surviving mules for two weeks and voted to dissolve September 13. Their quartermaster, Nat Seevers, offered to buy the goods that had been shipped to San Francisco. Bryarly, a doctor, began a successful practice in the mines and then in San Francisco, eventually becoming wealthy and returning to Maryland; Geiger did less well as a trader in Sacramento and then as a lawyer in Shasta City.[3] The members of Charles Parke's Como Company, after their crossing of the Donner Pass, traveled directly to Sacramento City, which they reached September 14. The company disbanded there, but four of their members, including Parke, formed the Union Bar Company with members of two other trail companies to work claims along the Feather River. Parke was only moderately successful and left the company August 25, 1850; after short visits to Sacramento and San Francisco, he left for home September 20, 1850.[4]

David Staples and Albion Sweetzer of the Boston-Newton Company came over Carson Pass and traveled directly to Sutter's Fort, which they reached September 27, 1849. Although there was no post office there at that date, they were able to receive their mail because the company had told their families to "direct . . . letters to Sutters Fort."[5] The company delegated three of the group, including Staples and Sweetzer, to go to San Francisco to collect the goods that had been shipped from Boston, a trip that took more than three weeks. During that time the rest of the company "sent parties in different directions to see of [they] could work together to advantage, and the committees reported that it was better to dissolve." They sold all their common property in Sacramento and disbanded October 25. Staples did not do well at mining but succeeded at hauling merchandise to the mines and then at ranching. Sweetzer began a construction business and then opened a store, both in Sacramento.[6] The Buckeye Rovers, Ezra Armstrong's company, took the Donner Pass and were also early, arriving at gold fields along the Bear River September 20, where they stopped to prospect before disbanding the company. The group stayed together longer than most, and all but three members wintered in Cold Spring, near Coloma. Armstrong mined with moderate success for two years and returned to Ohio in May 1852.[7]

The companies that took the Lassen Cutoff came in later and in worse shape than those that took the Sierra passes. Alonzo Delano and the Dayton Company, however, were well ahead of most of the groups that took the cutoff and arrived at Lassen's Ranch in fairly good shape on September 17. In that group, each mess (wagon) was fairly independent. With little property held in common, the company disbanded right away. Delano left for Sacramento with two others from the company to obtain provisions before beginning to mine, but most of the company left immediately for mines on the Yuba River. Delano became a merchant in various mining camps without much early success, but he did better in 1851 with a shop in San Francisco. He wrote his book there, and then he became a merchant and banker in Grass Valley.[8] Most of Charles Gray's Newark Company straggled into Lassen's Ranch on October 3, where they recruited and waited for the rest of the company to catch up. They disbanded October 9, with some of the company going south toward the Yuba River, and the rest going north toward the Trinity River.[9]

William Swain and the Wolverine Rangers reached Lassen's on November 8 "tired and worn down with toil and exposure but hardy, healthy, and in good spirits." However, they were "destitute of provisions, [and] without shelter."[10] The Wolverine Rangers had no property in common: "we have lost every thing—our wagons and horses, provisions, tools, and our private baggage. Most of us got in with the clothes we had on our backs."[11] Rather than formally dissolving, the members just drifted their own separate ways. William Swain, together with four others from the company formed a mining partnership that staked a claim at Long's Bar on the Feather River. After accumulating about five hundred dollars in a variety of mining places, Swain returned home in November 1850.

The last arrival of our sample of goldrushers was Goldsborough Bruff, whose odyssey at "Bruff's Camp" was told in chapter 4. Leaving Bruff to look after the company's common property on October 22, the members of the company disbanded and went their separate ways after arriving at Lassen's Ranch. They apparently did not believe that the property was worth going back into the mountains to collect and had no interest in rescuing Bruff. Bruff finally struggled into the Sacramento valley April 10, 1850.[12]

## The Marketplaces of Information in California, 1848–1851

Alonzo Delano described well the goldrushers frantic search for information when they first arrived at Lassen's Ranch:

> The emigrants, as a matter of course, were all anxious to find where the best mines were, and were busy seeking intelligence; but there seemed to be such a variety of opinions, nothing certain could be learned, and the consequence was that they scattered in all directions, as fancy dictated. . . . Some were arriving, some departing; and the camp and trading post looked more like the depot of an army, than the first halting place for the toil-worn emigrant.[13]

The passage indicates that the new arrivals had information of various sorts but had little ability to assess it. Because many felt deceived by the information sources they had on the trip, the credibility of these "opinions" was very important to the newcomers. Four available sources of information were maps, newspapers, books, and rumors; looking at how these sources developed and were used, one can observe a new credibility criterion becoming predominant, that of personal experience.

### *The Need for Maps*

In June 1849 one observer, Rev. Samuel C. Damon, commented in a letter:

> Although near three centuries have elapsed since California was discovered . . . and although much has been published about the country, yet its geography has been but imperfectly known. It is not until today, June 25 that I have met with anything like a tolerably well executed map of the country watered by the waters of the Sacramento and San Joaquin rivers, together with their numerous tributaries. This map was sketched by Colonel Frémont, or under his direction, still even this is far from being accurate.[14]

Damon was on a tour of communities in Oregon and northern California and had apparently seen a copy of the map in Frémont's 1848 *Memoir* (figure 3).[15] When one compares the California portion of the Frémont-Preuss map, with maps surveyed in 1849, it is clear that the Frémont-Preuss contained little detail about northern California; it named few of the rivers and none of the gold fields and showed no roads. This map was, however, the best available in early 1849. This situation changed rapidly in 1849 as the demand grew for maps showing

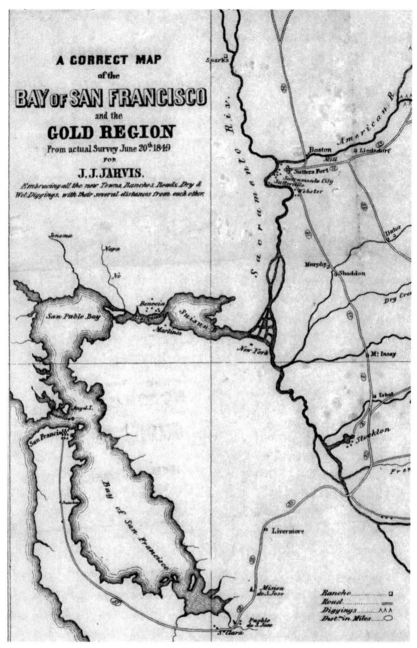

Figure 4. Detail from Map of Bay of San Francisco and the Gold Region by J. J. Jarvis, June 1849. Courtesy Yale Collection of Western Americana, Beinecke Rare Book and Manuscript Library.

the gold fields and the various rivers draining into the Sacramento and San Joaquin rivers.

Damon, who was not interested in and probably disapproved of the gold rush, thought there was one good thing about the gold rush: "every river and stream, mountain and hill, valley and canon, prairie and plain, will be explored, and accurately laid down upon the maps."[16] He was certainly right that goldrushers, the army, and others explored everywhere, but the plethora of maps that were published in 1849 and 1850 did not always result from those explorations and generally were not available to the goldrushers who traveled to California in 1849. Most of the California maps in those years were published in the East by copying from Ord or Frémont-Preuss (1848), and drawing a rough line around the "gold regions."[17] There were some new maps drawn by survey in 1849, however, showing more detail of the geography and locations of specific mines; until 1851, however, all of these maps were printed in the East.

In spite of these difficulties, goldrushers managed to get to specific mines. Many miners related the difficulty of traveling in the rough, unmarked terrain of the gold regions, but only a few worried about becoming lost.[18] It is a reasonable conjecture, therefore, that maps were in demand, and most likely some were available, perhaps hand-drawn since there were few printing presses in California.[19] Three maps that may have had an influence with the miners in 1849 and 1850 are the James Jarvis map (figure 4), the map "sketched" by Lt. George Derby (figure 5), and the map by William A. Jackson (figure 6). All three maps were drawn from surveys done in 1849, and although they were all printed in the East, it seems likely that copies of the drawings remained in California and were probably reproduced by hand. Each map showed the same relative positions of the rivers and the approximate locations and names of the mining camps existing in the summer of 1849; they differed significantly, however, in their coverage and detail, indicating that they were not copied from one another.

The importance of early maps as information sources extends beyond their use by goldrushers trying to get to specific mines. Early postmasters and express companies used maps to decide on new routes and where to locate offices, and place names and roads shown on maps provided an advertisement for new towns. Settlements were very often temporary, and getting them enshrined on an accepted map could make the difference between success and failure. One example is the location of Sutter's Mill, which in the earliest maps (Jarvis, for instance) was indicated by only "Mill." On the Derby map (surveyed only one month

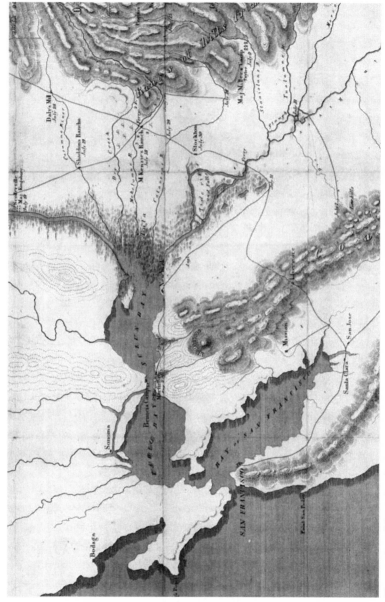

Figure 5. Detail from drawing by Lt. George Derby, "Sketch of General Riley's Route through the Mining Districts." Courtesy Yale Collection of Western Americana, Beinecke Rare Book and Manuscript Library.

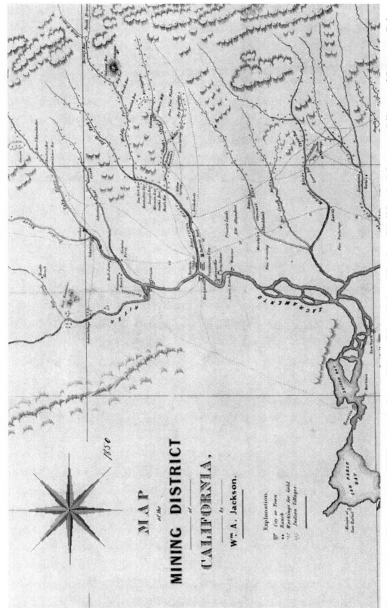

Figure 6. Detail from map by William A. Jackson, "Map of the Mining District of California." Courtesy Library of Congress Prints and Photographs Division, cat. #G4361, H2, 1850. J3 TIL.

127

later; figure 5) it received the name "Culloma," which was then repeated on the Jackson map (figure 6). It is worthwhile to take a closer look at the background of these three maps to gain an impression as to why they might have achieved credibility and consider clues as to whether they would have been available to goldrushers in the fall of 1849.

The Jarvis map provides clues as to the credibility sources and markers used on California maps in 1849 and 1850 and how they had changed from earlier maps. James Jarvis was the superintendent of the Royal Printing Establishment in the Sandwich Islands. He was on an official visit as a representative of the King of Hawaii to Boston and then to Europe when he stopped to survey the gold fields. Neither Jarvis's official position nor the status of his visit to California, appears on the map. What is prominent on the legend is "A Correct Map," and "From actual Survey, June 20th 1849." These are credibility markers in that they are written assertions of what the mapmaker thought the readers would want to know in order to assess the map. These statements can be compared to the legend of the Frémont-Preuss 1848 map, which emphasized "From the Surveys of John Charles Frémont and other Authorities. . . . Under the Order of the Senate of the United States." Claims of official sponsorship and the word "authorities," as well as Frémont's famous name, were in the view of that map publisher all that was needed to assess the reliability of the map. This represents an important transition: officialdom and authority as a source of credibility had been replaced by a declaration that the map was drawn from actual observation on a particular date.

Although officialdom as a credibility source was less effective than a year previously, a map done for the local military governor, the Derby map, could hardly avoid an official stamp. Yet even this map seems to downplay its official status by stating in the legend that it was "A sketch of General Riley's Route Through the Mining Districts July and Aug, 1849." It is hard to imagine either Frémont or Preuss calling their maps a sketch. Although the map is "a sketch," Lt. George H. Derby was a trained and competent topographer, and he put more detail and place names on his map than had appeared on any previous map. The map was drawn for Gen. Bennett Riley, who arrived in California April 12, 1849, to take over as civil governor of the Tenth Military Department, under the overall command of Gen. Persifor Smith.[20] In an effort to get a view of the rapidly changing and confused situation in California, Riley made a tour of the mines beginning July 5; the purpose of the map was to show the extent

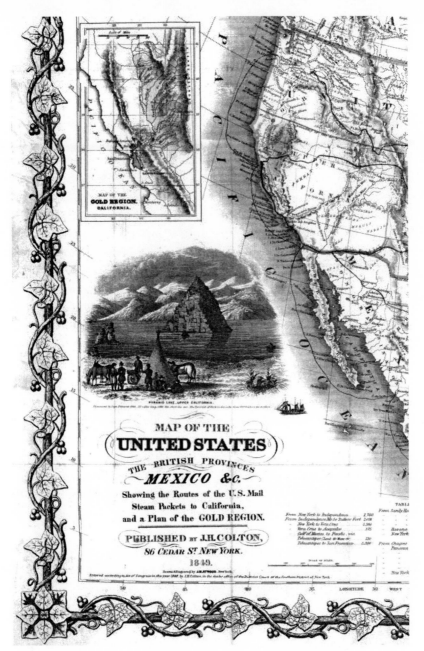

Figure 7. Detail from map by publisher J. H. Colton of New York, "Map of the United States, the British Provinces, Mexico &c: Showing the Routes of the U.S. Mail Steam Packets to California and a Plan of the Gold Region." Courtesy Library of Congress Prints and Photographs Division, cat. #G37UD 1849. A72 TIL.

of the mines and the route taken by the Riley survey. The Derby map seems to combine the credibility sources of officialdom with those of local expertise and experience. The map was eventually published by a New York lithographer in 1850. It seems likely that copies of the "sketch" remained in California and were recopied and sold to the miners.

A comparison of William A. Jackson's "Map of the Mining District of California," and the 1849 Colton "Map of the West and the Gold Region," published by J. H. Colton company in New York (figure 7), shows the clear distinction between maps sketched in California and those produced by well-known map publishers. Jackson's map, surveyed and drawn in 1849 and published early in 1850, like the Jarvis and Derby maps, was crude and looked hand-drawn with many blank spaces. It had, however, a more accurate representation of the various rivers and gold-bearing creeks than any other map of 1849, as well as more detail about the names and locations of gold-mining camps. The editor of the *San Francisco Alta California*, April 17, 1850, wrote that the Jackson map was the best map that he had yet seen, and the twentieth-century map historian Carl Wheat calls it the most important map of 1849.[21] The Colton map was an elaborately decorated pre–gold rush map republished with an insert marked "Map of the Gold Region." The insert showed few blank spaces and depicted the Feather River neatly slicing through a valley straight north almost to the Oregon border with unidentified streams draining into it from both east and west. The Jackson map showed the Feather River petering off into its east and west forks well short of the Oregon border. The emigrants who took the Lassen Cutoff knew perfectly well that the less-professional-looking Jackson map was more accurate; there were, in fact, one hundred miles of mountainous terrain from the Oregon border to the source of the Feather River, which twisted through another seventy to ninety miles of mountains before reaching the Sacramento Valley.

It is reasonable to conjecture that for goldrushers the rudimentary and hand-drawn look of these 1849 and early 1850 California maps, combined with detail relevant to them, would have created credibility for goldrushers.

### Newspapers in California, 1848 through 1851

It would be natural for goldrushers from the East to look to newspapers for information, but California's two newly established newspapers in San Francisco did not contain much information for the newly arrived goldrushers. A newspaper established in Sacramento in 1849 attempted at first to fill the mining information vacuum but did not maintain the effort. Difficulties in obtaining presses, distributing newspapers in the mining region, and finding credible and timely information about the fast-moving mining sector made newspapers an uncertain information source for the goldrushers.

California newspapers started slowly, in part, because there had been no newspapers in either Spanish or Mexican California and only one printing press, one brought over in 1834 from Boston by Augustin Zamorano, former secretary to the Mexican governor.[22] In 1846 Walter Colton and Robert Semple used Zamorano's printing press to publish California's first newspaper, the *Californian*, in Monterey and in the following year moved the press to San Francisco.[23] The first San Francisco newspaper, the *California Star*, was established in 1847 by the Mormons in California. It was owned by Samuel Brannon, who later played an important role in publicizing the gold rush. Both of these newspapers had to close in April 1848 when all their workers left for the gold fields. They were combined as the *Star and Californian* by Edward Kemble in November 1848 and then renamed the *Alta California* in January 1849. The *Alta* concentrated on "the work of forming a Provisional Government, and as zealously into the reform of municipal matters in San Francisco."[24] One goldrusher, writing to the *New York Tribune*, complained, "The *Alta California*, as you will see, says little of the gold diggings."[25] No other newspapers were established in San Francisco until August 1849 when the *Pacific News* began publication. It concentrated on politics and became an organ for T. Butler King and the Democratic Party in early state conventions.[26] Neither San Francisco newspaper focused on information for goldrushers.

Kemble saw the need for a journal aimed more at miners and in April 1849 took Zamorano's printing press to Sacramento to establish the *Placer Times*. The first issue, April 28, made it clear what the newspaper was about: "Having espoused the interest of the mining community, it [the *Placer Times*] will ever . . . cherish and defend them." In a column entitled "The Placer," the newspaper gave conditions in the mines. In April, for instance, it noted that "there [was] very little washing for gold . . . owing to high water." By the end of May, the first wave of new miners began to arrive from the East (those who had taken ships in December or early January), and "The Placer" column became an advice column for the arrivals. The May 26, 1849, issue is an example:

A report reached this place a few days since that new gold discoveries had been made on the Sacramento river near its head waters. . . . A gentleman from the American river *Dry Diggings* informs us that large accessions to the numbers already employed there have taken place of late . . . and gold has since been found over a large extent of country. . . . Hundreds have been flocking to the *Middle Fork* during the month . . . numbers are at work and doing well.

Kemble also knew his likely contributors and his audience; to obtain news of the diggings, he offered the only thing he had that was as good as gold: eastern newspapers.

We will be pleased to hear from the different gold diggings, the result of the labor, the news current, etc. Until we can employ regular correspondents, we will compensate the services of any who may undertake to perform the light task of an occasional contributor, *by supplying them with batches of Late State papers, and all other readable matter* received at this office.[27]

This promising start to an information source for newly arrived miners was not maintained. Kemble stayed with the *Placer Times* only two months, and he returned to San Francisco and the *Alta* in June. In spite of the name of the newspaper, the new editor, J. H. Giles, did not appear to be interested in the mines. "The Placer" column disappeared as a regular feature, and during the summer Giles printed very little about the mines. On August 18, 1849, just when the new mining season was getting started in earnest, there was an article entitled "The Mines," which stated, "We have seen several who have returned from the Placer within the past few days, but they bring no news of interest. They represent things favorably, as all do who have been successful." On September 1, 1849, the newspaper reported, "The waters are rapidly falling, but we do not hear of any company or organization that is taking out over a cart load of the dust per day." On September 9, the editor proclaimed, "All the *on dits* we get in regard to the Placer we shall publish without any investigation," reducing the newspaper's advice on the placers to the level of rumor. Giles was not interested in heightening the credibility of his reporting from the mines. In fact he published very little about gold finds that month, and on October 13, 1849, he published a letter from a miner at the Spanish Bar, advising the editor, "You are undoubtedly annoyed every day by new comers who wish to know the richest place. Give no advice at all; if my brother were to come to me with the inquiry, I could [would?] not give him the information required." Just as the number of goldrushers arriving in

California was reaching its maximum for 1849, the newspaper appeared to have taken itself out of the information marketplace for newly arrived miners.

The newspaper could not downplay interest in the mines for long. By November 1849 goldrushers from the States who expected information from newspapers formed the large majority of the population in northern California. There must have been complaints because, when the format of the *Placer Times* changed on November 17, the editor (still Giles) announced, "we shall, in this and subsequent numbers, devote more space to the subject of mining and mines. . . . [A]fter a succession of impartially written articles, perhaps the inquirer after correct knowledge will be able to deduct [deduce?] facts which will enable him to arrive at a correct conclusion in regard to this all-important topic [gold mining]." This was a complete turnaround from October 13; credibility was important, (the word "correct" was used twice in the one sentence), and the source of credibility was to be the recent experience of ordinary miners.

The article was a "mine" of information. It contained detailed advice about wintering in the mines, relative advantages of wet and dry diggings during the rainy months, road and trail conditions in specific locations, and advice as to where to purchase provisions. The tone and the detailed information in the article are very different from the newspaper during the summer. A week later, under the old heading "The Placer," the editor printed an article filled with the sort of advice a newly arrived goldrusher would have wanted:

> During the last ten days a large amount of provisions have found their way to the miners, although some teams have been on the road from twelve to sixteen days to the nearest diggings. . . . Our advices from the miners are on the whole favorable. From the streams up North we learn that many are doing exceedingly well. . . . People seem to be doing a better business on the Yuba than on the nearer streams. . . . While many do a flourishing business on the three Forks of the American river, others, equally deserving and industrious, hardly succeed in meeting their expenses.

The change in editorial interest is clear. The need for information by the goldrushers outweighed the reluctance of the editor to get involved in mining news.

The information marketplace became more competitive when the *Sacramento Transcript* appeared in April 1850 and a third Sacramento newspaper in October 1850, the *Settlers' and Miners' Tribune*. The difference between the newspapers was in large part political, related to the new status of California as a state.[28] The difference, however, also reflected the quest for readers among the new miners, who were arriving in even greater numbers in 1850 than the previous year. Probably the most innovative idea was a series of articles in the *Transcript* that was a kind of textbook for miners. They began July 23, 1850, with a clear purpose: "The writer proposes to indite a few chapters on the art of mining. Having spent several months in the diggings, during which time he was far more successful than the average, he thinks his advice will not be altogether worthless. Chapter No. 2 will be devoted to the subject of selecting proper places for digging." The author was identified only as "A Digger." The editor established credibility for the proposed series of articles by emphasizing local experience; this credibility criterion can be compared with the named and titled eastern "experts" and the inventors of mining machines who had been the eastern goldrushers primary source of information about mining.[29] The second chapter in the series appeared July 25 and fulfilled the promised textbook-like style, dividing gold-digging locations into five "branches," three types of wet diggings and two types of dry diggings, and proceeded to describe different mining techniques for each.

Distributing Sacramento newspapers in the mining region was very expensive. It was also slow, and therefore the information about new mines and successful strikes reached the miners too late to be useful. These factors must have limited the demand for local newspapers in the mines. Swain, for instance, in a letter to Sabrina in February 1850 exults that he has "seen two California *Tribunes*. . . . [and] learned something of the affairs of the States," but he does not mention San Francisco or Sacramento papers.[30] In the summer of 1850, the problem of too few newspapers was alleviated in part because some of the towns that were jumping-off points to the mines established newspapers. In Stockton the *Sonora Herald* and the *Stockton Times*, served the southern mines. In Marysville the *Marysville Herald* served the northern mines. Newspapers in the smaller mining towns were established all over the mining regions in 1851 and 1852.[31] Once editors realized the importance of the miners to their readership, they attempted to provide relevant and timely information to the newcomers and to establish credibility through claims of practical knowledge and local experience.

### The Beginnings of California Publishing and Bookselling

The gold rush migrations of 1849 through 1851 were some of the most literate large-scale migrations of the nineteenth century. The large majority of travelers were able and willing to read and write. Many overland travelers packed books about subjects other than mining to read along the journey, although unlike those who went by sea they had little time to read. Books were one of the first items to be thrown away. At least one goldrusher, Franklin Langworthy, viewed the discards as an opportunity. In 1850 he wrote, "Facilities for the acquisition of knowledge are becoming ample along these barren deserts. Lying by the wayside are a great variety of books, which their owners have thrown away to lighten their loads. From this extended library I frequently draw a volume, read and return it.[32]

Once in California, the goldrushers had more time to read, but the hard labor of mining combined with the high cost of candles were not conducive to reading books for information or as a pastime. Bayard Taylor said, "[I] saw many persons who had brought the works of favorite authors with them, for recreation at odd hours, but of all the works thus brought, I never saw one read."[33] In spite of Taylor's observation, Gary Kurutz provides evidence that reading books was a pastime for some, particularly at idle times such as recovery from illness.[34] Drinking and gambling, however, were more frequently described as recreations for the miners, both in the cities and in the mining camps.[35] Alonzo Delano described Sacramento in the spring of 1850 as a substantial city, but he said, "I regret to say, that gambling formed a prominent part in the business of the city. . . . These places of resort were daily and nightly thronged with men of all ages and conditions in life."[36] There were no bookstores in the town until August 1850.

Most of the books available to goldrushers were ones they had brought with them or picked up on the trail. There was, however, one book printed in California in 1849 written specifically to provide new arrivals with information about getting around California and about the art of mining; this was F. P. Wierzbicki's *California As It Is and As It May Be.*[37] The author purported to answer the questions of the new arrivals "by suitable information, upon which they can put at least some reliance," saying he was "neither a merchant, a trader, nor speculator in land or mines."[38] He claimed to write his book "to tell the truth about California" after seeing so many disillusioned by bad information.[39] Wierzbicki's assertion that he did not have a special interest was important in selling the book because the miners were wary of information providers who were actually selling something else. The example of Lassen was fresh in their minds. The statement, however, did not point to any credibility source, such as Wierzbicki's expertise or experience. The credibility marker was in the preface:

135

The residence of several years in the country together with his familiarity with its whole extent, not excluding the Gold Regions in which he passed more than four months rambling over its mountains, and even crossing the Sierra Nevada to the verge of the great Western Desert, give the writer of these pages a degree of confidence . . . [that] he supplies the desideratum [of information] so much needed at this moment.[40]

Wierzbicki did not mention titles nor official affiliation, nor did he provide any claim to expertise in mining or geology. His claim was only his own experience in California and beyond, that he knew the outer bounds of the gold fields because he went beyond them. This is another example showing that credibility sources had evolved from official titles, to claims of expertise (the trail experience of the mountain men leading the migration over new cutoffs), to personal experience.

Wierzbicki was a doctor from Poland who was practicing in Rhode Island when he joined the New York Volunteers in 1846. He was discharged in April 1847, went to the gold fields for four months the following year, and then settled into a medical practice in San Francisco. The book was similar in style to the better trail guidebooks, full of detailed and practical advice. It also contained a chapter on the gold region that provided a geography and related the prevailing theories concerning where the gold came from and how to find it.[41] Perhaps the chapter most useful to the neophyte miner was "Advice to the Miner," which described such details as what clothes and tools to take to the mines, how to build a rocker, what provisions to buy, what size partnerships were optimal, and what the difficulties were in traveling in various parts of the gold region.

The Wierzbicki book was immediately successful. The book sold in San Francisco for five dollars and went through two editions in three months (September and December 1849). According to Kemble, the editor of the *Alta*, "the sale is unprecedented for a first literary venture. It brings to the publisher some $8,000 to $10,000 . . . [the book] is all that it professes to be . . . it reviews the present condition of the country, its inhabitants and future prospects in a clear, concise and truthful manner."[42] Extracts of the book appeared in each of the San Francisco newspapers.

Wierzbicki's was the first and only book published in California in 1849 or 1850, although other books were available through early booksellers both in San Francisco and Sacramento.[43] Bookselling was a difficult business in those years in

California. John H. Still established the first bookstore in the state in September of that year, but his store was burned out in one of the many fires in San Francisco. He reestablished himself in 1850 as a bookseller for mining areas as well as the city when he advertised that he could supply "up to date country merchants, express riders and pedlars [*sic*] . . . with all the latest novels, magazines and newspapers on the most favorable terms."[44] From the point of view of this study, it is significant that his advertisement did not imply the bookstore was primarily a source of practical information. Rather, he supplied books for reading as recreation. In August 1850, Still left for Sacramento to establish the first bookstore in that town, Still, Conner and Company.[45] Another early San Francisco bookseller was Charles P. Kimball, nicknamed "Noisy Carrier," since he acted as a town crier while peddling newspapers.[46] His Noisy Carrier bookshop on Long Wharf in the city became successful in 1851, selling everything "from tomes in fine bindings to shells and slate pencils," but before then he had a difficult time as a peddler and a letter carrier from San Francisco to the northern mines."[47]

Within a few years, California's book trade blossomed with booksellers and publishers such as James Hutchings (publisher of the *California Illustrated Magazine*), Anton Roman (publisher of *Overland Monthly*, which published Bret Harte's famous short stories about California), and Hubert Howe Bancroft (whose library formed the basis of the Bancroft Library at Berkeley). Each of these literary entrepreneurs started in the mid-1850s. The San Francisco Merchants Library was formed in December 1852 "for the purpose of diffusing and promoting knowledge."[48] From the publication and bookseller evidence, it would seem that in the first two years of the gold rush, with the exception of Wierzbicki, books were not a major source of information for the early goldrushers.

### Rumors

In previous stages of their gold rush adventure, rumors played an important but secondary role as a source of information. Rumors of cholera in the trailhead towns, difficulties of crossing the Missouri River, Indian depredations on the trail, and the value or dangers of various cutoffs, all transmitted information (see chapters 3 and 4). They were usually supported or undermined by other information. In California, rumors played a primary role in the mines.

The miners seemed to be on the go much of the time, moving fairly long distances at a moment's notice on the basis of a rumor that the miners called "news." In describing mining along the Stanislaus River in May 1849, William Taylor wrote, "Three Americans, however, below Jamestown took out one piece of gold worth $278!! The news flew like wild fire."[49] Edward Buffum related in his book that in December 1848, while mining at Weaver Creek near Sutter's Mill, "the most extravagant reports reached us from the Middle Fork, distant in a northerly direction about thirty miles from Weaver's Creek. Parties who had been there described the river as being lined with gold . . . the news was too blooming for me to withstand. . . . I packed up and held myself in readiness to proceed by the earliest opportunity."[50] Walter Colton, one time *alcalde* of Monterey, trying his hand at mining in October 1848 also along the Stanislaus, related that a little girl picked up a "curious stone" that her mother found was a lump of pure gold: "The news of this discovery silenced all the picks here for half an hour, and set as many tongues going in their places. Twenty or thirty started at once to explore the wonders of this new locality."[51] The use of the word "news" to describe rumors was an indication that rumors were considered important and pertinent information.[52]

At times rumors spread with the retelling of a myth, such as the legend of the gold lake. In June 1850, Charles Parke, who was mining at Bidwell's Bar, reported, "Great excitement prevails along the river regarding the discovery of a certain 'gold lake' on the headwaters of the North Yuba river . . . six of our Company have packed the mules and gone in search of the hidden treasure."[53] Bidwell's Bar was on the middle fork of the Feather River and the headwaters of the Yuba was thirty to fifty miles south and east of the bar. The terrain in that part of the Sierra foothills (towards Downieville, California) is steep and difficult, and there were no detailed maps of the region, but the trip apparently fazed no one. Goldsborough Bruff first heard the story of the gold lake on June 20, 1850, at Lassen's Ranch. In the version circulating there, it was "a rumored discovery of immense deposits of gold, around a Lake, situate[d] somewhere between the upper waters of the Feather & Yuva rivers."[54] In the following days several pack teams were heading out to the rumored gold lake, and by July 12 Bruff was preparing to join Lassen with a large party for the search, although he wrote that he did "not believe the story." He thought instead, "we may be so fortunate as to find a rich gold place, if not a Gold Lake."[55] The expedition went through September, when dissension split the party, although "all firmly believe[d] in the existence of this '*Gold Lake.*'" Although there was no gold lake, perhaps it was not foolish to go look for it: the *Sacramento Transcript* reported on August 21, 1850, "two bars have lately been discovered of remarkable richness . . . they were discovered some five weeks ago by a party in search of Gold Lake."

Although rumors frequently caused stampedes to some new mining areas, some of the goldrushers understood that the purpose of those who spread rumors was not necessarily to convey accurate information. Bruff blamed the gold lake "hoax" on a Bostonian he named Gibbs whom he felt profited from supplying the prospectors. Wierzbicki also emphasized the dangers of ignorance and self-interest among rumormongers:

> Interest and ignorance frequently conspire in circulating extraordinary stories of success, on very slender foundation, for some never have been in the mines at all, and have not the slightest idea of them, crediting everything they hear; others have *their* [trading] posts established on some particular spot, where, of course, the mines *must be very rich*.[56]

In spite of the repeated failure of rumors to "pan out" and the fact that many goldrushers realized, or read, that rumors were not spread by disinterested people, rumors continued to be a major source of information for the goldminers all during the gold rush years. In 1852, when more miners had considerable experience, Louise Clappe, described the continued penchant of miners for following rumors, even when they were working a satisfactory claim:

> Our countrymen are the most discontented of mortals. They are always longing for "big strikes." If a "claim" is paying them a steady income, by which, if they pleased, they could lay up more in a month than they could accumulate in a year at home, still they are dissatisfied. . . . Sometimes, a company of these wanderers will find itself upon a bar where a few pieces of the precious metal lie . . . the news spreads that wonderful "diggings" have been discovered at such a place . . . and lo! As if a fairy's wand had been waved above the bar, a full-grown mining town hath sprung into existence.[57]

This survey of information sources about mining in California in 1849 and 1850 shows that useful printed information existed but was not timely and was not widely disseminated at the mines. Rumors, however, were followed almost blindly. Rumors may have been unverified, but they were timely. Also, credibility now depended on perceived practical experience, which was a characteristic of miners' rumors. With so few alternate sources of credible information, one might as well follow rumors as anything else. The fact that rumors were unverified might not have bothered miners as much as when they were on the trail, because they realized that finding gold was "a lottery," as much a matter of luck as skill and good information.[58]

## Communications with Home: Letters and Gold

There were similarities and substantial differences between the marketplaces for information and communications in the early gold rush years of 1849 through 1851. In both there was a slow development of traditional mechanisms: newspapers and books for information and the Post Office for communications. Unlike information, however, communications developed an alternative that grew fast and achieved the confidence of goldrushers. This was the express industry in the West.

### Mail and the Post Office: Control from Washington

Other than finding gold, nothing was more important to the goldrushers than receiving mail from home. Whether they came by sea or overland, they had been out of touch with home for six to nine months, and in some cases more. Almost every miner who wrote about his experiences in California mentioned the importance of receiving letters and their disappointment at not receiving expected letters. One eloquent statement about goldrushers' letters was written by Luther Melancthon Schaeffer in 1860:

> There is one source of happiness to the Californian, which can never be fully understood by friends at home: I allude to letters—to a sheet of paper, scribbled over, perhaps, carelessly by a friend, who little thinks how each word, each crossing of the T, or dotting of an I, will be dwelt upon; how every sentence is remembered, and how the rough miner throws his body down on his hard pallet, with his letter secreted in his bosom, and dreams, perchance, of the writer, or of the pleasure of returning home.[59]

William Swain, writing to Sabrina February 17, 1850 (four months after he arrived in California), complained, "I cannot express the disappointment I have experienced in not as yet having received any letters from either you or George. I am as well satisfied that there are a dozen for me at Sacramento City as I am of my existence."[60] He was right about her sending many letters; beginning May 27, 1849, when William was barely a week out of Independence, she and his brother George began sending letters regularly, at least one per month, addressing them to Sutter's Fort, California. Eventually, he received twenty-nine letters, but when he finally received his first letters, March 3, 1850, there were only two. Swain wrote, "they were the most precious tidings I have ever known and double pay for the disappointment of looking and expecting anxiously the arrival of some note of absent and loved relatives."[61] Swain was typical in his reaction to the receipt of letters and the fact that he was so frequently disappointed about not receiving the letters he expected.

Many goldrushers who complained about not getting letters blamed the Post Office. Daniel Robinson, writing to his sister in October 1849, lamented,

> We are all sadly disappointed in getting no news from home. But one letter from Bloomington [Indiana] has reached this office for any of our company. The Post Office at San Francisco is the most corrupt and miserable affair of the kind in the world. I learn they have more letters there than can be stored, yet they will not send them to this office without the postage is paid there in advance.[62]

Aaron Hyde wrote to his parents in 1851:

> I write at periods of three or four months and wait for answers. But having had but one letter . . . which letter I received about 15 months ago. I have watched the Post Office and advertised lists, waited hopefully and still hope that I may have a letter somewhere between the digings [*sic*] in the vicinity of Sonora Southern mines and Danverse, Sandwich, [in New Hampshire, where his parents lived] or wherever you may live, if indeed you are living, but who knows.[63]

The goldrushers' anguish was made worse by the fact that they did not know whether the mail did not get through or people at home had forgotten them. John Stacey sent his wife Clarinda many letters and $150 during 1850 but had not heard from her: "I hope I shall get a letter from you at that time as I shall otherwise think that I am entirely forgotten or forsaken. Still I can't help thinking that you have written & they have miscarried, but I think I have got all but one that you have written previous to the first April."[64] These examples could be multiplied many times.

Newspapers also complained about the Post Office. The most severe complaints were from Sacramento, which was dependent on letters being sent from San Francisco. An August 18, 1849, an editorial in the *Placer Times* complained, "the regular mail is a regular humbug, it's stuck in the mud half the time and might as well be the other half." The Sacramento Post Office would send lists of names of people for whom letters should be forwarded to Sacramento, but they were not sent: "By the last mail from San Francisco not a single letter was there re-mailed for our Post Office, though the Postmaster here has forwarded to the Office below upward of 2,400 names . . . only the letters originally directed to this point came."[65] As mail failures continued, the complaints grew more heated, as in this editorial in the *Placer Times*, November 3, 1849: "It is certainly one of the most outrageous grievances that ever any people suffered to be so long deprived of the receipt of the regular mails from the United States. . . . To the ordinary business and corresponding relations of a community, the failure of two successive monthly mails is an almost incalculable evil."

The failure of the post office in 1849 and 1850 was caused in large part by the fact that eastern control of the agency did not allow postmasters or carriers to be paid California wages. The situation in California was new and completely different than the national managers of the Post Office had seen before. Routes, rates of pay, and rates paid to carriers were all regulated at the national level, while the local Post Offices were directed to cover their own costs. The *Placer Times* put its finger on the main problem in an editorial September 1, 1849:

> We are informed that the Government Post Office . . . is in admirable confusion. Somewhat less than ten Postmasters have been appointed in as many weeks, succeeding each other with a rapidity peculiar to the lively state of affairs in California. . . . For the benefit of the people the Government appoint Postmasters for California, and for the same excellent reason either neglect or absolutely refuse to pay them. . . . A Postmaster is sent to San Francisco with a salary of $2,000, when at the same time the Postmaster General knew, or should have known, that such pay would scarcely furnish clean linen for the incumbent.

Centralized control dated back to the Post Office Act of 1792 when Congress delegated to itself the authority to designate every postal route in the United States.[66] Congress passed an act to install post offices in California August 14, 1848, three months after it ratified the treaty of Guadalupe Hidalgo, ending the Mexican War and annexing California to the United States. The postmaster general appointed William Van Voorhies as "special agent" for California in November 1848 to establish post offices and appoint postmasters in San Diego,

San Pedro, Santa Barbara, San Luis Obispo, Monterey "and at such points on the Pacific, at which the United States steam mail packets shall touch." Voorhies's instructions mandated postal charges at forty cents per single letter to and from the Atlantic coast, and twelve and one-half cents between any places on the Pacific. No specific interior routes were created by Congress, but Voorhies was allowed to establish them provided that the specified mail charges were maintained, that annual compensation for weekly horseback conveyance of the mail would not exceed six dollars per mile and, most important, "each office situated in the interior [was] conditioned upon the expense thereof being defrayed out of the net proceeds of such office."[67] These instructions might have been appropriate for Dana's California, but in gold rush California they made mail delivery impossible when average wages were sixteen dollars per day and transportation charges were many multiples of regulated rates.

The Taylor administration replaced Voorhies with R. T. P. Allen, who arrived in San Francisco June 13, 1849, and quickly informed Washington of the situation with regard to prices and wages and of the need for large supplementary payments. He assumed that Washington would meet the need, and he began planning for service to towns in the interior by appointing postmasters and letting contracts for carrying the mail to Sacramento, Coloma, Stockton, and Monterey. The contracts totaled $62,400 per year, and the postmaster general refused payment. Few mail deliveries were made beyond San Francisco, and even in San Francisco all mail came to the Post Office and had to be picked up there.[68] The Sacramento postmaster's plan to send names of people in Sacramento for whom mail should be forwarded from San Francisco, as described in the August 18, 1849, *Placer Times*, had no hope of being fulfilled.

Although mail did not get delivered within California, it did reach the Pacific coast through Panama in these early years of the gold rush. In March 1847 before the United States annexed California, Congress passed an act to build four naval steamships that, among other duties, would transport mail to the Pacific coast (Oregon was more on their minds than California).[69] Two ships were to operate between the east coast and Panama, and three were to run on the Pacific side; two companies were organized to carry mail, freight, and passengers: the United States Mail Steamship Company and the Pacific Mail. The timing was remarkable because the first of these ships, the *Falcon*, went into service in December 1848, just as the first wave of goldrushers took to the sea. Unfortunately, the ships on the Pacific side were not in service as quickly, which resulted in the backup of goldrushers and mail in Panama City (see chapter 1).[70] The mail sent out on these ships was accompanied by agents charged with protecting the mail bags and seeing that they were transferred through Panama. Most of the early agents were postmasters on their way to California, but in November 1849, two permanent agents were appointed for one thousand dollars per year, for "the charge and re-assortment of the mails between New York and Panama."[71] By mid-1850, the mail was reaching San Francisco on a regular basis.

It took several years for the postal service to improve to the satisfaction of the California residents. By 1851 the postal service had established, on paper at least, about sixty post offices, but many in California continued to consider the mail service unreliable.[72] The June 11, 1853, *San Francisco Alta California* complained about the U.S. mail: "It has been so useless that business men place no reliance on it," and two years later (July, 13, 1855) the newspaper was still complaining, "The Post Office system as far as California is concerned, is a humbug and a nuisance. . . . It does not facilitate intercourse between different parts of the state, but impedes it."[73]

### The Express Companies: From Pack Mules to International Banking

By the end of 1849, the communications gaps unfilled by the Post Office left unsatisfied a huge demand for better communications. In addition to about eighty thousand emigrants clamoring for mail, a burgeoning but chaotic commercial sector required contact with suppliers in the States. It was also imperative that a reliable and safe method could be found to transport gold to the East. These demands were met by private carriers, known collectively as express companies.

The *Placer Times* looked around for an answer to the problem and decided, "We had about made up our mind to let the Post Office arrangements for California go to 'grass' their own way, hoping that there would be private enterprise enough to eclipse that shabby concern altogether."[74] In the same issue there was a large advertisement from Angle, Young and Company's Express. The advertisement covered a wide range of services from picking up letters at the post office in San Francisco to sending "Letters, Packages and Gold Dust" within California or to the east coast of the United States and other countries. The ad tried to instill confidence by proclaiming that "Competent Men" were engaged, that an agent would accompany all shipments, and that the firm had the "exclusive right of carrying Gold Dust or Express matter" on a particular steamer, the *Senator* (a river steamer which went from Sacramento to San Francisco).

144

Angle, Young and Company was not the first express to operate out of Sacramento, although it may have been the first to offer a full range of express services.[75] Less ambitious enterprises were organized earlier, consisting of individuals who would carry letters. This was an employment that anyone could do, and many did when mining was not going well. The experience of Charles Kimball, before he established his Noisy Carrier Bookshop, illustrates the job of carrying letters. Kimball arrived in San Francisco July 6, 1849, from Boston, where he had been a peddler and bookseller. He tried his hand at mining and peddling and carrying letters and packages for individuals; it was a hand-to-mouth existence. On October 1, 1849, he wrote in his diary, "I have got 25 and 40 orders for letters and several other things . . . which pays my board here . . . what I shall do next time I do not know."[76] He arrived in San Francisco October 4 and was back in Sacramento October 11, where he wrote that he would, "make but one trip more with the Express," since he had not made more than his costs for the trips up and down the American River. On October 19 he wrote, "I have given up my Express business. . . . I have Peddled to day," and he was still not quite making his board in Sacramento. On October 22 a Mr. Tiffany from Wells and Company Express asked him to take over seventy letters up to seven different mines. He made his deliveries and got back to Sacramento October 30. He then left for San Francisco again and by November 17 established his "stand" which eventually grew into the Noisy Carrier Bookstore.

Many men who started a small-scale letter delivery business were more successful than Kimball. In July 1849 in the southern mines, Alexander Todd was having no luck mining and his health could not take the hard physical labor, so he started a "letter express".[77] He took the names of miners expecting letters in San Francisco, charging one dollar for each name, traveled to the city, collected what letters he could, carried them back to the mines, and charged again for delivery. He paid the postmaster twenty-five cents per letter to be allowed to go into the office and get his letters out quickly. After his first trip, merchants in Stockton approached him to carry gold dust to San Francisco, which he did, for 5 percent. The business grew until he carried fifteen hundred to two thousand letters per trip and had offices in many mining camps, using merchants as his agents. Also miners began coming to him. He wrote, "the miners had no opportunity for taking care of their dust, and we were obliged to have safes at our different offices, and our express business soon merged into a banking business."[78] At the height of his business he was making one thousand dollars per day, although he stated he was robbed several times by his clerks and he was burned out in May 1850. By 1851, Todd's main competitor was the largest express company, Adams Express.

The expressmen provided more than a means to send letters, packages, and gold dust; they were a network of communications among mining camps. In their travels they stayed in miners' tents and cabins, in hotels, and at ranches and were conveyors of news, information, and rumors. One of the few extant diaries of an expressman is that of James S. Tolles, which was published in the *Marysville Democrat*, in February and March 1930.[79] Tolles began his one-man express business December 7, 1849, possibly influenced by Todd's success, but he was neither enormously successful like Todd nor a relative failure like Kimball. His handbill gives a good impression of his business and the way expressmen connected the isolated mining camps, particularly in the winter:

> James Tolles Express from the Feather River to San Francisco . . . Calling at Brown's Bar, Boone's Bar, Stringtown, Fairfield Bar, Bidwell Bar, Long Bar, Marysville, Vernon and Sacramento . . . Monthly to catch the steamer. . . . Starting from Mountain Cottage kept by A. Tolles & Co., eighteen miles above Bidwell's Bar on the Ridge Road from Marysville to Slate Creek.[80]

Tolles's diary described his trip to San Francisco beginning December 7, 1849, with his list of names for whom he would be picking up mail; the trip is a detailed illustration of how expressmen provided communications in the mining areas and in the towns. On December 7 he said, "procured shelter in a wagon, and had tolerable lodgings. Met quite a number of teams going up to the mines with provisions." The next day he was at "Charlie's ranch," and December 9, "Nichol's ranch." He stayed at the "U.S. Hotel" in Sacramento December 10 and arrived in San Francisco on the twelfth where he went straight to the Post Office, presumably to deposit letters from the miners. On the thirteenth he "had good success in getting into the office for my list of names" and planned to be "ready to start home in a few days." He got back to Sacramento on the nineteenth and "walked from the city up to Frémont . . . having to go through brush and water, traveling 30 miles."[81] Fortunately he "had a very comfortable place to stay over night at a house kept by a man of family from Oregon." In spite of bad weather and flooding, he got to Yuba City by Christmas and back to the mining camps December 26.

Tolles not only provided a delivery service and was able to talk to people where he stayed, he also must have communicated with other expressmen in

San Francisco since most had to time their trips to the city to meet the monthly steamer. The clear similarities between Tolles's and Todd's way of operating in San Francisco is another indication of communication among the expressmen. In this way the network of communications operated not only among the camps visited by a single letter carrier but among mining regions.

Letter carrying became a common occupation, and the number of these carriers, along with the growth of numerous small express companies, indicates the extent of the express companies' communications network in the mining regions. E. Wiltsee identifies eleven very early one-man express companies in different mining regions, mostly from handbills, advertisements, or the rare letter with a frank of the expressman. Within a year, the one-man expresses began to grow or sell out; many of the men who ran the initial start-ups became owners or agents of larger companies.[82] From 1850 to 1853 there were ninety separate express companies operating in six mining regions, not counting the one-man companies or the national companies.[83] Not all these companies operated all the time, and most of them operated a particular route on which they distributed letters and packages. Some connected specific camps; for example, in Nevada and Sierra counties, Angier's Express operated from North San Juan to Humbug, and Sam Abbey's Express from North San Juan to French Corral. Others defined their routes a little more generally, such as Green's Express, which went from "Nevada City to camps on the ridge." There was considerable competition in connections from the towns servicing broader mining areas, such as Marysville; there were four express companies operating from Marysville to Downieville and three from Marysville to various points on the Feather River. Single expresses operated from Marysville to Bidwell's Bar, to Nevada City, to Foster's Bar, to Gibsonville Ridge, to Rich Bar, and to Oroville. Other mining regions were equally densely serviced by express companies identified by Wiltsee. These companies filled the communications gap left by the Post Office.

California newspapers understood very well the importance of the express companies. In the same issue of the *Placer Times* that lamented that the "regular mail is a regular humbug," they pleaded, "who will establish an express? And who will not give a dollar for every letter promptly delivered?"[84] In July 1850 the *San Francisco Alta California* acted as cheerleader:

> We scarcely know what we should do if it were not for the various Express lines established, enabling us to hold communication with the mines.

147

... [O]ur enterprising express agents, however, supply the deficiency, and by the promptitude with which they attended to the transmission of letters and packages, and the fidelity with which they conducted all business entrusted to them, are justly entitled to the confidence and support of the community.

Alonzo Delano, writing to the *New Orleans True Delta*, effused,

Almost every bar and diggings beyond the reach of mail arrangements has its connecting express line, and the glistening eye of the sunburnt miner, as through them he receives the missive of love from home, attests the estimation in which they are held in California. But for them, how many hearts would be sad—how many hopes disappointed![85]

Most miners were not as effusive as the editorial writers or Delano, but there are many references from miners about using the expresses to carry letters. On January 16, 1850, from the South Fork of the Feather River, William Swain sent one of his first letters home via an expressman to San Francisco who charged two dollars per letter. William Murray, in January 1850 from Sacramento, decided to send duplicate letters, one by "private conveyance" and the other by the Post Office so his wife "might have two chances to hear from [him]."[86] Three months later, in Sacramento, he had to pick up his mail at the "Express office" and complained that he had to pay both postage and express fees.[87]

Murray was complaining about how the Post Office tried to counteract competition from the express companies. The Post Office had a monopoly for letter delivery. The illegal competition of the express companies greatly concerned the postal officials in Washington because it resulted in lost revenue. In response, the postmaster general issued orders on November 15, 1849, that agents on ships and in Panama should confiscate letters in express mail, charge them with postage, and treat them as if they had been conveyed in the mail. These letters, then, would be charged double and faced "the hazard of never reaching their destination."[88] These measures were ineffective, however, as goldrushers would not trust the Post Office and placed more and more faith in private carriers.

Carrying letters and providing communications among mining towns were only some of the services provided by express companies. As the larger national companies came into the business, they expanded into a sophisticated international banking service to provide a relatively safe way for miners to send money back home. William Swain in June 1850 had accumulated enough gold to send some home but did not even consider sending it via the Post Office. A Mr. Chadwick, who established a small store at Swain's mining location on the Feather River, was returning to the states and offered to carry letters and gold. Swain accepted the offer for letters but wrote to his brother, George, "I might send $500 by Chadwick, but I prefer the responsibility of Adams & Company's Express to that of an untried stranger."[89] Most of the gold sent east by goldrushers went by two express companies, Adams Express in the early years and Wells, Fargo and Company after 1855.

Adams Express, founded by Alvin Adams in Boston in 1840, was one of the first express companies in the country and the first to contract with the U.S. Treasury to carry government money between the New York Customhouse and the U.S. Mint in Philadelphia.[90] This experience was well advertised and helped build confidence for their business among the goldrushers. Adams Express also had extensive national and international connections by acquiring the first express in the country from W. F. Harnden, who in addition to carrying packages and undoubtedly letters, ran a business issuing bills of exchange using banks in cities where he had agencies.[91] These bills were receipts of payment in which a customer in one city would pay a sum of money to an agent and send the bill to a recipient in another city. The recipient would present the bill to the agent in his city and receive payment. The transfers would then be cleared through Harnden's bank correspondents in both cities. This operation was used by Harnden to finance European immigration (he called it his "Foreign Passenger Express") and was adapted by Adams to transfer gold from California. Miners would deposit gold dust at Adams's agencies in California who would issue certificates for the amount that would be sent by Adams Express to recipients in the East, who could claim payment at an Adams office. Adams offices in California would consolidate gold deposits and ship them, under guard, to the mint in Philadelphia.

The operation described above worked and provided the most secure means of communication, transportation, and finance between California and the East. It was fraught with risk, however, for both the miner and the company. First there was the question of trust. Frequently the miners would not be able to get to an Adams agent and would use a local express rider, like Todd, to take the gold.[92] The miners had to trust the local expressman, the national express company, and the local agent at the miners' homes in the states. Second there was the risk of loss through theft or ships lost at sea. Gold shipments were usually insured, but a large loss could bankrupt an insurance company and international reinsurance was not available. Third, there was a measurement risk. Since gold was a physical commodity whose value was dependent on weight and purity, the gold had to be weighed and assayed in every stage of the transaction. If at any stage the recipient decided there was less gold or it was less pure than the conveyor claimed, the sender would receive a smaller payment. Given the difficulty of communications, it was very hard to go back through the transaction chain to obtain approval for corrections. The miner was at risk until Adams office issued a receipt (or certificate) and, if there was a discrepancy, would not know if the original measurement was wrong, the expressman had stolen a bit, or he was being cheated by the Adams agent who claimed there was a shortfall. Once the certificate was issued, Adams was at risk if the mint decided there was a shortfall.

A transaction by Francis Post, whose certificate is shown in figure 5, is an example of the measurement risk.[93] In this case, Adams was simply conveying his package of gold dust to one Cranston Wilcox and not assuming any risk. The certificate, which was issued July 28, 1851, simply states, "One package addressed Mint Phil, order Cranston Wilcox, New Bedford & said to contain coin and dust: Value Two thousand." Because Adams was not at risk, their fee, $60.00, or 3 percent, was considerably less than the typical 5 percent charge. Wilcox, the beneficiary of the gold shipment, received a remittance from the mint for only $1,183.65, so he wrote to Post on October 9, 1851, "It seems there is a deficiency in the gross weight." Wilcox claimed in his letter to Post that when he complained to the mint of a deficiency in payment, the mint wrote back that "the bag was in good order and the seal not mutilated; and the bag would not have held the $2,000." On November 25, Post wrote to Adams Express in San Francisco, "There appears to have been a mistake made at your office in weighing, or marking some Gold Dust for me on the 28th of July last." In this letter, Post diplomatically suggests, "It seems that there must have been a mistake in putting up the package—but I think it most likely the wrong package was marked for us. Perhaps you can find the mistake." He did not want to accuse them of stealing, but he was short $876.35. Since Adams had not insured it, however, and was not at risk, as it would have been had he deposited the amount with the company, Post most likely recovered nothing.[94]

An indication of the risk of the express business was that Adams Express did not survive intact. In 1854, Adams reorganized its California operation and

Figure 8. Adams and Company's Express Certificate for $2,000 in gold. Courtesy American Antiquarian Society, Worcester, Massachusetts.

turned it over to D. H. Haskell, who had managed the firm in California since 1849. Later that year, in a robbery on the Sonora stage, they lost twenty-five thousand dollars, and there was a run on Adam's offices in the southern mines; finally in 1855, the largest bank in San Francisco, Page, Bacon and Company, closed its doors and there was a more serious run on Adams, which had to close two days later.[95] After the failure of Adams Express, the consolidation of express companies in California accelerated, with Wells, Fargo and Company absorbing most of the competitors and taking over most of the business.

## Conclusion

During 1849 and 1850 printed information sources in California had little credibility among the goldrushers, and the new miners lost whatever confidence they might have had in the primary communications mechanism, the Post Office. This is a turnaround from the situation in the East. There, printed newspapers, books, and maps provided most of goldrushers' information, and they had so much confidence in the Post Office that they were sure that they would have many letters waiting for them in San Francisco or Sutter's Fort. The printed information sources had, however, misled them on the trail, and the letters were not waiting for them. The primary story of this chapter is how goldrushers, now miners, merchants, tradesmen, shippers, and every kind of worker, substituted rumors for untimely printed information and utilized express companies in favor of the Post Office.

*Information and Communications in California*

A fundamental aspect of these developments in communications and information dispersal was a change in commonly accepted sources of credibility. Goldrushers learned on the trail that claims of official information sources and of personal expertise were unreliable indicators of good information. New credibility criteria emphasized personal experience. It is likely that many goldrushers now trusted oral communications more than print. This led the new emigrants to follow rumors delivered by other miners like themselves, whom they could look in the eye and question. To an extent, this indicates a reversion to eighteenth-century methods of information assessment when most information was transmitted orally.[96]

By 1852, the official sources of communications and information began to catch up, and the difficulties of private communications services and rumors became more apparent. Wages declined in California, and the Post Office rescinded some of its rigid administrative regulations so that post offices could expand and be more effective in delivering mail. Post roads helped connect isolated mining communities, and newspapers appeared in small towns and even mining camps, which allowed much faster dissemination of information in print. California publishing and bookselling grew with the success of such prominent figures as Joseph Hutchings, Anton Roman, and Hubert Bancroft. These changes coincided with changes in mining as quartz mining and large firms began to dominate the industry. The story of the first two years, however, remains an important example of the role of credibility criteria and confidence building in new and difficult situations where the traditional forms of information dispersal and communications did not function well.

# CHAPTER SIX

# The Gold Rush in 1850
## *Private Communications and Public Information*

While California was developing its own information and communications infrastructure, news of the West continued to be important to newspapers and book publishers in the East. The controversy over slavery in the new conquests obtained from Mexico kept California in the news, and continued gold fever maintained the demand for information. Gold fever in 1850 differed from that in 1849 because there was more information about California and gold and because the information was considered more reliable. For the first time people could obtain information directly from goldrushers in the form of letters and in several books published in 1850 to 1851 by returned miners and reporters. New maps appeared in print, including the Jarvis, Derby, and Jackson maps described in the previous chapter. Letters from California played a key role in the information marketplace by late 1849 and in 1850 to 1851. These communications, in print or in private letters, provided a new means of assessment that made extravagant claims and fraudulent guidebooks easier to spot.

Communications from the West to the East not only allowed a means of cross-checking facts, they also changed the way people who did not go to California in 1849 perceived the gold rush, and they affected the credibility criteria with which easterners assessed gold rush information. The personal experiences described in goldrushers' writings became an important source of credibility. Goldrusher information also influenced the decisions of easterners of whether to go west in 1850. This effect was substantial because the 1850 emigration was almost double the size of 1849's. The great influence of these communications did not always work to the advantage of the 1850 goldrushers, because the substantial delay in letters, or in book and map publications, meant that their information was always out of date. Since conditions on the trails and in the mines changed rapidly, the second wave of goldrushers at times got in trouble because they utilized obsolete advice.

Although there were several reporters among the emigrants who wrote for publication, most letters from goldrushers were private, written to their families and friends in the East or business letters written to suppliers and partners.[1] Private letters became, however, public information when published in newspapers. Letters were in great demand by newspaper editors, who would ask families if they would allow letters they received to appear in their newspapers. In other cases, the letter writers stipulated that the letter was for publication, or the recipients of letters would send them to the local newspapers on their own initiative.

Goldrushers' letters were distinctive for two main reasons. First, these letters represented a firsthand source of information from individuals who had made the trip successfully and were still there trying to mine gold, practice a profession or trade, or sell merchandise. Second, and more important, many goldrusher letters were printed in local newspapers, and the readers knew, or at least knew of, the letter writers. This source influenced how the information they contained was interpreted, and it made the information more credible. The questions of those who did not go in 1849, possibly because they did not trust the information available at the time, now could be answered with more assurance: Was there really gold obtainable in California? Was the trip practical with the resources at hand? Did health improve or deteriorate with the travel? Could a professional, tradesman, craftsman, storekeeper or laborer really make more money in California than in the East? When answers to these questions came from a husband, brother, son, friend, or business partner who had actually made the trip, they were likely to be more credible than information from a newspaper article copied from the exchanges or a book written by an author not known to the reader.

An important effect of the published and unpublished letters of the first year's goldrushers was that they decreased the uncertainty about the feasibility of the trip. No matter how harrowing the letter writers described the journey, they were there—the trip was possible. Goldrushers' letters also decreased the uncertainty about the existence of gold and whether it was possible for individuals or small groups with little or no capital to mine successfully. Even letters discouraging people from coming admitted that there was a great deal of gold in California. The information in these letters also stated, or implied, that although most goldrushers did not strike it rich, some did. Even if one was not lucky, however, it was still possible to work at wages or for profits that far outstripped anything one could make in the East doing similar jobs.

Business communications were entirely by letter, and business success, particularly for merchants, was strongly affected by the timing and uncertainties of mail and freight delivery. Goldrushers who were merchants in the East saw the fabulous opportunities for profit afforded by the extremely high gold rush prices. They would quickly set up stores and write their suppliers in the East to send those articles that were most in demand when they wrote the letter. As in most other aspects of the gold rush, many people did the same thing simultaneously. By the time the business letters reached the East and goods were ordered and shipped to California, the market would be flooded with these items and the merchants would go bust. There were many gold rush journals that described a miner who was sure that he could make much more money in commerce than in mining, only to lose his stake or go deeply into debt because prices changed when he finally had goods to sell. There were merchants, however, that became fabulously wealthy. These were people like Sam Brannan, who was there first, or Collis Huntington and Chester Crocker, who were good at guessing what would be scarce in the future.

Goldrushers wrote books as well as letters, and some letter writers, like Bayard Taylor who wrote for the *New York Tribune*, turned their letters into a book. Taylor returned east after only four months in California to report to Greeley, and he quickly prepared his book manuscript. Published in the fall of 1850, it became one of the most popular of the contemporary gold rush books. In our group of travelers, the book-writing goldrushers were J. Goldsborough Bruff of the Washington DC company and Alonzo Delano of the Dayton, Illinois, company. Bruff stayed in California until June 1851 and spent his last several months there preparing his manuscript. He was sure of his writing and drawing talents. According to his statement in a letter to the Society of California Pioneers in 1869, "In Sacramento [1850] I was offered Ten Thousand dollars cash, for my rough sketches of the overland Travel: but declined it, for obvious reasons."[2] The editors at Harpers, to whom he submitted his manuscript for publication, were apparently less impressed, and they wrote, "it is full of romantic and thrilling adventures," but it needed thorough revision. The book went through several rewritings, including one edited by Richard Locke, the editor of the *New York Sun* but was not published until Read and Gaines's two volume publication in 1944.[3] Alonzo Delano was a professional journalist before coming to California

155

and published his book, although he never moved back east. After unsuccessful mining in 1849, he set up a shop in San Francisco and later moved to Grass Valley to become a merchant and banker. During this time he turned his journal into a book.[4]

There were others who had been in California before the gold rush who published books in 1850. One of the most successful of these authors was Edward Gould Buffum, a member of the New York Volunteers, who finished his manuscript in January 1850 and sent it to Philadelphia in time for Lea and Blanchard to publish it that year. Walter Colton, former *alcalde* of Monterey, was another such author. He toured the gold mines in 1848 and returned to Philadelphia in early 1849 to publish his book by mid-1850.[5] These were the best known of the early books written by goldrushers, but there were many more published from 1850 to 1851.

This chapter will illustrate how private letters became important public information for potential goldrushers in the East, how business success was determined in part by the constraints of cross-country communications, how the markets for books adapted to the new information, and how letters and books influenced the size and travel of the overland migration in 1850.

## Private Letters in the Public Domain
### Letters of the Wolverine Rangers

The Wolverine Rangers Company was organized by James Pratt, the editor of the *Marshall (Michigan) Statesman*, in part to record the trip through letters sent back to his newspaper. Unlike Bayard Taylor, Pratt was a goldrusher, interested in being a lawyer and making money in California as well as in telling the story of the company and the gold rush through the pages of the *Statesman*.[6] The newspaper covered the organization of the company in January 1849, printed its articles of agreement, and advertised the company throughout mid-Michigan. Pratt traveled ahead of the company to arrange its outfitting and provisioning in Missouri, and the *Statesman* printed the nine letters it received from Pratt during his trip to the trailhead in Independence, Missouri. These early letters not only described the progress of the company but were a kind of travelogue for the readers back in Michigan. For example, Pratt wrote from Chicago, "We arrived at this city yesterday. . . . There are some delightful residences, particularly along the beach of the lake. The river is full of shipping, and preparations are busy for early navigation. . . . There are several splendid public houses."[7] He named the newspapers of the city and described the politics as well as the cost and convenience of outfitting in the city (the Rangers outfitted in Independence). Subsequent letters described his trip through Illinois to St Louis and Independence.[8] The readers of the newspaper must have felt they were sharing in Pratt's trip as, vicariously, they would share in the great adventure over the next year.

Pratt was not the only member of the company to write to the newspaper, and one letter by Horace Ladd on May 14, 1849, illustrated well the intersection of private communications and public information in these letters. Ladd wrote what appeared to be a very personal letter to the brother of Charles Palmer, who was the company's doctor: "DEAR SIR: It falls to my lot to convey to you the mournful intelligence of the death of your brother, Dr. Palmer. He died this morning at 4 o'clock of the Cholera."[9] The letter went on to describe in great detail Palmer's rather gruesome symptoms. Palmer apparently contracted the disease while attending another cholera sufferer (whom, the letter stated, he cured). The letter was full of names of people from the community who were in the company and was written in such a way that it was both personal and part of the public story. The letter connected the company with the community back home. An example was in the last paragraph: "During the afternoon he said to Mr. E. S. Camp, (who was with him at the time,) here is my watch (handing it to him) which I wish you would take care of until I get well, but if I should not get well, give it to my sister. This was all he said on the subject of his death at any time."[10] Most of the readers of the *Statesman* probably knew Palmer or members of his family, so this rather touching last paragraph appeared to be written both to Palmer's family and to the community.

Letters designed to provide an ongoing record of the company for the community continued to arrive until the company reached Fort Kearny and, after a hiatus of two months, from Fort Laramie, carried mostly by go-backers. A letter from Herman Camp, one of two Camp brothers in the company (the other was Elmon), made clear the relationship between private letters and public information.[11] The letter read like a public letter, filled with many names of people in the community, vignettes of a buffalo hunt and a strong storm, and a description of their Fourth of July celebration. Most of the names of people in the company that Camp mentioned were people from the community; he did not mention William Swain, who was a newcomer to the company from New York.[12] When he published the letter, the *Statesman*'s editor wrote, "We are particularly requested to publish the following long letter describing their trip so far." The Camp family apparently sent the letter to the newspaper so the entire community could read it. These letters were at once personal and public, meant to bind the community to the enterprise and provide information about how the company was coping with the difficulties of the trip.

The editor of the *Statesman* worried when no letters were received from the company after they began the western part of the trip.[13] On December 26, 1849, he wrote, "We have been anxiously looking for the past week for letters from some of the 'Wolverine Rangers,' but have been disappointed. . . . Great anxiety is manifested for their welfare, by their friends in this place." Finally, two weeks later, Horace Ladd's wife Ann sent to the newspaper a letter from Ladd from a "Camp on the Pitt River, 150 miles north of Sutter's Fort."[14] The letter was short, and it only mentioned that they were safe and had been "grossly deceived by going a new route from the Humboldt to the North or Lawson's Pass." Three weeks later the newspaper published another letter from Ladd to his wife from a mining site on the Feather River that was also a personal letter. It requested that she "please call on Mrs. Allcott, by George's request, and tell her that George is well and healthy, also on Mrs. Camp and tell her that Elmon will write in a few days," and added, "Mr. Jas. Pratt and all the Marshall boys are well and in good spirits."[15] She probably fulfilled the request to make personal visits, and she went a step farther by sending the letter to the *Statesman* for publication.

Although the company broke up after reaching California, the *Statesman* continued to publish many letters of the travelers from Marshall, thus continuing the relationship between the town and the goldrushers. The February 20, 1850, issue of the *Statesman* was devoted almost entirely to letters from two members of the former company sent to the newspaper by family members who had received them. In this issue the editor described the public service component of these letters:

> Through the kindness of Messrs. George S. Wright and H. A. Woodruff we are enabled to publish the following highly interesting letters from two of the Marshall company. The great anxiety of the numerous relatives and friends of the 'Rangers' will be relieved by these more full particulars of their safe arrival, and their present health and success. . . . The letter from James Pratt, Esq., being partly upon private business, shows an apparent want of connection, as we publish only what would interest the community generally.

The letters in the February 20, 1850, issue, and in subsequent issues for the next several months, not only described the hardships of the trip over the Lassen Cutoff and the beginning of the writers' mining experience, they also provided for the first time credible information about whether one could make money in California. Various letters published from February through April 1850 appeared in time for people to decide whether they wanted to make the trip in that year. In the small town of Marshall, Michigan, they probably provided the bulk of the information that the community had about the gold rush and formed the basis of information on which potential 1850 goldrushers decided on whether or not to go to California.

The letters of James Pratt from San Francisco were good examples of apparently private letters becoming public sources of information. Pratt was no longer connected with or obligated to write for the *Statesman*, but in long letters to his family that he may have expected to be published in the *Statesman*, he described his personal experiences setting up as a lawyer and businessman. In spite of his possible expectation of publication, the letters read like private family correspondence. If he was dissimulating, he was very skillful.

Pratt wrote he arrived in San Francisco December 8, 1849: "a stranger, penniless, at a season when it is crowded and thronged by a population ready to snatch at the first chance of labor of any kind—my heart sank within me, and I felt how utterly desolate was my condition."[16] He managed to partner with a lawyer acquaintance from Michigan and lived in the "'law offices,' two small rooms, a mere shell of a building—[renting for] $400 per month!" Although he was living on borrowed money and had no clients, his letter was optimistic: "There is a world of legal business doing and to be done here . . . when a United States court shall be established here, it will continue to be as it is now already becoming, one of the most splendid cities for the legal profession in the world." The letter also contained news of some of the former Rangers who were wintering in the mines and were "in good health and spirits . . . scattered all around on the river [the Feather River]."

Pratt wrote again in January, by which time he had new quarters: "in my little office, 10 feet by 12! The ground is half covered with boards for a floor," but he still had no clients. The tone of this letter is also optimistic and reflects the excitement he still felt:

This is a great city. There must be now at least 60,000 people here. Vessels from all parts of the world are at anchor in the splendid harbor. The confusion of tongues at Babel was never greater than here. All day passers by converse and jabber in the peculiar language of the country; and at all hours of the night the unceasing jargon is heard outside the place of one's rest. . . . My office is near the corner of Pacific and Montgomery sts. The latter is one of the heaviest business streets in the city and it is the muddiest and most disagreeable. . . . I went into the court . . . and heard a case tried . . . his lawyer charged $150 for his services. So you see if one gets into a good law business here he can live even at California prices for board, rent. &c.[17]

On January 10, Pratt moved into his new offices, and on the twelfth he got his first client:

a gentleman with whom I became acquainted on the frontier of Missouri called upon me . . . [they] made six thousand dollars, and are still digging successfully. He has concluded to leave $3,000 . . . with me to invest and speculate at my own discretion, and he will lend me as much more money for the same purpose, if I desire. Money loans here at 10 per cent a month. It can be used so advantageously.[18]

Pratt was on his way. He closed his letter, "My health and spirits are good. I shall labor to render a good account of myself." The effect of this letter on professionals reading the *Statesman* must have been startling, and because they knew, or knew of, Pratt, they probably found it believable. A professional in a small town in 1850 made between three and five hundred dollars per year; after only two months, starting from nothing, Pratt appeared to be making much more.

The newspaper reported success at mining as well as Pratt's success in San Francisco. Horace Ladd and another former Ranger, Tom Manser, were mining at the Feather River. Ladd kept his wife Ann informed of their progress, and Ann turned over the letters (presumably edited) to the *Statesman*. The first was written on January 9, 1850, and printed by the newspaper March 20. They were living in "a tent which [was] large and good" and, in spite of the high cost of tools, clothing and provisions (they had lost everything on the Lassen Cutoff) wrote, "we have $500 worth of gold dust on hand; all this we have dug ourselves, and no thanks to any one for assistance." Although it was the rainy season, he said, "When we do work in the mines we get pretty well paid; some days we get $25, and others $100." Not everyone made money though: "there are a great many here that do not make a living nor never did at home . . . a poor man that will not work cannot expect to get rich here or at home either. Tho's and I have worked hard . . . any man of good and enterprising character can do well here."[19] The former Rangers were scattered up and down the Feather River, and Ladd reported that all seem to be healthy and doing well: "I wish you could see the Marshall boys now; they are all so fat you would not know half of them. . . . There is no sickness here this winter . . . all are healthy and able to work when the weather will admit."[20]

The Camp brothers also kept their family informed, and their letters were printed in the *Statesman*. In a letter dated January 9, 1850, Elmon Camp reported that he deeply regretted losing on the Lassen Cutoff Dr. Palmer's gold watch that he was carrying for Palmer's sister.[21] The letter described how they arrived at the mines with one dollar and no supplies, but were able to borrow three hundred dollars to build a winter quarters (a stone house, which was much better shelter than most miners', who typically had only a tent or a log cabin) and begin mining: "We then commenced mining and have succeeded in obtaining a sufficient amount of gold to pay all our debts, and purchase a supply of provisions for the winter." Apparently Elmon was sickly back in Michigan and wrote that mining was hard physical labor: "You may think if such be the case, I could not accomplish much; but you will think differently when I tell you that I am stout, rugged and healthy. I never was so strong before . . . the journey over the plains has completely restored my health." The letter continued in this optimistic vein: "The amount of gold in this country fully realizes my anticipations."

An important theme in Ladd's and Camp's letters from the mines was that success resulted from patient hard work, which resulted in a steady income many times what someone could earn back in Michigan. Ladd wrote that a healthy man willing to work hard could make "ten times as much . . . as he would be [making] at home." Camp agreed that there was "certainly a fortune . . . for every honest, industrious, hard working young man." They were telling their friends back in Michigan that real mining success was the result of "patient industry" and that in good weather a miner would be "sure of washing out his ounce per day."[22] One ounce was worth sixteen dollars and this amount was considered average by miners in the winter of 1849, and many decided it was inadequate and left mines producing at that rate to go prospecting for richer sites. It compared extremely well, however, with average wages in the states of between one and three dollars per day.[23]

The good experiences of the Rangers continued to be reported through April

1850, and the credibility of their reports of success was enhanced when they sent gold back to Michigan. In a February letter Ladd reported to his father, "I have made up a package of one pound of gold dust, and put it into the hands of a gentleman going to San Francisco, to be sent by express to Ann."[24] The gold was worth about $256 at $16 per ounce, and the express charges were about 5 percent, so Ann should have received about $240. This was the ultimate justification of the trip. Ladd was a saddler in Marshall, whose annual income probably did not exceed $300 per year. In a few months of mining, after arriving in California with nothing, he paid his debts, financed provisions for the winter when mining was slow, and still saved and was able to send home almost his annual income. Also, his expectations were high for the new mining season to start soon: "I am now connected with a company of 10, going up the river some 25 miles for the purpose of damming and draining the river so as to dig in the bed of the stream." The effect of this news must have been very positive for those readers still thinking about going to California. Here was an ordinary local person who had had a terrible trip across the country and lost everything, who had not been extraordinarily lucky, but who was still apparently doing much better in California than he would have done in Michigan.

The letters of the Wolverine Rangers illustrated, in microcosm, several ways in which private letters from California changed the public information that people in the East obtained about the gold rush. First, these letters were personal and from local people known to many of the readers; this increased substantially the credibility of their information. Readers could now assess the credibility of the information based on their knowledge of the individuals. Second, the letters provided a connection between the local goldrushers and the community that made the gold rush story, at least in part, a local story and vividly concrete. The adventures, hardships, and successes of their friends and neighbors became more real and more believable when it was related by people they knew. Third, in terms of influencing potential 1850 goldrushers, the letters were a great incentive to go in part because they showed that with hard work and perseverance, one could make much more money in California than in the States even if one did not strike it rich in the mines.[25]

### Information through the Mail

Although the letters printed in the *Marshall Statesman* did not contain much explicit advice about outfitting, provisioning, the overland route (other than one should not take the Lassen Cutoff), or the specifics of mining or working in California, other published letters were written for the purpose of giving guide-book-like information and advice. Also, some letter writers were explicit about whether or not their friends or neighbors should follow them to California.

Many letters containing advice about the overland trail were sent to and published by Missouri newspapers since that was where so many goldrushers purchased outfits and provisions. Some were meant solely to provide public information, such as a January 24, 1850, letter from "M. M." sent to Chambers and Knapp, the publishers of the *St. Louis Missouri Republican*. The letter begins, "I do not advise any man to come, rich or poor, but to those who will come, I can give them a little good advice, especially if they come by land." He goes on to recommend ox teams over mules and taking only a very light wagon, no "heavier than a light two horse wagon": "it should be new, or as good as new. . . . To each team there should be not less than four yoke of oxen. . . . To each team 1,600 pounds are all that should be put on."[26] The recommendation of 1,600 pounds was considerably less than the 2,000-pound recommendation of Gilpin and others the previous year. Many emigrant letters described the enormous waste of food and material on the trail in 1849 and recommended light loads. John Crigler, of Howard County, Missouri, wrote to his father in a letter that was printed in the *Missouri Republican* that he would recommend only 1,000 pounds per wagon.[27] A letter written by Simeon Switzler to his son and published in the January 25, 1850, *Missouri Statesman* contradicted M. M.'s advice about oxen and style of wagon (he recommended mules and a heavy one-horse wagon) but agreed on the light loads, writing, "some thousand of heavy wagons, with their cargoes thrown away are being strewed over the Plains."[28]

Advice letters published in Missouri newspapers in the late winter and spring of 1850 covered almost every aspect of the trip. M. M., who clearly thought of himself as writing a guidebook-like letter, gave advice on topics no 1849 guidebook touched on. For instance, he recommended against "joint-stock messes" in which four or five men jointly owned the wagon, animals, and provisions that made up the equipment of their mess.[29] He felt that one man should own the wagon, animals, and cargo, and the others should pay him (in advance) as much as $350 dollars to belong to the mess. That way, if the mess broke up, as many did, there was no problem about how the commonly owned outfit and provisions should be split. One can imagine that M. M. had exactly this problem. He gave recommendations about cooking: "the way to cook beans on the road . . . is to stew them; but they must be boiled in fresh water until they are soft, before any salt or bacon be put into them," and advised, "every mess should have a guide book, and the best are the Mormon books." He told the readers never to hurry their teams and to travel slowly for the first six hundred miles. He also advised that during long, forced drives (such as over the deserts) travelers should not make the animals travel faster but should cut down on the stops and make them travel longer. M. M. recommended leaving early, even if the grass was not up, and taking extra feed, since the weight would decrease as the grass grew. He gave detailed directions about cutoffs and corrected guidebook inaccuracies such as Ware's statement that it was thirty-five miles across the Sublette Cutoff. He warned against the Lassen Cutoff, and recommended the Carson Pass instead of the Donner Pass.[30] Many advice letters recommended forgetting the firearms. A Mr. Taylor of Roanoke, Missouri, writing to his brother, stated that if he were to do it over, he would bring "a small rifle, if . . . any at all—no pistols, and but little powder and lead."[31]

Big city newspapers also printed letters sent from goldrushers but concentrated more on gold rush and California news than on creating a connection between the gold rush companies and local readers or on giving guidebook-like advice about the trip. For example, in the first three months of 1850 the *Boston Evening Transcript* published no articles or letters describing the progress of Boston-based gold rush companies or giving advice about the trail. California was prominent in the newspaper, however, because it printed articles announcing ships arriving from California and giving the amount of gold they were carrying, articles about the prospects of a St. Louis to San Francisco railroad, reports of fires in San Francisco and Sacramento, reports of the progress of the government in California, and almost daily reporting on the congressional debates on California statehood. The *Transcript* also published letters from California that described the success or failure of individuals' gold mining or merchandising ventures, but they had a different style from those in the *Marshall Statesman*. For example, the newspaper published a letter from "an intelligent journeyman carpenter" who described in quite personal terms an illness, and his living conditions and added, "carpenters can do first rate here, especially in the summer season. Any man who is a good carpenter, I would advise to come out here."[32] This good news for carpenters contemplating going to California may not have had the same credibility as, for instance, Pratt's description of his success as a lawyer in San Francisco, because the *Transcript* neither gave the letter writer's name nor where he was from.

In New York, James Gordon Bennett's *Herald* and Horace Greeley's *Tribune* continued to cover the gold rush, including publishing letters sent directly to their newspapers and from the exchanges. Like the *Boston Transcript's*, however, the gold rush coverage of the New York newspapers was less personal and less advice-driven than that of smaller town newspapers like the *Marshall Statesman*, or the Missouri newspapers. Also, a greater proportion of the coverage of the New York newspapers was general news about California, such as how much gold had been shipped, questions of land settlements, the development of San Francisco and other towns in California, and, most important, politics.

The November 12, 1849, issue of the *New York Herald* contained news of both the Monterey convention and accounts from the gold region that covered the entire front page and about one-third of the second page. The headlines were a list of items in the upper-left-hand column that indicated the relative importance that James Gordon Bennett gave to the kinds of news from the state. The list included, in descending order:

Highly Important Intelligence
Proceedings of the State Constitutional Convention
Slavery Prohibited in California
Accounts of the Gold Region
Arrival of Gold Diggers with their Pockets Full of Rocks
Over Half a Million in Gold in the Empire City
Marriages and Deaths [in California—one marriage and twenty deaths]
Shipping Intelligence

There were personal stories printed in the *New York Tribune*. Bayard Taylor, the author and reporter sent out by Horace Greeley for the purpose of writing to the newspaper, wrote many letters during his trip through the Panama Isthmus and on his arrival in California. His first letters from the gold region were from the southern mines and were dated late August and early September 1849. They read like personal letters, written in the first person with many descriptions of people he stayed with and places he visited, always in a light and interesting style. For instance, in describing his trip from "the hospitable oaks of Maj. Graham's camp" to the diggings along the Calaveras River, he wrote, "for the first time in several days, we slept in a bed—the bed of the Calaveras River, and in the deepest hollow of its gold-bearing sands. . . . Heaping the loose gravel for pillows, we enjoyed a delightful sleep, interrupted only once by the howling of a large gray wolf."[33] His letters were amusing and detailed; the content, however, was different from Pratt's because he was reporting the event as an observer rather than relating his success or failure as a goldrusher. Also, he gave no advice for potential goldrushers. For this reason these letters had quite a different informational and communications function than the letters published by the *Statesman* or the Missouri newspapers.

Readers of the New York newspapers wanted information about going to California and what to do when they got there. Many editors, however, did not oblige. Horace Greeley, for example, unlike in the previous year, did not see that providing information was the major purpose of his articles and editorials about California. In November 1849, Greeley wrote in the *Tribune*, "We have received a large number of letters asking information in regard to the best route and cost of getting to California—and having no time to reply to them by letter we take this method of giving the information asked."[34] "This method" consisted of the article that followed containing one paragraph about fares to Chagres and the Pacific steamers, one sentence about ships going around the Horn, and nothing at all about the overland trip. Information in newspapers for potential New York goldrushers came from published letters, particularly in November and December 1849.[35] Except for Bayard Taylor and Theodore Johnson, these letters, however, generally were not signed and did not create credibility by personalizing the gold rush in the way that was done by the *Statesman*.

Private letters that were not published also had a public information effect because receivers shared the letters or talked about a goldrusher's success or failure to family and friends. Many letters seemed to be written explicitly to provide information and advice to several people who were named in the letters. For example, Daniel Robinson, of Bloomington, Indiana, wrote to his sister and brother from the trail and from California with letters filled with names of goldrushers from Bloomington.[36] Presumably, he expected his siblings to convey the information to the individuals' friends and family and, it is reasonable to assume, to the rest of the town. Sometimes letter writers requested that their receiver convey information. Thus, David Campbell, traveling with his brother, James, made a request of his father: "send word down to Elizabeth [James's wife] that all is well. Tell her . . . she will hear from James in a few days."[37] At other times, a goldrusher would write to several people expecting them to share information, as Swain did when writing to his wife, Sabrina, and his brother, George, about different aspects of his life on the Feather River mines.[38]

Many letter writers gave advice about whether family or friends should come to California. Naturally, such advice was more personal than they would write in letters they thought would be published. The criteria most often mentioned for joining the goldrusher were the related issues of health and money. For example, John Ingalls, in writing to his brother, stated:

> I tell you honestly that I should not like to advise you to come though I have not the least doubt but that you would make money here if you had your health. There are thousands of persons here that hardly ever saw a sick day in the States that are completely broken down and many of them, if they live, never will fully recover their health. . . . You are just the man to make money here but these dull sleepy fellows that can't turn around once a week had better stay at home.[39]

Given this very ambiguous advice, Ingalls's brother never went to California, at least during the gold rush, but John Ingalls's wife, Anne, went west in January 1851 and joined him in Marysville, where he owned a store.

## The Letters of Merchants, Tradesmen, and Contractors
### Rewards and Risks of Mining the Miners

Many goldrushers tried merchandising, plying a trade, practicing a profession, or going into business when either the hard physical labor of mining got them down or they simply found no gold. It seemed to many early goldrushers that a store was a sure thing if one had merchandise to sell. Alternatively, if one had a useful trade or profession such as carpentry, cooking, law, or medicine, wages and prices of services were so high that one could not fail to make a great deal of money. At the high prices and wages in California in 1849, many miners thought that the merchants, tradesmen, and professionals were the ones collecting most of the gold. In a letter dated March 13, 1849, at a time when miners were making very good money, "McK" wrote, "From all that I can learn, the traders and merchants at this place make more money than the miners do. Goods sell enormously high here, but I am told that everything is four hundred per cent higher at the mines."[40] Cities were being built seemingly overnight, and building lumber and carpentry skills were scarce. As a result, lumber and ready-to-assemble buildings were being shipped from the East to be sold at prices, hopefully, that were many multiples of the suppliers' cost of material and transportation. Boardinghouses were making money: D. D. McDonald wrote to his brother in Plattsburg, Missouri, in the spring of 1850, that by keeping a hotel in Marysville he "expect[ed] to clear, in the fall and winter, about fifteen or twenty thousand dollars . . . [and] return to the States."[41] Doctors were also doing well according to William Royall, who in a letter published in the *Missouri Statesman* wrote, "physicians are all making fortunes in this country; they hardly look at a man's tongue for less than an ounce of gold!"[42]

Merchandising, trades, and professions, however, were not a sure track to riches largely because so many tried to do the same thing at the same time and because of difficulties in communications and information. Merchants had to obtain supplies from the East, and their primary means of communication with suppliers was by letter. As we have seen in chapter 5, most goldrushers considered the mails to be slow and unreliable, and while expresses were much better, they were expensive. Some letters written to newspapers in 1849 and 1850 warned eastern merchants of the danger of fluctuating prices. In the same issue of the *Missouri Republican* in which McK's letter was printed, a letter from "V. J. F." asserted, "the price of goods, of every description is falling rapidly, and it is feared that the market will soon be glutted. It is believed that heavy losses will be sustained by those sending or bringing in cargoes from abroad."[43] J. D. Stevenson, writing to his son-in-law in New York City, warned him against shipping to California in April 1949: "From all the accounts we receive from the States, large quantities of goods must be coming out here; and I apprehend the shippers will suffer severe losses. I hope not; but I do assure you that there is a great danger."[44] With regard to the professions, Franklin Street wrote in a book about his experiences in California that, by 1850, "The professions [lawyers and doctors], as may readily be supposed, are completely full in California, and that of physicians is crowded to overflowing."[45]

Many tradesmen's problems were also caused by communications and information difficulties. Knowing what jobs enjoyed high wages in various places at particular times was extremely difficult. Tradesmens' frustrations were increased by the fact that competition would fluctuate greatly. Goldrushers would change from merchandising, to trades, to laboring, and back to mining very quickly, and labor markets suffered large short-term fluctuations. Carpenters were a good example of this effect. The many fires that destroyed property in San Francisco and Sacramento required a great deal labor for rebuilding; wages for carpenters would skyrocket at those times. The news of the fires would get to the mines some time afterward, and many miners who were not prospering would come to the cities to hire out as carpenters, although they may not have had many qualifications for the trade. This would rapidly drive down the wages of carpenters in the cities.

### The Problems of Albion Sweetzer

One of the goldrushers we have been following, Albion Sweetzer of the Boston-Newton Company, went to California primarily to work at his trade, carpentry, and to run a store. He had experience in both of these occupations in New England, and he had arranged that when he arrived in California, he would contact Littlefield and Blood of Boston about shipping goods to California. Sweetzer frequently changed businesses and occupations, always making enough to get by but never meeting his expectations. He wrote to Littlefield and Blood every month from April 1850 through February 1851.[46] Sweetzer's story, told in these letters is an excellent illustration of how the difficulties of timing, information, and communication, complicated the life of gold rush tradesmen and merchants.

Sweetzer's first attempt at business was a store at a mining camp on the North Fork of the American River, but he abandoned this early in 1850 because of the difficulties in transporting merchandise to the mines. He went to Sacramento in the spring of that year to try his hand at carpentry and contracting. Littlefield and Blood had shipped a prefabricated building to him, but in April 1850 Sweetzer wrote to them that this may have been a mistake. In this letter he indicated that timing and communications problems would plague their business relationship: "I am sorry to learn that you have sent the Building as they are selling very low at present but in all probability it will fetch more when it arrives than at present . . . the market is [so] fluctuating that I advise you not to make any more shipments."[47] The next month he wrote to Littlefield and Blood that he could not pay them, presumably for the building. Although only a few months previously, Sacramento had been a city of tents with a tremendous demand for buildings; Sweetzer wrote, "as I stated before it is not safe to send any goods here as the market is very fluctuating . . . one year ago this place was a wilderness and now it is literally covered with Buildings to 3 stories high."[48] A month later things were better: "I have just made a contract to put up a building 20 by 72½ feet and 3 stories high." In this letter he seemed pleased: "there has been another great fire at San Francisco and it is estimated that 3 millions of property is destroyed, which will probably affect the price of lumber."[49] He was also finally able to send them some money: $250 of gold dust in May, $350 in July, and $250 (no date stated), all sent by local express to San Francisco, and then to Boston by Adams and Company.

Business, however, kept fluctuating, and even getting jobs at carpentry became difficult because "carpenters [were] so thick that jobs [were] taken low." He tried mining and purchased a claim with a partner, but this did not last long. In September he moaned, "I have but little to do at present—people are all short of cash or dust . . . many of the miners that have worked a number of months have lost all of their labour; and I know of a number that could have sold their claims from $1500 to $3000 that have failed entirely."[50] He then went back to merchandizing in Sacramento and expected a shipment from Littlefield and Blood, but he was pessimistic: "this is the hardest market in the world to keep the run of things. For instance you will recollect that I wrote to you that 8 oz tacks were sold @2.50 [*sic*] cts. per paper; now they are Back to the old price again, 50 cents per paper." When the goods did arrive, some were damaged and other commodities were not profitable, such as jewelry (too high quality for the market), oats (cost more to put them in sacks than he could get for them), and boots (too small, miners only wanted very large sizes). He wrote in October, "my invoice as a whole was a very hard one and I should have been hundreds of dollars better off had I not received them. . . . I have lost a good deal of money of late."[51] At the height of the 1850 mining season, October and November, he went into partnership for a store at the mines, and he did better. In one of his few positive letters, he wrote, "we have a Team [they were shipping his merchandise to the mines] and I can sell goods faster than the team can haul them in." He complained, however, that his suppliers were still sending the wrong goods at the wrong time to Sacramento.[52]

Littlefield and Blood must have been getting tired of Sweetzer's whining letters and may have been losing money on what they sent him. In October 1850 Edwin Littlefield decided to come out to California to see for himself. Sweetzer tried to discourage him: "this is a bilious climate and you know that warm climate[s] are not thought to be so good for the Liver complaint, and I think that if I was as well situated as you are and doing as well that I should not come." This must have seemed at bit disingenuous because Sweetzer made it clear that he was staying in California and was looking for a wife. Littlefield came early in 1851 and wrote to Sweetzer from San Francisco in January on a letterhead showing prominently

Sam Brannan's very successful store in San Francisco.[53] Sweetzer went to see him. Apparently, Littlefield and Sweetzer patched up their problems, and the business relationship continued, but Littlefield now wanted payment in advance.

There are a few other letters from Sweetzer in the Huntington collection, but they add little to the Sweetzer saga. His letters in 1850 provided a personal and clear example of the interrelated problems of competition, information, and communications that plagued businesses in the early years of the gold rush. They were, in part, similar to the informational problems of miners described in chapter 5. Sweetzer, neither a total failure nor a great success, kept changing occupations and locations, much like the miners who kept moving about on the basis of rumors. Sweetzer survived as a businessman, and he eventually prospered. He married in 1853 and stayed in Sacramento, becoming one of the founding members of the Society of California Pioneers. He died on August 29, 1910, nearly ninety-one years old.[54]

## Books for the Goldrushers of 1850

Although letters were a new and valuable source of information for potential goldrushers, books about California continued to be a major resource for eastern readers. These books, however, differed in several respects from those available in 1849 because the demand for information had changed, and the information marketplace responded to that change. The major difference was that the information from goldrushers about the trail and California reduced the demand for guidebooks, and few were published in 1850.[55] In place of guidebooks, travelogues written by people who had just returned from the trip became popular. These descriptions of trips to the West in 1849 and of gold mining were generally taken from the goldrushers' journals and, frequently, were published privately or through local newspapers. Fiction and humor were other new categories of gold rush books. Also, unlike in late 1848 and early 1849, there were publications that considered California as a place of settlement and discussed how it was to be integrated into the United States. Finally, there were three influential books published in 1850, which were not written by goldrushers, that included the authors' views on the effects of the gold rush on California. Two were travelogues: Bayard Taylor's record of his trip, essentially his letters to the *Herald* published in book form, and Walter Colton's comparison of California before and after the gold rush. One was an official government report: Thomas Butler King's report to Congress.[56]

The various types of books described above differed greatly in their approach and subject matter. They all, however, dispersed information about the gold rush to prospective goldrushers and those who stayed home. Unlike the goldrushers' changing perception of information on the trail, in California and in the goldrushers' letters, books did not show the sharp changes in credibility sources from authority to personal experience. In addition to the importance of personal experience of ordinary people emphasized in some of the travelogues, official sponsorship—as in the case of Thomas Butler King, and individuals' titles, such as Rev. Walter Colton's, alcalde of San Francisco—still mattered to book publishers. Since the King and Colton books were very successful, these criteria must have mattered to readers as well.

### Travelogues

Most goldrusher travelogues were personal journals of ordinary people who went west, and many were self-published.[57] Rather than emphasizing great feats of exploration and discovery as did Frémont or Bryant, these publications reflected the sights and atmosphere experienced by thousands. Many were designed to enable readers to visualize California, a fact that was emphasized in the titles of their books.[58] Some were originally written for local newspapers to describe the progress of a member of the community in the gold rush. An example of this is the book of "sketches" (all word descriptions) by Leonard Kip, which he introduced by writing,

> The author of these Sketches being applied to by friends, who wished *reliable* information on California, hastily compiled these Recollections of the Country.... [T]hey were intended for one of the daily papers, but the friend to whom they were sent (in the absence of the author), has assumed the responsibility of publishing them in this form, for the benefit of those who are meditating a voyage to the El Dorado of the West.[59]

Other authors took more literally the idea of providing images of the gold rush. William M'Ilvaine Jr. published *Sketches of Scenery and Notes of Personal Adventure in California and Mexico* in 1849, which consisted of sixteen lithographs with printed descriptions on the overleaf. The images were of the most famous sites, such as San Francisco with lots of ships in the harbor. The captions were comments on the images that read as if he were presenting them as stereo slides in his parlor. For instance, the caption for his view of Sacramento read,

"The board house on the extreme right is the store of Mr. Brannan, a very rich merchant, who was the first to carry to San Francisco the news of the discovery of gold;" and for Sutter's Fort he wrote, unnecessarily, that it was "in a dilapidated condition."[60] From the point of view of gold rush communications, these travelogues were another indication of a significant shift from the grand narrative of large expeditions, such as Frémont's, Wilkes's, and Bryant's, to smaller stories of ordinary people.

Several of the 1850 travelogues were written by professional journalists such as Bayard Taylor and Theodore Johnson. Edward Buffum published one of the first popular travelogues of the early gold rush.[61] Buffum was a New York journalist who worked for Bennett's *Herald*. Unlike Taylor or Johnson, Buffum traveled to California before the gold rush, not to report for the newspaper, but to join the New York Volunteers and fight in the Mexican War. He saw action at La Paz in Baja, California, and was discharged in September 1848. He went immediately to the gold mines where he was successful and stayed for six months until he became ill with scurvy. Buffum finished his manuscript in San Francisco in January 1850, but it was not published until May of that year.[62] The time pressure felt by the publisher (Lea and Blanchard of Philadelphia) was evident from the "Publisher's Notice" at the front of the book, which stated that the work had "been hurried through the press, without the revision expected by the author [who was still in California]." As the title indicated, his book was primarily a narrative of his mining experiences, but he also provided a description of the towns and camps and was optimistic about the prospects in California. In spite of that, he "advise[d] all who [were] in good positions at home to remain there." His reason was one that was repeated in many of the publications about the first years of the gold rush: that the soft eastern urbanite would not be able to take the hard physical labor of mining gold: "Many a fine, spruce young clerk coming to California with golden dreams of wealth before him has proved, to his sorrow, that the crowbar is heavier than the pen."[63]

Walter Colton's travelogue of California differed from the travel journals of the goldrushers and the adventures of Buffum in that Colton lived in California for several years before the gold rush. He also wrote many letters to eastern newspapers during the late months of 1848 and early 1849 so readers may have been familiar with his name. Colton's *Three Years in California* predominantly told the story of California before 1848 and the changes wrought by the gold rush.[64] Thus, the book provided some context for readers. Colton wrote with some authority; he was an ordained minister educated at Yale who became a navy chaplain and alcalde in pre–gold rush California. Colton's book also exhibited a kind of early California boosterism. To prospective goldrushers, it provided the view that there was more to California than gold and that, although the gold rush changed the land forever, the non-mineral wealth of the state might again predominate. California was a place for settlement as well as mining.

> California will be no more what she has been: the events of a few years have carried her through the progressive changes of a century. . . . But the gifts of nature here are not confined to her sparkling sands and veined rocks, they extend to the productive forces of her soil; they lie along her water-courses, through her verdant valleys, and wave in her golden grain.[65]

This theme, that California was forever changed because of the gold rush but that its future was not dependent on gold, became popular in the next few years and was repeated in various formats from sermons to guidebooks.[66]

### Humor

Humor was a new class of publication about the gold rush that became prominent after the first wave of goldrushers. This genre, predominantly aimed at urban readers in the East, was used to spoof those who were considering going to California. Although it was not designed to provide information about the gold rush, most of the humor directly or indirectly conveyed a message similar to that of Buffum's: eastern urbanites were not suited to be goldrushers.

Cartoonists had fun lampooning goldrushers. In one lithograph by Nathaniel Currier, a goldrusher was depicted sitting on a hill of gold that he had put on a barge that was being towed by a whale in harness; in another, a cartoonist spoofed Porter's ad to fly to California in a kind of zeppelin.[67] One of the most popular humorous books about the gold rush was entitled *Journey to the Gold Diggings by Jeremiah Saddlebags*, published by Stringer and Townsend in late 1849.[68] This was an early comic book composed of cartoon-like pictures with captions. The sequence of pictures told a story of Jeremiah Saddlebags, a soiled urban dandy living in a loft room, who inherited five hundred dollars and "invested" in a trip to the gold mines, which he found out about reading an issue of the *Herald*. His adventures included being captured by pirates in Panama, buying a baby's cradle when he heard about mining gold with a cradle, finding a huge lump of gold that he lost gambling, and getting captured by Indians on his return. The book satirized

Figure 9. "The Independent Gold Hunter on His Way to California." Source: Courtesy American Antiquarian Society, Worcester, Massachusetts.

a middle-class urban man attempting to become a western traveler and goldminer. This was a popular theme for humor. In a well-known lithograph, an upright, cigarette-smoking man with a neatly trimmed beard and glasses was depicted walking resolutely toward "California, 1700 miles" (figure 9). The humor of the image stems from the juxtaposition of urbanity (he was wearing a suit and carrying a suitcase) and silly gold rush accessories (a pan on a long handle slung over his shoulder, a shovel under his arm, and weapons stuck in his pocket).[69]

Given the success of many of these humorous books, the exaggerated caricatures of middle-class urbanites and respectable tradesmen or farmers who turned themselves into "wild westerners" must have reflected a type of person well known to many easterners. Most of the actual urbanites who went to California in 1849, however, did not stumble into the misadventures of Jeremiah Saddlebags but made it to California, found some gold and, according to most of the communications of 1849 and early 1850, did better during those years than if they had stayed in the East.

## The Official Report

One of the most influential books on the gold rush in 1850 was not written by a goldrusher or a reporter, but was a report to Congress on the newly conquered region and the gold fields by Thomas Butler King. Although born in Pennsylvania, King was in 1849 a Georgia congressman whom the new president, Zachary Taylor, appointed as an official agent of the federal government to California. The Thirtieth Congress of 1848–49, could not agree to establish California as an organized territory because of the dispute over slavery in the new regions. Taylor, although a southerner and a slaveholder, favored admitting California directly as a state and would have accepted any position regarding slavery chosen by its citizens.[70] King, who had decidedly more proslavery views than Taylor, was sent to California, in part, to deliver this message. He arrived in San Francisco June 4, 1849, gave his initial address and then made an elaborate show of touring the mines.[71] He became ill while visiting the mines and did not attend the September 1849 Monterey convention, during which the participants wrote and adopted a state constitution forbidding slavery. King returned to Washington after the convention and prepared his report to Congress, which was published in book form in March 1850.

King's report was the most thorough description of California since the discovery of gold. It was the first to give serious consideration to economic development

176

other than mining and to the crucial public-policy issues of land titles, mining licenses, and taxation. He began with a geography and gave a very optimistic report on the productive potential of the region, particularly for commerce and agriculture. He was one of the first writers to recognize the importance and potential of large-scale irrigation in California. His chapter on the gold region included technical descriptions of mining methods and was optimistic about the continued productivity of the mines. Perhaps his most important comments were about land policy and taxation. Although most of the gold-bearing lands were in the public domain, he cogently argued against land sales or taxation of land. He urged the appointment of a mining commissioner to license miners and use the money to build roads and bridges and pay down the Mexican War debt. These recommendations appeared sensible, but they were not followed, because there was no administrative structure that could implement them. He wanted to discourage the export of gold from California and to establish a mint in San Francisco to regularize the use of gold as a medium of exchange. King's chauvinistic prejudices came through in his deprecation of foreigners in the camps, whom he wanted to tax, and his comment "gold is a common treasure of the American People." King's report to Congress and the book that followed provided for the first time an official document that took California seriously as part of the country and more than just a place to go temporarily to get rich quick.

## The Gold Rush of 1850

The personal and generally optimistic communications from California along with the large amount of more credible information decreased uncertainty about the trip. These communications and better information were important reasons that the overland migration to California of 1850 was much larger than in 1849. They also spurred other western travel since Oregon and Utah also had a larger emigration in 1850 than in the previous year.[72] Another important difference between the years was that time horizons had changed. The goldrushers of 1850 had had a year to think about and plan for going rather than the two or three months of their predecessors. All of these factors helped tip the balance for those who wanted to go in 1849 but could not convince their family and friends that they should do so or those who could not prepare in time. Better information and more time to prepare established a solid basis for gold fever in 1850.

Despite the worsening of cholera on the trail, the overland route in 1850 was easier to travel than in 1849.[73] There were some changes in preferred trailhead towns and routes, although the primary route along the Great Platte River Road, the Sublette and Hudspeth cutoffs, or the Salt Lake alternative, and the Humboldt River trails were still by far the most heavily traveled byways. The most important change was the elimination of the Lassen Cutoff, which became known as the "Greenhorn Cutoff."[74] The Carson Pass became the preferred route over the Sierras. Kanesville, Iowa, took a larger proportion of non-Mormon trailhead traffic than in 1849, but St. Joseph still outfitted the largest number of emigrants.[75] By the spring of 1850, St. Joseph had grown to about 3,500 residents with four hotels, twenty-six stores, twelve blacksmith shops, eight wagon makers, and several warehouses and bakeries. Even so, the merchants were not adequately prepared for the migration's almost doubling in size: the local newspaper estimated thirty-thousand travelers left from the city in that year.[76] The more southern trailhead towns (Independence, Westport Landing, and Westport) lost California business compared to St. Joseph and Kanesville but continued to prosper as the Santa Fe trade revived.[77] More ferries were added for crossing the Missouri River, and improved ferries were established, mostly by Mormons, at the North Platte River west of Fort Laramie, the Green River beyond South Pass, and the Bear River between Fort Bridger and Salt Lake City.[78] Finally, the emigrants of 1850 utilized trail improvements made by the travelers of 1849, such as grades down to the fords of the smaller rivers and creeks and a few bridges.

Some aspects of the migration of 1850 were more difficult than in the previous year, in part because the information obtained from the travelers in 1849 inadvertently misled those who followed. One of the major problems was that so many writers in 1849 emphasized that they took too much food and too many supplies. The emigrants of 1850 took the explicit and implied advice to heart and packed less food. The conditions in 1850, however, were different than in the previous year. First, the spring was later, delaying the start for the majority of the travelers. Heavier rains during the spring and summer also made for more difficult traveling. Most important, there were many more travelers. Therefore, supplementing food from hunting was more difficult in the latter year because animals, including the buffalo, were more scattered across the plains and were pursued by more hunters. Many goldrushers ran out of food supplies on the last leg of their trips. The privation was made worse by the fact that the number of travelers on the trails along the Humboldt River in 1850 was larger not only because of the larger overall migration but because none were lured off the river trails by the Lassen Cutoff. Thus, the density of travelers from the beginning of the Lassen Cutoff to the Humboldt Sink and in the deserts beyond to the Truckee and the Carson rivers was much greater than in 1849. These were areas in which it was almost impossible to supplement food supplies by hunting. George Stewart describes the conditions in 1850:

> On the lower Humboldt half the people were reported to be destitute and starving. Thousands were on foot. . . . Desperate and starving people sometimes took food, or appropriated cattle for slaughter, by what was the equivalent of highway robbery. . . . The horrors of the desert crossing to the Carson River were worse than ever. A count recorded the bodies of 9,771 dead animals. . . . Traders, exploiting the emergency, went out with water, and sold it, according to an eyewitness, at fifteen dollars a glassful. . . . Again, relief parties pushed out from California, but one can scarcely maintain that the catastrophe was averted.[79]

Although there were few new guidebooks published in 1850 because most goldrushers had confidence in alternative sources, many still wanted more information about the trails west of South Pass. Thus, guidebooks describing these areas played a role in providing information to goldrushers in that year. In particular, the handwritten Mormon guidebooks were in demand, and guidebook writers were pleased to serve the market. Also, the advice offered by the Mormons must have changed after 1849 because several companies that went via Salt Lake City took the old, discredited Hastings Cutoff, going south of the Salt Lake.[80]

There is some confusion in the historical record about the use of Mormon guidebooks by travelers on the Hastings Cutoff. Sarah Royce, who took the Hastings Cutoff, wrote, "our only guide from Salt Lake City consisted of two small sheets of note paper, sewed together, and bearing on the outside in writing the title, 'Best Guide to the Gold Mines, 816 Miles, by Ira J. Willis, GSL City.'"[81] Was this the same Ira J. Willis guide of 1849? If so, Royce must have been confused since the Willis guide of 1849 described the Salt Lake Cutoff north of the lake. Madison Moorman, who also took the Hastings Cutoff, had a copy of Clayton and of Frémont, 1848, and he apparently purchased the same guide as Royce.[82] Perhaps the enterprising Mr. Willis wrote out and sold several guidebooks describing different routes west of Salt Lake City.

Another aspect of the continuing uncertainty of goldrushers west of Salt Lake City, and their search for information, concerned companies and individuals who stayed in that city at least part of the winter of 1849. These companies did not receive the information in letters, newspapers, and books that were published in the East, and they provided a market for guides hired in Salt Lake City.[83] These guides led companies that wished to continue the trip during the winter on a trail called the "Mormon Corridor" that went south from Salt Lake along the Virgin River to Vegas Springs (now Las Vegas) and across the Mojave Desert to San Bernardino, California.[84] Riley Senter was a goldrusher of 1849 who reached Salt Lake City too late cross the Sierras that year. He joined a company that formed in Salt Lake to continue their trip and hired a Mormon guide to take them down the Mormon Corridor. He wrote of his experiences to his cousin Ordelia in upstate New York.[85] He related to her in October 1849, "A man by the name of Hunt has undertaken to guide a company through a new route which if successful in going, it is expected to be but some 600 to 700 miles. . . . When a company is ready in some 3 weeks, or perhaps more, we intend to go on it."[86] Senter did not make the Hunt train, the "Sand Walking Company" of one hundred wagons. By the time he was ready, Senter joined a small company of fourteen people and four wagons. They followed Hunt's trail. They reached Vegas Springs after some hardship but in good condition and then prepared for the Mojave crossing by ditching their wagons and packing on oxen. It rained before they crossed, and they had no trouble, reaching San Bernardino the last day of January 1850.

## Conclusion

The gold rush of 1850 highlighted the importance of communications and information flows that came from the goldrushers of 1849. These new information sources, in particular the letters and books of the 1849 goldrushers, had a profound effect on the decisions of the travelers in 1850. Communications could also create close connections between gold rush emigrants and their eastern communities, such as in Marshall, Michigan. New information was disseminated quickly due to the responsiveness of the publication marketplaces, in particular newspapers and books, to the changing needs for information. Some communications difficulties, however, could not be overcome, such as the time it took for letters to cross the country. That problem, combined with the problems of information dispersal in California discussed in chapter 5, exacerbated the difficulties of commerce and business in California.

Important differences between early 1849 and 1850 in the available information concerning California illustrate how information was assessed and used in the two years. In 1849, newspapers and guidebooks were the primary forms from which goldrushers obtained information, and the most influential sources of credibility were claims of officialdom and expertise. A year later, newspapers and books still dispersed information, but the content and style had changed drastically; and a new medium, letters, had a profound impact. These letters, although private, became a source of public information by being printed in newspapers and published in books. Although they were for the most part not written for publication, they substantially influenced the marketplaces of information. They also influenced credibility criteria with which readers assessed printed information about the gold rush. Credibility criteria that were crucial in 1849 carried less weight in 1850, and a new source of credibility, the personal experience of ordinary people, became important.

# Conclusion

One of the most fascinating aspects of history is that stories from the past can be retold many times, and each time new lessons can be learned and new aspects of the stories can be highlighted. The California gold rush is an excellent example. Except for the major wars, few events in American history have been retold as many times and for as many reasons as the gold rush. Gold rush stories have illustrated in a dramatic microcosm broad aspects of American history such as geographic and technical discoveries, the exploitation of natural resources, mass migration, repression of Native Americans and other ethnic groups, and the painful process of learning to live with diverse peoples. This history of the gold rush is similar; it is a series of tales of communications and information dispersal in a situation in which good information was desperately needed but difficult to assess, and communications were restricted by technological, geographical, and institutional limitations.

This study fits into and contributes to both California gold rush history and the history and analysis of communications and information. With respect to the gold rush, communications and information dispersal were crucial elements explaining many goldrushers' decisions. The lemminglike throng of some ten thousand goldrushers on the Lassen Cutoff seems mysterious or irrational unless one considers the constraints on communications, the availability of information, and the difficulties of information assessment. The apparently irrational chasing of wild rumors in the gold fields while ignoring the information of printed sources is another example. Emphasizing the importance of communications constraints also helps explain the rapid and innovative growth of the express business in the gold fields.

With respect to the history and analysis of communications and information, this work is a case study demonstrating the importance of information assessment in studies of communications and information dissemination.[1] The gold rush is very useful for this purpose: there are probably few historical episodes in which information was needed as quickly and was so difficult to assess as the early months of the gold rush. The study shows that to understand the ways in which information and communications affect decision making, the way information was assessed was as important as the communications channels through which it was disseminated.

The example of the gold rush also shows that one cannot analyze the effects of communications and information on decision making only through general principles: the particularities of time and place matter. In terms of this case study, these include institutional constraints, such as the "one-way valve" of the booksellers' markets; political and social constraints such as southern editors' preoccupation with the effects of the gold rush on slavery; physical constraints such as the impossibility of receiving mail on the trail; economic constraints such as the inability of the Post Office in California to pay wages appropriate for California; and technological constraints such as the long time period for commercial information to travel from California to the East. The microcosm of the gold rush illustrates the historical contingency of information analysis and indicates that the approach used herein is an appropriate methodology for this subject.

In spite of the importance of the specific attributes of historical situations to the analysis of communications and information dispersal, one can make useful generalizations. First, the constraints of information marketplaces can adversely affect the distribution of information, for example, the inability of western publishers to market their guidebooks in the mainstream book markets resulted in eastern goldrushers not having access to the best guidebooks in early 1849. Second, timeliness can be more important than content, as shown by the inability of the Sacramento newspapers to provide information to miners. Third, information production is easier than information assessment. Most importantly, this study—as well as others such as in Richard Brown's *Knowledge Is Power*—shows the importance of these factors in explaining key elements of historical events. The implication is that these factors should feature heavily in accounts of historical change.

The problems of how best to use communications mechanisms to obtain more or better information and how to assess the information exist in all time periods including the present. Whether on the battlefield, in the boardroom, or at home, making decisions under uncertainty is a key human problem that can be alleviated by obtaining better information. Problems of information assessment may be more acute now than in most periods because so much more information is produced and is obtainable so much faster and more cheaply. Although ways in which goldrushers attempted to assess information says little about what to make of the barrage of information coming over television, radio, print, and the internet, it does provide a context within which to study the modern problems of information. It shows how ubiquitous the problems have been and that, in the absence of appropriate filters and credibility criteria, people will invent their own assessment methods, which may be worse than discarded credibility criteria. This case study of gold rush communications and information dispersal not only provides a better understanding of the past but also, by providing an historical context for the discussion of these issues, connects to the present.

# Selected Booksellers' Catalogs, 1844–1847

## *Titles Concerning the West*

SOURCE: AMERICAN ANTIQUARIAN SOCIETY

**1844 Bartlett and Welford, part 2 (New York City)**
*"Part II" of their catalogue, on "American History." It started with "Works on America Generally—Voyages Around the World—Biographical Works—Atlases, etc.*

George Catlin, *American Indians, etc.* 2 vols. (New York, 1842): $6.50.

Ross Cox, *Adventures on the Columbia River,* (New York, 1833): $1.50.

Timothy Flint, *Geography and History of the Western States* 2 vols. (Cincinnati, 1828): $4.00.

Robert Greenhow, *Memoir on the North West Coast of America, and adjacent Territories* (New York, 1840): $1.50.

J. Gregg, *Commerce of the Prairies* 2 vols. (no city, 1844): $2.50.

Capt. Basil Hall, *Travels in North America* 2 vols. (Philadelphia, 1829): no price.

Judge Hall, *Letters from the West* (London, 1828): various fanciness: $.75, $1.25, $1.75 (in Morocco).

Judge Hall, *Sketches of History, Life, and Manners in the West* 2 vols. (Philadelphia, 1835): $1.50.

Judge Hall, *Statistics of the West, at the Close of the Year 1836* (Cincinnati: 1837): $.75.

W. Irving, *Astoria* 2 vols. with map (Philadelphia, 1836): $2.50.

W. Irving, *The Rocky Mountains . . . Adventures of Capt. Bonneville* 2 vols. (Philadelphia, 1836): $2.00.

Edwin James, *Expedition* 3 vols. (London, 1823): $5.00.

Kendall, *Narrative of the Texan Santa Fe Expedition* 2 vols. (New York, 1844): $2.50.

B. von Langsdorff, *Voyages and Travels in Various Parts of the World from 1803 to 1807, Including California and the Western Coast of North America* (Carlile, 1817): $1.75.

M. Lewis, *Travels of Lewis and Clarke* (London, 1809): $2.50 (calf).

M. Lewis and W. Clarke, *History of the Expedition* 3 vols. (London, 1814): $7.50, or $9.00 (hf. calf, very scarce).

Major Stephen Long, *Account of an Expedition* 2 vols. (Philadelphia, 1823): $5.00.

Maximillian, Prince of Wied, *Travels in the Interior of North America* (London, 1843): $15.50 (half Morocco, gilt edges).

Samuel Parker, *Journal of a Tour beyond the Rocky Mountains in 1835–37* with map (Ithaca, 1838): $1.25.

*Pike's Expedition to the Sources of the Mississippi* 1 vol. with maps (Philadelphia, 1810): $1.50 (sheep).

## 1847 D. Appleton and Co., New York City

*A "Library Manual" that contained a "Catalogue Raisonne of upwards of Twelve Thousand of the Most Important Works in Every Department of Knowledge in all Modern Languages," including a detailed subject list and an index. It was a huge volume of 434 pages plus 50 more pages of advertisements. It proclaimed its aim was not to be exhaustive but "to exhibit under each head the extent of its literature, so far as it might serve the purposes of the general reader." It was not restricted to Appleton publications.*

## North America, Geography

Maximilian, Prince of Wied, *Travels in the Interior of North America* with 81 elaborately colored plates (London, 1843): £2 12s. 6d.

### American Indians

George Catlin, *Letters and Notes on the North American Indians* £7 7s.
George Catlin, *The N.A. Indian Portfolio* £7 7s.

### California

J. Coulter, *Adventures on the Western Coast of South America and the Interior of California, etc.* 2 vols. (London, 1847): no price.

M. Duflot de Morfras, *Exploration du territoire . . .* with atlas (Paris, 1844): 8of.

Duhaut-Cilly, *Voyage autour du monde, principalement a la California . . .* (Paris, no date): 14f.

A. Forbes, *California: a History of Upper and Lower California from their First Discovery . . .* (London, 1839): 14s.

R. Greenhow, *The History of Oregon and California . . .*

M. Venegas, *A Natural and Civil History of California* translated from Spanish (London, 1759).

### Guidebooks
None featuring the West, California, or Oregon

### Oregon
Duflot de Mofras, *Exploration du territoire . . .* (Paris 1844) f8o.

J. Dunn, *History of the Oregon Territory and British North American Fur Trade . . .* (London, 1846) 2s. 6d.

P. J. Farnham, *Travels in the Great Western Prairies . . .* (New York 1843).

Fedix, *L'Oregon et les Cotes de l'Ocean pacifique du Nord* (Paris, 1846) f7.

J. C. Frémont, *Exploring Expedition to the Rocky Mountains . . .* (Washington, 1845).

R. Greenhow, *Geography of Oregon and California* (D.A. and Co., 1845).

R. Greenhow, *History of Oregon and California.*

Nicolay, *The Oregon Territory* (London, 1845) 1s. 6d.; (Knight's Weekly Volume).

T. Twiss, *The Oregon Question examined . . .* (London and New York, 1846) 7s.6d.

Geo. Wilkes, *History of California, Geographical and Political* (New York 1845).

### Texas
R. Green, *Journal of the Texan Expedition against Mier* (New York).

G. W. Kendall, *Narrative of an Expedition across the Great Western Prairies from Texas to Santa Fe* (New York, 1845).

### Voyages and Travels
None on the West; most are on round-the-world trips.

### Back Pages
R. Greenhow, *The History of Oregon and California* (Librarian and Translator to the Dept. of State) with map, $2.50. "This history presents accounts, clear and

sufficiently detailed, of all the discoveries and settlements made and attempted in the countries to which it relates, and of all disputes, negotiations and treaties between the governments of civilized nations respecting them; with abundant notices of facts and authorities."

T. Twiss, *The Oregon Territory* (Professor of Political Economy in the University of Oxford) $.75, "This work is written in a dignified and impartial style, and cannot fail to command the attention of all interested in the settlement of this important national question."

Marshall, *The Farmer's Hand-Book* $1.00. "This Manual is the result of much experience, observation and research, and as such is confidently recommended to all Farmers and Emigrants, to whom it will teach wisdom and ensure comfort"—*Evening Mirror.* "One of the most useful books we ever saw."—*Boston Post;* "Mr. Marshall's Manual explains about fifteen hundred different subjects—and from a close research of them, it seems difficult to specify what additional information a farmer can require a hand-book of experimental and practical intelligence upon agricultural topics."—*Cincinnati Atlas;*

C. Frémont, *Oregon and California Expedition.* "Capt. Frémont is not only one of the most courageous and intelligent travelers of the day, but one of the most graphic and admirable writers of the country; and his work has been universally and justly welcomed as deeply interesting, and containing an immense amount of novel information not elsewhere accessible."

### 1848 John Doyle, New York City
*A very large catalog of "Ancient and Modern Books, in every department of Human Knowledge, for sale at extremely low prices for cash at the Cheap, Ancient and Modern Bookstore—the Moral Center of the Intellectual World."*

*Voyages and Travels—American Books*
*Apparently this means books about America. There were about 260 titles. Among these, the following are books about the American West.*

Rev. P. J. De Smet, *Oregon Missions, and Travels over the Rocky Mountains, in 1845–46* (New York: 1847): $1.00.

J. C. Frémont, *Exploring Expedition* (1845): $1.50.

P. Gass, *Journal of the Voyages and Travels of a Corps of Discovery . . . in 1804–5–6* (Philadelphia, 1812): $1.00.

A. M. Gilliam, *Travels over the Table Lands, and Cordilleras of Mexico, including a Description of California* (Philadelphia, 1846): $1.00.

R. Greenhow, *History of Oregon and California* (New York: 1845).

Alex de Humboldt, *Political Essay on the Kingdom of New Spain* (New York: 1841): $2.00.

W. Irving, *The Rocky Mountains, or, Scenes Incidents and Adventures in the Far West* (Philadelphia: 1837): $1.25 [*Capt. Bonneville*].

S. H. Long (compiled by W.H. Keating), *Narrative of an Expedition* . . . (Philadelphia: 1824): $3.00.

H. Martineau, *Retrospect of Western Travel* (New York: 1838): $2.00.

Rev. S. Parker, *Journal of an Exploring Tour beyond the Rocky Mountains in 1835–36* (Auburn: 1846): $.63.

C. Wilkes, *Narrative of the Exploring Expedition* 5 vols. with illustrations and maps (Philadelphia: 1845): $8.75.

## 1847 Daniels and Smith, Philadelphia
*This store advertised itself as "The Cheap Book Store—Small Profits and Quick Returns." It specialized in history, theology, and school books. In the American history section it had only Catlin on American Indians, and in biography it had nothing on the West.*

### Voyages and Travels
Kendall, *Santa Fe Expedition.*

Irving, *Astoria,* and *Rocky Mountains.*

Farnham, *Travels in the Rocky Mountains.*

Lewis and Clark, *Travels.*

Dana, *Two Years.*

Wilkes, *Exploring Expedition.*

Frémont, *Exploring Expedition,* "Oregon and California."

Townsend, *Journey to the Rocky Mountains.*

Lyell, *Travels in the United States.*

Pike, *Expedition to the West.*

Pattie, *Narrative of his travels in the West.*

Coxe, *Expedition to the Columbia River.*

Mrs. Farnham, *Prairie Land.*

# Prices and Wages in the Gold Rush

One can imagine the kind of calculations many individuals made in early 1849, when newspapers reported that most miners could average about one ounce of gold per day but that one could not mine during the rainy season (roughly December through April). The cost of shelter and food could run as high as $4.00 per day. Assuming the trip itself would cost around $400.00 each way, would it be worth it if the prospective goldrusher did not get very lucky and strike it rich? Some of the men contemplating going to California would perhaps put together something like the following figures:

| | |
|---|---|
| Gross annual earnings as a miner: | |
| 250 mining days @ $16 per day: | $4,000 |
| Less cost of provisions and upkeep: | |
| $4.00 per day for 350 days: | $1,400 |
| Estimated savings at end of a year: | $2,600 |
| Cost of transportation to mine fields: | |
| $400 each way, total: | $ 800 |
| Net savings from gold rush in one year: | $1,800 |

How would prospective goldrushers compare this bottom line to what a man could make in various occupations in the East? In 1848 the average wage for an unskilled laborer in the Northeast was less than $1.00 per day and, for an artisan, less than $1.50; average income for a white-collar worker was around $500.00 per year.[1] Robert Margo shows that, after adjusting for room and board, a farm laborer's wages were similar to those of an unskilled urban laborer. A small family farm averaged about $200.00 per year in net income. Therefore, even if one did not strike it rich and earn the fabulous sums that some lucky miners did, one could still come back with cash equal to the fruits of many years of labor in the East.

These kinds of numbers, for California earnings and prices, appeared in eastern newspapers early in 1849, but were the projections realistic? Rodman Paul, in his book, *California Gold: The Beginning of Mining in the Far West*, the most comprehensive work published on the economics and technology of mining in the gold rush, estimates the average daily take in mining was $20.00 in 1848 and $16.00 in 1849. He estimates wages at similar levels.[2] Robert Margo, using the pay records at military forts, has calculated (using an indirect method) that California's nominal wages in 1849 were considerably lower than Paul's estimate: $7.17 per day for common laborers and $12.01 per day for artisans.[3] The problem with Margo's estimates, however, is that the military did not pay competitive wages in 1849, which led to numerous desertions and the complete abandonment of some military installations and warships. Therefore, market wages in California in 1848 to 1849 were probably closer to Paul's estimates than to Margo's.

It is more difficult to estimate the actual cost of provisions and shelter. Though extraordinary amounts were quoted in newspapers, magazines, and guidebooks, $4.00 per day is probably reasonable. For example, in December 1849 Edward Buffum and his companions purchased $600.00 worth of provisions in Coloma and took them to their mining site at Weaver's Creek. He claimed that these provisions were sufficient for sixty days for the six of them (that is, less than $2.00 per day per person).[4]

If these estimates are reasonable, then, why were so many goldrushers disappointed and, by 1851, destitute? As described in chapter 6, most goldrushers were not disappointed in 1849, and they wrote back to their friends and relatives in the East that they were doing as well as they expected. Many had accumulated money but they did not return to the East with their savings. The miners assumed that the following year would be even better because they would start the year better off and with some experience. The problem was that gold fever, stimulated in part by their own communications home, induced such a large number of people to travel to California in 1850 that the average gain from mining and labor dropped drastically. Merchants' high profits of 1848 and 1849 encouraged such an increase in the number of traders that prices and returns to storekeepers dropped substantially by 1850. If one got sick there was no income and expenses went up. During the snowy season, maintenance costs increased, and at the mines, $4.00 per day was insufficient. Finally, many of the men were not frugal and subsisted on rudimentary provisions and upkeep during the lonely winters of 1849 and 1850; gambling, liquor, and prostitution took many miners' accumulated money and forced them into debt. By the time they could start mining again in the summer of 1850, many had run through their savings and were starting over.

# Classification of Kurutz Bibliography

Thanks to Dr. Gary Kurutz and the California State Library for granting permission to republish portions of his bibliography. Gary Kurutz, *The California Gold Rush: A Descriptive Bibliography of Books and Pamphlets Covering the Years, 1848–1853* (San Francisco: Book Club of California, 1997). Numbers in parentheses indicate bibliography entry number.

## 1848

### *United States*

**GUIDEBOOKS**

Bryant, E. *What I Saw in California*. New York: D. Appleton (95).

Foster, G. *The Gold Regions of California*. New York: Dewitt and Davenport (250).

Sherwood, E. *California: Her Wealth and Resources*. New York: George Nesbitt (581).

Simpson, H. I. *An Emigrants' Guide to the Gold Mines*. New York: Joyce (584).

**TRAVELOGUES**

Damon, S. C. *A Trip from the Sandwich Islands to Lower Oregon and Upper California*. Honolulu: Polynesian Office (168).

Frémont, J. C. *Geographical Memoir of Upper California*. New York: D. Appleton (256).

Kells, C. E. *California, from Its Discovery by the Spaniards to the Present Time, with a Brief Description of the Gold Region*. New York (369).

**FICTION AND OTHER**

Kent, E. *Instructions for Collecting, Testing, Melting and Assaying Gold . . . by Edward N. Kent, Practical Chemist*. New York: by author, Van Norden (374).

*Appendix C*

*Germany*

GUIDEBOOKS

Kunzel, H. *OberCalifornien Eine Geographische Schilderung Fur Den Zweck Deutscher* . . . Darmstschet: C. W. Leske (385).

Schmolder, B. *Neuer Pracktischer Wegweiser fur Auswanderer Nach Nord America*. Mainz: Selbstverlagdes Verfassers (562).

1849

*United States*

GUIDEBOOKS

Bryant, E. *What I Saw in California*. New York: D. Appleton (95).

*California Gold Regions, with a Full Account of Their Mineral Resources, How to Get There, What to Take* . . . New York: F. M. Pratt; W. H. Graham, agent for supplying the trade (107).

Colton, J. *Particulars of Routes, Distances, Fares to Accompany Colton's Map of California*. New York: J. Colton (149).

Disturnell, J. *The Emigrants' Guide to New Mexico, California and Oregon*. New York: J. Disturnell (196).

Duganne, A. J. H. *California and Her Gold Regions*. Philadelphia: G. B. Zieber, Ag't. (208).

Foster, C. *The Gold Placers of California*. Akron: H. Canfield (249).

Hastings, L. W. *A New History of Oregon and California*. Cincinnati: George Conclin (320).

Jefferson, T. H. *Accompaniment to the Map of the Emigrant Road*. New York: by the author (359).

Mitchell, S. A. *Description of Oregon and California Embracing an Account of the Gold Fields*. Philadelphia: Thomas Cowperthwait (447).

Robinson, F. *California and Its Gold Regions*. New York: Stringer and Townsend (539).

Seymour, E. S. *Emigrants' Guide to the Gold Mines*. Chicago: R. L. Wilson, Daily Journal Office (568).

Steele, O. G. *Steele's Western Guidebook and Emigrants Directory*. Buffalo: Oliver G. Steele (600).

Walton, D. *The Book Needed for the Times, Containing the Latest Well Authenticated Facts from the Gold Rush*. Boston: Stacy, Richardson (658).

Ware, J. *The Emigrants' Guide to California*. St. Louis: J. Halsall (663).

Wierzbicki, F. P. *California as It Is and as It May Be, or A Guide to the Gold Region.* San Francisco: Washington Bartlett (678).

**TRAVELOGUES**

Farnham. *Life, Adventures and Travels in California.* New York: Nafils and Cornish (233).

Folsom, J. L. *A Short Account of the Gold Region of California.* Maysville KY: Eagle Office (247).

Hall, J. L. *Journal of the Hartford Union Mining and Trading Co.* On board ship *Henry Lee*: J. B. Hall (305).

Johnson, T. T. *Sights in the Gold Region and Scenes by the Way.* New York: Baker and Scribner (363).

Revere, J. W. *A Tour of Duty in California.* New York: C. S. Francis (529).

Thornton, J. Q. *Oregon and California in 1848.* New York: Harper and Brothers (631).

Wilkes, C. *Western America, Including California and Oregon.* Philadelphia: Lea and Blanchard (679).

**FICTION AND OTHER**

*Amelia Sherwood: or Bloody Scenes at the California Gold Mines.* New York: C. W. and G. E. Kenworthy (13).

Anstead, D. *The Gold Seekers Manual.* New York: D. Appleton (19).

Averill, C. *Kit Carson: The Prince of the Gold Hunters.* Boston: George H. Williams (25).

Averill, C. *Life in California, or Treasurer-Seekers Expedition.* Boston: George H. Williams (26).

Comstock, J. *A History of the Precious Metals.* Hartford: Belknap and Hamorsley (154).

Greenleaf, B. *The Californian Almanac.* Boston: Geo. C. Rand (293).

Harris, J. M. *A Paper upon California; Read Before the Maryland Historical Society, March 1849.* Baltimore: printed for the society (314).

*Outline History of an Expedition.* New York: H. Long and Bro. (474).

Peck, G. W. *Aurifoding, or Adventures in the Gold Region.* New York: Baker and Scribner (490).

Perkins, G. W. *An Address to the "Pacific Pioneers."* Meridian CT: E. Hinman's Office (495).

Porter, R. *Arial Navigation: The Practicality of Traveling Pleasantly and Safely from New York to California in three Days.* New York: H. Smith (513).

Read, J. A. and D. F. *Journey to the Gold Diggings by Jeremiah Saddlebags*. Cincinnati: U. P. James (524).

Tibbits, H. J. *Statement of Hall J. Tibbits, Master of the American Ship Pacific as to His Removal from Command*. New York: George F. Nesbit (634).

### COMPANY PROSPECTUSES

American Quicksilver Co. New York: Pubney and Russell (14).

Beverly Joint Stock San Francisco Co. Salem MA: Register Press (53).

Brothers Mining and Trading Co. New Haven CT (82).

Bunker Hill Trading and Mining Association. Boston: Mudge and Carliss (98).

Cayuga Joint Stock Co. Auburn NY (122).

Colony Guard. New York: William J. Spence (147).

El Dorado Association for Trading and Mining. Boston: Donnell and Molore (219).

Frémont Mining and Trading Co. Hartford: J. Gaylord Wills (257).

Granite State Trading and Mining and Agricultural Co. Hanover NH (285).

Gronton California Co. New London CT: D. J. Ruddock (297).

Hartford Union Mining and Trading Co. Hartford CT: Elihu Ceer (316).

Massachusetts and California Co. Northhampton MA: J. L. Metcalf (430).

Mechanics Mining Co. New York: Israel Sackett (435).

New England and California Trading and Mining Association. Boston: J. B. Chisholm (460).

New York and California Mining and Trading Association. New York (461).

New York Commercial and Mining Association. New York: John Belcher (462).

New York Excelsior Trading and Mining Association. New York: H. Cogswill (463).

New York Mining Co. New York: J. P. Pnall (464).

Pittsburg and California Enterprize Co. Pittsburgh (507).

Rhode-Island Working Men's Mining Co. Providence RI: H. H. Brown (531).

Rising Sun Mining and Trading Association. New York: Geo. B. Maigues (537).

Sagamore and California Mining and Trading Co. Lynn MA: C. and H. J. Butterfield (549).

Tallman Mining and Trading Association. Providence RI: M. B. Young (616).

### SERMONS

Brigham, C. *An Address Delivered to the Companies of California Adventurers of Taunton*. Trenton NJ: C. A. Hasck's Book and Job Office (73).

Cleaveland, E. L. *Hasting to be Rich*. New Haven CT: J. H. Benham (139).

Day, G. *Address to the Holyoke Mining Co.* (172).

Frothingham, N. *Gold: A Sermon*. Boston: John Wilson (261).

Johnson, S. R. *California: A Sermon*. New York: Stanford and Swords (362).

Lunt, W. P. *The Net That Gathered of Every Kind*. Boston: Dutton and Wentworth (410).

Shepard, G., and S. L. Caldwell. *Addresses of the Rev. Professor George Sheppard and Rev. S. L. Caldwell*. Bangor ME: Smith and Sayword (575).

Worcester, S. M. *California: Outline of an Address before the Naumkeag Mutual Trading and Mining Co.* Salem MA (701).

## Australia

### FICTION AND OTHER

*The Digger's Hand Book and Truth about California*. Sydney: F. M. Stokes (195).

## England

### GUIDEBOOKS

Bryant, E. *California, Texas and the Gold Region*. London: J. Field (94).

*Emigration to California*. London: Thomas Harrild (223).

*Guide to California*. London: Effingham Wilson (298).

*The Penny Guide to California*. London: John Cleve (492).

Thompson, G. A. *Handbook to the Pacific and California Describing Eight Different Routes by Sea*. London: Simkin and Marshall (629).

Thurston, W. *Guide to the Gold Regions of Upper California with a Map*. London: J. and D. A. Darling (633).

Vizetelly, H. (J. Tywhitt Brooks, pseud.). *Four Months among the Gold Finders in Alta California*. London: David Bogue (653).

### TRAVELOGUES

*California: Its Gold Mines*. London: The California Agency (108).

Ward, J. Perils, *Pastimes and Pleasures of an Emigrant in Australia, Vancouver's Island and California*. London: Thomas Cautley Newby (661).

**FICTION AND OTHER**

Forrester, A. (Alfred Crowquill, pseud). *A Good-Natured Hint about California*. London: D. Bogne (248).

Wyld, J. *Geographical and Mineralogical Notes to Accompany Mr. Wyld's Map of the Gold Regions*. London: James Wyld (702).

## France

**GUIDEBOOKS**

Rossignon, J. *Guide Practique des Emigrants en Californie*. Paris: Adophe Rene (544).

Villars Miette et Clerambaut, M. M. de *Manuel des Emigrants en Californie*. Paris: Chez L'Auteur (442).

**TRAVELOGUES**

Boudracourt, C. *Notice Industrielle Sur La Californie*. Paris: F. Mathias (67).

Thornton, de Mouncie, T. *De La Californie et Des Cotes de L'Ocean Pacifique*. Paris: Comptoir des Imprimours-unis (631).

Delessert, B. *Les Mines D'Or de La Californie*. Paris (184).

Denis, F. *La Californies, L'Orgon et L'Amerique Ruse*. Paris (186).

La Coste, A. *Californie: Fragments Inedits du Voyage Autour du Monde*. Paris: Chez L'Auteur (387).

**FICTION AND OTHER**

Cretenier, A. *La Caliornia: Ou Documents Historiques, Authentiques et Officiels . . .* Paris (163).

*Documents Generaux, Officiels et Complet Sur La Californie*. Paris (198).

## Germany

**GUIDEBOOKS**

*Californien's Gold—Reichthum*. Leipzig (113).

*Calfornien Und Seine Goldminen*. Kuenzuach: R. Voigtlander (112).

*Das Goldland Kalifornien*. Leipzig (278).

Gerstacker, F. *Kaliforniens Gold*. Leipzig (269).

Hartmann, C. F. A. *Geographisch, Statistiche Beschreiburg Von Californien*. Weimer (317).

Hoppe, Janns and Erman, Adolph. *Californiens Gegenuart und Zukunft.* Berlin: G. Reimer (341).

Morton, C. *Califorien, Das Neue Goldland.* Grimma, Druck und verlag deg Verlagg-Comptoires (455).

Osswald, H. F. *Californien, Und Seine Verhaltnisse . . .* Leipzig: K.F. Kohler (473).

Weik, J. *Californien Wie Es Ist, Oder Handbuck Von Californien.* Leipzig: Ernst Schefer (669).

**TRAVELOGUES**

Uhlenhuth, E. *Rathgeber Fur Auswanderer Nach Californien.* Bremen: A. D. Geisler (645).

**FICTION AND OTHER**

Krakenfuse, A. *Munchhausen in Californien.* Bremen: Franz Schlodtmann (384).

Schwarz, J. *Briefe Eines Dutscher Aus Kalifornien . . .* Berlin: W. Adolf und Comp (564).

## Holland
**GUIDEBOOKS**

*Gids Naar Californie.* Amsterdam (273).

Lauts, G. *Kalifornia Door den Hoogliersar.* Amsterdam: R. Stimvers (394).

Plasburg, C. L. *Californie, Beschrijuing Van Dot Land.* Arnheim: J. G. Stenfert Kroese (508).

Van Lennep, J. *Een Droom Van Californie.* Amsterdam: P. Meijers Warnars (397).

## Norway
**GUIDEBOOKS**

*Beretning Om Californie.* Christiana: C. Wulfsberg (50).

## 1850
## United States
**GUIDEBOOKS**

Buffum, E. *Six Months in the Gold Mines.* Philadelphia: Lea and Blanchard (97).

Delavan, J. *Notes on California and the Placers, How to Get There, and What to Do Afterwards, by One Who Has Been There.* New York: Long and Brother (183).

Gregory, J. *Gregory's Guide for California Travellers.* New York: Nafis and Cornish (294).

Isham, G. S. *G. S. Isham's Guide to California.* New York: A. T. Houel (356).

Taylor, B. *El Dorado, or Adventures in the Path of Empire.* New York: Geo. P. Putnam (618).

### TRAVELOGUES

Colton, W. *Deck and Port: Incidences of a Cruise.* New York: A. S. Barnes (231).

Colton, W. *Three Years in California.* New York: A. S. Barnes (151).

Frost, J. *Frost's Pictoral History of California.* Auburn NY: Derby and Miller (260).

Kip, L. *California Sketches, with Recollections of the Gold Mines.* Albany NY: Erastus H. Pense (379).

McNeil, S. *McNeil's Travels in* 1849. Columbus OH: Scott and Bacon (425).

M'Collum, W. S. *California As I Saw It.* Buffalo NY: George Derby (417).

M'Ilvaine, W. J. *Sketches of Scenery and Notes of Personal Adventure.* Philadelphia: Smith and Peter (420).

Root, R. *Journal of Travels from St. Joseph to Oregon.* Galesburg IL Gazetteer and Intelligencer (543).

Taylor, J. *A Journal of the Route from Ft. Smith, Arkansas, to California in the Year* 1849. Bowling Green MO, Job Office (619).

Tyson, J. L. *Diary of a Physician in California.* New York: D. Appleton (642).

### FICTION AND OTHER

Beschke, W. *The Dreadful Sufferings and Thrilling Adventures of an Overland Party of Emigrants to California.* St. Louis: Barklay (52).

Brock, J. C. *A List of Persons from Nantucket Now in California.* Nantucket MA: Jeethro C. Brock (75).

Coyne, S. *Cockneys in California.* New York: Samuel French (160).

Eckfeldt, J. R. and Dubois, W. *New Varieties of Gold and Silver Coins, Counterfeit Coins and Bullion.* Philadelphia: C. Sherman (217).

Edelman, G. W. *Guide to the Value of California Gold.* Philadelphia: G. Appelton (218).

Elton. *Far from the Atlantic to the Specific Oceans*. New York: Eldon (221).

Jackson, W. A. *Appendix to Jackson's Map of the Mining District of California*. New York: Lambert and Lane (358).

King, T. B. *Report on California*. Washington, DC: U.S. House of Representatives, Gridern (377).

Parburt, G. R. *Oration Delivered on Board the Ship Sylph*. New York: I. and S. H. Parker (480).

Tyson, P. T. *Report of the Secretary of War, Communicating Information in Relation to the Geology and Topography of California*. Washington DC: U.S. Senate (643).

COMPANY PROSPECTUSES

The Rocky-Bar Mining Co. California (no city mentioned) (541).

SERMONS

Farley, C. A. *The Moral Aspect of California*. New York: Henry Spear (231).

## Australia

TRAVELOGUES

Jewetp, W. C. *California, Its Present Condition and Future Prospects*. Adelaide: Andrew Murray (360).

## Chile

FICTION AND OTHER

Vicuna, P., Felix. *Consideraciones Sobre La Alta California*. Valparaiso: Mercurio (652).

## England

GUIDEBOOKS

*The Californian Hoax*. London: W. G. Kerton (109).

Flemming, E. A. *California: Its Past History, Its Present Position, Its Future Prospects*. London (242).

*The Illustrated Year-Book of Wonders, Events and Discoveries*. London: Arthur Hull, Virtue (352).

Melvin, J. W. *The Emigrants' Guide to the Colonies*. London: Simpkin, Marshall (437). London: William Shober (548).

FICTION AND OTHER

*Adventures of a Gold-Finder, Written by Himself*. London (5).

*Appendix C*

COMPANY PROSPECTUSES

Anglo-California Gold Mining Co. London (17).

Ryan, W. R. *Personal Adventures in Upper and Lower California in 1848–49.*

## France

GUIDEBOOKS

Faugere, P. *La Merville du Siecle: Les Richesses de Californie.* Paris (234).

Ferry, H. *Description de la Nouvelle Californie Geographique, Politique et Morale.* Paris: La Coeur et Cie. (236).

Mithouard, J. *La Californie Documents Officiels et Renseignments.* Paris: Chez L'Auteur (448).

Treny. *La Californie Devoilee ou Verities Irrecusables.* Paris: "Chez tous les libraries" (637).

## Germany

GUIDEBOOKS

Muller, J. *Das Goldland Californien.* Leitmeritz: C. W. Merdan (456).

Fleischmann, C. L. *Neueste Officielle Berichte an die Regierang Der Vereinigten Staaten.* Stuttgart (241).

## Monaco

TRAVELOGUE

Caccia, A. *Europa Ed America, Scene Della Vita.* Monaco (103).

## Poland

GUIDEBOOKS

*Opis Kaliforni, Pod Wzgleden, Jeograficznyra, Statystycgnyn, Geologicznyn.* W. Krakowie: W. Drukarni Josefc Czecha (471).

## Russia

GUIDEBOOKS

Blokot, G. K. *Karatkoe-Geografichaske Statistichesho.* St. Petersburg: V. Moveiskai Tipografii (61).

## 1851

### United States

GUIDEBOOKS

Cain, J., and A. Brower, *Mormon Way-Bill to the Gold Mines.* Salt Lake City: Deseret, W. Richards (104).

Hall, J. B. *An Account of California and the Wonderful Gold Fields.* Boston: J. B. Hall (304).

Shepherd, J. S. *Journal of Travel Across the Plains and Guide to the Future Emigrant.* Racine WI: Mrs. Rebecca Shepherd (576).

Street, F. *California in 1850, Compared to What It Was in 1849, with a Glimpse at Its Future Destiny.* Cincinnati OH: R. E. Edwards (607).

## TRAVELOGUES

Brown, A. M. *The Gold Region and Scenes along the Way.* Alleghany PA: Purviance (83).

Clapp, J. T. *Journal of Travels to and From California.* Kalamazoo PA: Geo. A. Fitch (132).

Hale, J. *California As It Is . . .* Rochester, NY: by the author (301).

Keller, G. *A Trip across the Plains and Life in California.* Massillon: White's (367).

Kip, L. *The Volcano Diggings: A Tale of Californian Law.* New York: J. S. Redfield (380).

Miles, W. *Journal of the Sufferings and Hardships of Captain Parker H. French's Overland Expedition to California.* Chambersburg: Valley Spirit Office (443).

## FICTION AND OTHER

*Adventures of the Firm of Brown and Jingo in California.* San Francisco: Cooke and Lecount (7).

Billings, Eliza A. *The Female Volunteer.* Ohio: H. M. Rulison (58).

Gibbes, C. D. *Accompanyment to Gibbes New Map of the Gold Region of California.* Stockton CA: J. Drayton Gibbes (270).

Ringgold, C. *A Series of Charts with Sailing Directions.* Washington DC: Jhn. T. Towers (536).

Slater, N. *Fruits of Mormonism.* Caloma, CA: Harmon and Springer (585).

Vance, R. H. *Catalogue of Daguerreotypes: Panoramic Views in California.* New York: Baker, Goodwin (649).

Worth, J. J. *A Dissertation on the Resources and Policy of California.* Benecia, CA: St. Clair and Pinkham (670).

Woods, D. B. *Sixteen Months at the Gold Diggings.* New York: Harper and Brothers (696).

## COMPANY PROSPECTUSES

Burns Ranche Gold Mining Co. New York: John F. Trow (100).

Grass Valley Gold Mining Co. New York: E. Winchester (287).

Ural Mining Co. San Francisco: Franklin Book and Job Office (648).

*Appendix C*

*Belgium*

**TRAVELOGUES**

Bellemare, E. L. G. *Impressiones Des Voyages et Adventures* . . . Brussels (46).

*England*

**GUIDEBOOKS**

Shaw, W. *Golden Dreams and Waking Realities.* London: Smith, Elder (572).

**TRAVELOGUES**

Brodie, W. *Pitcairn's Island.* London: Whittacker (77).

Kelly, W. *An Excursion to California.* London: Chapman and Hall (370).

Lucett, E. *Rovings in the Pacific from 1837–1849.* London: Longman, Brown, Enean (?) and Longmans (409).

*France*

**FICTION AND OTHER**

*Alanach Californien Pour* 1851. Paris: Chez Martinon (11).

Fournier de Saint-Amant, M. P. C. *Voyages en Californie, 1850–51.* Paris: Chez Garnier Freres (550).

*Germany*

**FICTION AND OTHER**

Ballenstedt, C. W. T. *Beschreihung Meiner.* Schoningen (33).

*Holland*

**GUIDEBOOKS**

*Californie in 1850–51.* Utrecht: Kenick and Zion (110).

**TRAVELOGUES**

*Californie Tot* 31 *December* 1850. Amsterdam (111).

Oregon-California Guidebook Title Pages

# REPORT

OF

# THE EXPLORING EXPEDITION

TO

## THE ROCKY MOUNTAINS

IN THE YEAR 1842,

AND

## TO OREGON AND NORTH CALIFORNIA

IN THE YEARS 1843-'44.

BY

### BREVET CAPT. J. C. FRÉMONT,

OF THE TOPOGRAPHICAL ENGINEERS,

UNDER THE ORDERS OF COL. J. J. ABERT, CHIEF OF THE TOPOGRAPHICAL BUREAU.

---

PRINTED BY ORDER OF THE HOUSE OF REPRESENTATIVES.

---

WASHINGTON:
BLAIR AND RIVES, PRINTERS.
1845.

1. John C. Frémont, *Report of the Exploring Expedition to the Rocky Mountains.* Courtesy Library of Congress Prints and Photographs Division, cat. #F542.F83.

30th Congress,     [ HO. OF REPS. ]     Miscellaneous.
2d Session.                           No. 5.

# GEOGRAPHICAL MEMOIR

UPON

# UPPER CALIFORNIA,

IN ILLUSTRATION OF HIS

# MAP OF OREGON AND CALIFORNIA.

BY

## JOHN CHARLES FRÉMONT:

ADDRESSED TO THE SENATE OF THE UNITED STATES.

WASHINGTON:
PRINTED BY TIPPIN & STREEPER.
1849.

# WHAT I SAW IN CALIFORNIA

BEING THE

## JOURNAL OF A TOUR

BY THE EMIGRANT ROUTE AND SOUTH PASS OF THE ROCKY MOUN-
TAINS, ACROSS THE CONTINENT OF NORTH AMERICA, THE
GREAT DESERT BASIN, AND THROUGH CALIFORNIA,

IN THE YEARS 1846, 1847.

"All of which I saw, and part of which I was."—Dryden

By Edwin Bryant
Late Alcalde of San Francisco

## THE FINE ARTS PRESS
Santa Ana, California, 1936

3. Edwin Bryant, *What I Saw in California: Being the Journal of a Tour.* Courtesy Library
of Congress Prints and Photographs Division, cat. #F864.B804.

THE

# GOLD REGIONS

OF

# CALIFORNIA:

BEING A SUCCINCT DESCRIPTION OF THE

## GEOGRAPHY, HISTORY, TOPOGRAPHY,

AND

## GENERAL FEATURES OF CALIFORNIA;

INCLUDING A CAREFULLY PREPARED ACCOUNT OF

## THE GOLD REGIONS

OF THAT FORTUNATE COUNTRY.

PREPARED FROM OFFICIAL DOCUMENTS AND OTHER AUTHENTIC SOURCES.

EDITED BY G. G. FOSTER.

New York:
DEWITT & DAVENPORT,
TRIBUNE BUILDINGS.
1848.

4. George G. Foster, *The Gold Regions of California*. Courtesy Library of Congress Prints and Photographs Division, cat. #F865.F74.

# CALIFORNIA

AND ITS

# GOLD REGIONS;

WITH A

GEOGRAPHICAL AND TOPOGRAPHICAL

VIEW OF THE COUNTRY,

ITS MINERAL AND AGRICULTURAL RESOURCES.

PREPARED FROM

Official and other authentic Documents;

WITH

A MAP OF THE U. STATES AND CALIFORNIA,

SHOWING THE ROUTES OF

THE U. S. MAIL STEAM PACKETS TO CALIFORNIA,
ALSO THE VARIOUS OVERLAND ROUTES.

BY FAYETTE ROBINSON,

AUTHOR OF "MEXICO AND HER MILITARY CHIEFTAINS," ETC. ETC.

NEW YORK:
STRINGER & TOWNSEND, 222 BROADWAY.
1849.

5. Fayette Robinson, *California and Its Gold Regions*. Courtesy Yale Collection of Western Americana, Beinecke Rare Book and Manuscript Library.

# THE EMIGRANT'S GUIDE TO THE GOLD MINES.

## THREE WEEKS IN THE GOLD MINES,

### OR

### ADVENTURES WITH THE GOLD DIGGERS OF CALIFORNIA

#### IN AUGUST, 1848:

TOGETHER WITH

## ADVICE TO EMIGRANTS,

### WITH FULL INSTRUCTIONS UPON THE BEST METHOD OF GETTING THERE, LIVING, EXPENSES, ETC. ETC., AND A

## Complete Description of the Country.

### WITH A MAP AND ILLUSTRATIONS.

### BY HENRY I. SIMPSON,

OF THE NEW-YORK VOLUNTEERS.

### NEW-YORK:

### JOYCE & CO., 40 ANN STREET.

1848.

Price with the Map, Cents.                    Price without the Map, 12½ Cents.

6. Henry Simpson, *The Emigrant's Guide to the Gold Mines: Three Weeks in the Gold Mines.*
Courtesy Library of Congress Prints and Photographs Division, cat. #F865.s6.

*Accompaniment to the*

# MAP OF THE EMIGRANT ROAD

## FROM INDEPENDENCE, MO.,

### TO

### ST. FRANCISCO, CALIFORNIA

#### BY

#### T. H. JEFFERSON

---

*Brief Practical Advice to the Emigrant*
*or Traveller*

THE JOURNEY is not entirely a pleasure trip. It is attended with some hardships and privation—nothing, however, but that can be overcome by those of stout heart and good constitution. A small party (10 or 20) of the *proper* persons *properly* outfitted might make a pleasure trip of the journey. Large parties are to be deprecated.

There are two modes of outfit—one with horses, called "packing," the other with wagons, drawn by oxen.² The first perform the journey in from 60 to 90 days; the second from four to six months. A walk is the usual gait of all parties. Packing is the

1

7. T. H. Jefferson, *Accompaniment to the Map of the Emigrant Road from Independence, Mo., to St. Francisco, California.* Courtesy Library of Congress Prints and Photographs Division, cat. #F593.J4.

THE

# EMIGRANTS' GUIDE,

TO

# OREGON AND CALIFORNIA,

CONTAINING SCENES AND INCIDENTS OF A PARTY OF

OREGON EMIGRANTS;

## A DESCRIPTION OF OREGON;

SCENES AND INCIDENTS OF A PARTY OF CALIFORNIA

EMIGRANTS;

AND

## A DESCRIPTION OF CALIFORNIA;

WITH

A DESCRIPTION OF THE DIFFERENT ROUTES TO

THOSE COUNTRIES:

AND

ALL NECESSARY INFORMATION RELATIVE TO THE
EQUIPMENT, SUPPLIES, AND THE METHOD
OF TRAVELING.

———————

BY LANSFORD W. HASTINGS,

Leader of the Oregon and California Emigrants of 1842.

———————

CINCINNATI:

PUBLISHED BY GEORGE CONCLIN,

STEREOTYPED BY SHEPARD & CO.

1845.

8. Lansford W. Hastings, *The Emigrants' Guide to Oregon and California*. Courtesy Yale
Collection of Western Americana, Beinecke Rare Book and Manuscript Library.

THE

LATTER-DAY SAINTS'

# EMIGRANTS' GUIDE:

BEING A

## TABLE OF DISTANCES,

SHOWING ALL THE

SPRINGS, CREEKS, RIVERS, HILLS, MOUNTAINS,

CAMPING PLACES, AND ALL OTHER NOTABLE PLACES,

## FROM COUNCIL BLUFFS,

TO THE

## VALLEY OF THE GREAT SALT LAKE.

ALSO, THE

## LATITUDES, LONGITUDES AND ALTITUDES

OF THE PROMINENT POINTS ON THE ROUTE.

TOGETHER WITH REMARKS ON THE NATURE OF THE LAND,
TIMBER, GRASS, &c.

THE WHOLE ROUTE HAVING BEEN CAREFULLY MEASURED BY A ROADOME-
TER, AND THE DISTANCE FROM POINT TO POINT, IN
ENGLISH MILES, ACCURATELY SHOWN.

BY W. CLAYTON.

ST. LOUIS:

MO. REPUBLICAN STEAM POWER PRESS—CHAMBERS & KNAPP.

1848.

9. William Clayton, *The Latter-Day Saints' Emigrants' Guide*. Courtesy Library of Congress Prints and Photographs Division, cat. #F593.c61.

# THE
# EMIGRANTS' GUIDE
## TO
# CALIFORNIA,

CONTAINING EVERY POINT OF INFORMATION FOR
THE EMIGRANT—INCLUDING ROUTES, DISTANCES,
WATER, GRASS, TIMBER, CROSSING OF RIVERS,
PASSES, ALTITUDES, WITH A LARGE MAP OF
ROUTES, AND PROFILE OF COUNTRY, &C.,—
WITH FULL DIRECTIONS FOR TESTING AND
ASSAYING GOLD AND OTHER ORES.

## BY JOSEPH E. WARE.

## PUBLISHED BY J. HALSALL,
### No. 124 MAIN STREET,
## ST. LOUIS, MO.

10. Joseph E. Ware, *The Emigrants' Guide to California*. Courtesy Yale Collection of Western Americana, Beinecke Rare Book and Manuscript Library.

# Notes

## Introduction

1. I use the term "goldrushers" as a collective noun meaning people who left their homes to travel to California either to mine gold or to make money off the goldminers. Although I concentrate on 1849, I have avoided the term forty-niners because many goldrushers, in the sense I use the term, came in 1850–51. Since I frequently refer to this group, I also call the goldrushers emigrants and travelers. This is done only for the sake of varying the style, and in this study the meaning of the three terms is identical.

2. A good historigraphical essay on the gold rush is in Malcolm Rohrbough, *Days of Gold: The California Gold Rush and the American Nation* (Berkeley: University of California Press, 1997), 295–308. Since Rohrbough's book, there has been much work published on the gold rush. See for example Kevin Starr and Richard Orsi, *Rooted in Barbarous Soil* (Berkeley: University of California Press, 2000); Brian Roberts, *American Alchemy: The California Gold Rush and Middle-Class Culture* (Chapel Hill: University of North Carolina Press, 2000); Susan Lee Johnson, *Roaring Camp: The Social World of the California Gold Rush* (New York: W. W. Norton, 2000); and H. W. Brands, *The Age of Gold: The California Gold Rush and the New American Dream* (New York: Doubleday, 2002). The recent studies of the gold rush are framed chronologically in California history by two excellent collections of articles in the "California History Sesquicentennial Series" published by the California Historical Society and the University of California Press. For the period before the gold rush, Ramon Gutierrez and Richard Orsi, *Contested Eden: California before the Gold Rush* (Berkeley: University of California Press, 1998); for the period just after the gold rush, John Burns and Richard Orsi, *Taming the Elephant: Politics, Government, and Law in Pioneer California* (Berkeley: University of California Press, 2003).

3. The joint product and pricing problem is discussed theoretically in Richard Stillson, "An Analysis of Information and Transactions Services in Financial Institutions," *Journal of Money, Credit and Banking* 6, no. 4 (1974): 58–34. An historical example of the problem is described and analyzed in Richard Stillson, "The Financing of Malayan Rubber, 1905–1923," *Economic History Review* 24, no. 4 (November 1974): 589–98.

4. At times I refer in the text to credibility sources, meaning credibility criteria that are embodied in a source, such as officialdom.

5. Most overland goldrushers organized themselves into companies that were usually formal organizations created for the purpose of the trip across the country. They wrote, and frequently published, prospectuses that specified officers, financing, organization, and what each member was required to bring to the group, for example, a wagon, guns, provisions, and money. Everyone joining the company would have had to agree to these provisions and sign the prospectus.

6. There was a great deal of information about the California gold rush published in other countries in 1849–51. See appendix C, which classifies by year, country, and type of publication the excellent bibliography of gold rush publications compiled by Gary Kurutz: *The California Gold Rush: A Descriptive Bibliography of Books and Pamphlets Covering the Years 1848–1853* (San Francisco: Book Club of California, 1997).

7. See Johnson, *Roaring Camp*, for a history of the difficulties of several non European American groups in the southern mines. Sucheng Chan analyzes racial and ethnic repression in his article: "A People of Exceptional Character: Ethnic Diversity, Nativism, and Racism in the California Gold Rush," in, Starr and Orsi, *Barbarous Soil*, 44–85. James Sandos focuses on the problems of Californios and California Indians in "Because He Is a Liar and a Thief: Conquering the Residents of 'Old' California, 1850–1880," in Starr and Orsi, *Barbarous Soil*, 86–112. For a history of California Indians see Albert Hurtado, *Indian Survival on the California Frontier* (New Haven: Yale University Press, 1988).

8. J. Sabin, *Bibliotheca Americana: A Dictionary of Books Relating to America from Its Discovery to the Present Time* (New York: Bibliographic Society of America, 1868–1936). This is a standard bibliographic reference for nineteenth-century books about America. Sabin's list is made much easier to use because of an index by John Edgar Molnar, *Author-Title Index to Joseph Sabin's Dictionary of Books Relating to America* (Metuchen NJ: Scarecrow, 1974).

9. The catalogs were Bartlett and Welford, New York, 1844; D. Appleton, 1847, New York; John Doyle, New York, 1848; and Daniels and Smith, Philadelphia, 1847. D. Appleton was one of the largest publishers and booksellers in the country, and its book-length catalog contained some twelve thousand entries. Bartlett and Welford and John Doyle were smaller but still notable New York bookstores, and Daniels and Smith was a Philadelphia bookstore that advertised itself as "The Cheap Book Store—Small Profits and Quick Returns." These catalogs are in the extensive collection of nineteenth-century American book catalogs at the American Antiquarian Society in Worcester, Massachusetts.

10. The initial publication was followed by another Washington edition in that year, and editions in Boston in 1807 and 1808. See Sabin, *Bibliotheca,* entry 40824 for the various editions. A London edition of Jefferson's "Communications to Congress" was published in 1807 and again the following year by a different publisher.

11. Nicholas Biddle, *The Expedition of Lewis and Clark* (Philadelphia: Bradford and In-skeep, 1814).

12. An example of an unauthorized version of the *Travels* was William Fisher, *The Travels of Captains Lewis and Clark by Order of the Government of the United States . . .* (Philadelphia: H. Lester, 1809). Fisher cashed in on the interest in the expedition by publishing three versions of his spurious account with different publishers in Philadelphia and Baltimore. The

first and best-known of the books by other members of the expedition was Patrick Gass, *A Journal of the Voyages and Travels of a Corps of Discovery, Under the Command of Captain Lewis and Captain Clark . . .* (Pittsburgh: David M'Keehan, 1808), a book that was republished in London in 1808 with subsequent editions published in Philadelphia by Mathew Carey in 1810, 1811, and 1812. See Sabin, *Bibliotheca*, 26741.

13. Meriwether Lewis, *Journal of Lewis and Clark to the Mouth of the Columbia River . . . New Edition with Notes, Revised, Corrected and Illustrated . . .* (Dayton OH: B. F. Ellis, 1840); Meriwether Lewis, *History of the Expedition* (New York: Harper and Brothers, 1842).

14. Zebulon Pike, *Expedition to the Headwaters of the Mississippi River through Louisiana Territory and in New Spain during the Years 1805–06* (Washington: U.S. Senate, 1807); also published in Philadelphia by C. and A. Conrad, 1810, and in London by Longman, Hurst, Rees, Orme and Brown, 1811.

15. Wilkes's expedition was an enormous around-the-world trip the report of which was published in 1845 as a five-volume set: Charles Wilkes, *Narrative of the United States Exploring Expedition,* 5 vols. (Philadelphia: Lea and Blanchard, 1845). Long's expedition was recorded by the botanist of the expedition, Edwin James. James's book was published in 1823 and was still for sale in the bookseller catalogs of the mid-1840s: Edwin James, *Account of an Expedition from Pittsburgh to the Rocky Mountains Performed in the Years 1819 and 1820* (Philadelphia: H. C. Carey and J. Lea, 1823).

16. William Emory, *Notes of a Military Reconnaissance from Fort Leavenworth, in Missouri to San Diego, in California* (New York: H. Long and Brothers, 1848). The map of the expedition, drawn by Joseph Welch, was published separately in 1847 (Washington DC: C. G. Graham, Lith.) and in 1848 (Washington DC: Wendell and Van Benthuysen).

17. John C. Frémont, *Report of the Exploring Expedition to the Rocky Mountains in the Year 1842. To Oregon and North California in the Years 1843–44* (Washington: U.S. Senate, Gales and Seaton, printers, 1945) and (U.S. House of Representatives, Blair and Rives, printers, 1845). It was also published in New York by D. Appleton, 1846. Frémont's *Report* described two of his expeditions, the first in 1842 along what became "the Great Platte River Road," and his explorations of the Wind River mountains in the current state of Wyoming; and the second in 1843–44, in which he explored the Great Basin in the current states of Utah and Nevada and crossed of the Sierra Nevada mountains of California.

18. Frémont, *Report*, 61–62. Some historians attribute this style to his wife, Jessie Hart Benton, who acted as Frémont's secretary, writing what he dictated. See, for example, Richard White, *It's Your Misfortune and None of My Own: A New History of the American West* (Norman: University of Oklahoma Press, 1991), 123. For a discussion of Frémont's style and Jessie's "eager help," see Bernard DeVoto, *The Year of Decision, 1846* (New York: St. Martin's Griffin, 2000), 39–40.

19. Three works on the mountain men are Le Roy Hafen, *The Mountain Men and the Fur Trade* (Glendale CA: Arthur Clark, 1965); William Goetzmann, *The Mountain Man* (Cody WY: Buffalo Bill Historical Center, 1978); and Robert Utley, *A Life Wild and Perilous: Mountain Men and the Paths to the Pacific* (New York: Henry Holt, 1997).

20. Smith's discovery of South Pass was reported by the *St. Louis Enquirer*, August 30,

1824, and repeated in *Niles Weekly Register* in Baltimore, Maryland, which provided national coverage of the event and the people involved. See John D. McDermott, *The Frontier Reexamined* (Urbana: University of Illinois Press, 1967), 63.

21. Timothy Flint, *The Shoshonee Valley: A Romance* (Cincinnati OH: E. H. Flint, 1830). This was the first novel in which mountain men appeared as characters and was still on bookseller catalog lists in the mid 1840s. Two other novels depicting mountain men that were published before 1848 were an English-language version of a German novel, Charles Sealsfield [Karl Anton Postl], *Life in the New World; or, Sketches of American Society* (New York: J. Winchester, 1844) and a fictional account dressed up as nonfiction: David H. Coyner, *The Lost Trappers: A Collection of Interesting Scenes and Events in the Rocky Mountains Together with a Short Description of California* (Cincinnati OH: J.A. and U.P James, 1847). See Henry Nash Smith, *Virgin Land: The American West as Symbol and Myth* (Cambridge MA: Harvard University Press, 1950), 81–89, for a discussion of the mountain man as mythical hero and a comparison of their depiction to Daniel Boone, the eastern frontier hero.

22. Biddle, *Expedition of Lewis and Clark,* 166. The original version by Lewis said only, "a curious custom with the Souix as well as the rickeres is to give handsom squars to those whome they wish to Show some acknowledgements to. The Seauex we got clare of without taking their squars, they followed us with Squars two days." Frank Bergon, ed., *The Journals of Lewis and Clark* (New York: Penguin Books, 1995), 63.

23. Edwin James, *Account of an Expedition from Pittsburgh to the Rocky Mountains Performed in the Years 1819 and 1820,* in *Early Western Travels, 1748–1846,* vol. 19, ed. Reuben Gold Thwaite (Cleveland: Arthur H. Clark, 1905), 204–6.

24. There were many editions of Catlin's books: the one available in the Appleton, and Bartlett and Welford, catalogs was George Catlin, *Letters and Notes on the Manners, Customs and Condition of the North American Indians . . . With Four Hundred Illustrations, Carefully Engraved from his Original Paintings* (New York: Wiley and Putnam, 1842). This was his primary book of engravings of North American Indians and was republished many times both in the United States and London. The Smithsonian has published an excellent book on Catlin, including many reproductions of his images of Indians as a catalog to an exhibition of his paintings at the Renwick Gallery in 2002–2003: Brian Dippie, and others, *George Catlin and His Indian Gallery* (Washington DC: Smithsonian American Art Museum, 2002). Wied, Maximilian, Prinz von, *Prince of Wied's Travels in the Interior of North American* (London: Ackerman, 1843). This book was listed in the catalogs of Bartlet and Welford (1844) and D. Appleton (1847).

25. A good review of newspaper accounts of Oregon and the Oregon Trail in the early 1840s is in John Unruh, *The Plains Across: The Overland Emigrants and the Trans-Mississippi West, 1840–60* (Urbana: University of Illinois Press, 1973), pp. 28–61.

26. Washington Irving, *Astoria, or Anecdotes of an Enterprise beyond the Rocky Mountains* (Philadelphia: Lee and Blanchard, 1836; London: Richard Bentley, 1836; and New York: G. P. Putnam, 1836 and 1849). Washington Irving, *The Rocky Mountains; or Scenes, Incidents and Adventures in the Far West; Digested from the Journal of Capt. B. L. E. Bonneville . . .* (Philadelphia: Lea and Blanchard, 1837; London: Richard Bentley, 1837; and New York: G. P. Putnam, 1837).

27. See Unruh, *Plains Across*, 45–47.

28. Robert Greenhow, *The History of Oregon and Calif.... Accompanied by a Geographical View and Map of Those Countries* (New York: D. Appleton, 1844; Boston: Little and Brown, 1844; and London: John Murray, 1844). This book had four editions in Boston and two in London. Greenhow followed up with *The Geography of Oregon and California and the Other Territories of the Northwest Coast of N. America* (Boston: printed for the author by Freeman and Bolles, 1845; and New York: M. H. Newman, 1845). Although these titles included California, Greenhow was primarily a booster of the Oregon emigration. These books were available in the book catalogs of 1847.

29. Henry Dana, *Two Years before the Mast* (New York: Harper Brothers, 1840; and London: Edward Moxon, 1840).

## 1. Newspapers

1. Almost every gold rush history begins with some description of the spread of the gold rush news to the East; for example see John Caughey, *Gold Is the Cornerstone* (Berkeley: University of California Press, 1948), chap. 3; and Malcolm Rohrbough, *Days of Gold: The California Gold Rush and the American Nation* (Berkeley: University of California Press, 1997), chap. 2. The earliest, and still the most thorough research on newspaper reporting of the gold discovery is Ralph Bieber, *Southern Trails to California in 1849* (Glendale CA: Arthur H. Clark, 1937), chap. 2; and Ralph Bieber, "California Gold Mania," *Mississippi Valley Historical Review* 35, no. 1 (June 1948): 3–48. Ralph Bieber donated his research materials in the form of a large selection of newspaper clippings from every state to the Huntington Library where it is maintained as the Bieber Collection.

2. Richard Brown, *Knowledge Is Power: The Diffusion of Information in Early America, 1700–1865* (New York: Oxford University Press, 1989), 279.

3. Traditional historiography of journalism and newspapers emphasized the role of individual newspapers and editors in developing the modern form of American newspaper and style of journalism. See, for example, James Melvin Lee, *History of American Journalism* (Boston: Houghton Mifflin, 1917) and Frank Luther Mott, *American Journalism: A History, 1690–1960* (New York: Macmillan, 1962). More recent work on newspaper history has substantially altered the focus of these traditional "Whig" histories, emphasizing objectivity, journalistic standards, and the business of newspapers. See, for example, Daniel Schiller, *Objectivity and the News: The Public and the Rise of Commercial Journalism* (Philadelphia: University of Pennsylvania Press, 1981); Hazel Dicken-Garcia, *Journalistic Standards in Nineteenth-Century America* (Madison: University of Wisconsin Press, 1989); Michael Schudson, *Origins of the Ideal of Objectivity in the Professions: Studies in the History of American Journalism and American Law, 1830–1940 (New York: Garland Publications, 1990)*; and Gerald J. Baldasty, *The Commercialization of News in the Nineteenth Century* (Madison: University of Wisconsin Press, 1992).

4. Journalism historians have extolled the penny press as a revolutionary development in American newspapers, and Bennett and his *New York Herald* are prominent in this historiography. See Schudson, *Origins*, chap. 2; Baldasty, *Commercialization of News*, chap.

2; and Mott, *American Journalism*, chap. 12. For a contrary view, see John Nerone, "The Mythology of the Penny Press," *Critical Studies in Mass Communication* 4, no. 4 (December 1987), 376–404.

5. Don Carlos Seitz, *The James Gordon Bennetts, Father and Son* (Indianapolis: Bobbs-Merrill, 1928); Oliver Carlson, *The Man Who Made News, James Gordon Bennett* (New York: Duell, Sloan, and Pearce, 1942); and James L. Crouthamel, *Bennett's* New York Herald *and the Rise of the Popular Press* (Syracuse NY: Syracuse University Press, 1989). Bennett's memoirs, originally published in 1855, have been reprinted: Isaac C. Pray, *Memoirs of James Gordon Bennett and His Times* (New York: Arno, 1970).

6. Crouthamel, *Bennett's* New York Herald, 25–26.

7. Bieber, *Southern Trails*, 19–22.

8. Crouthamel, *Bennett's* New York Herald, 40.

9. *New York Herald*, November 28, 1848. Bennett published a *Baltimore Sun* account of Mason's report on November 30, 1848. Loeser's trip and the story of the official report and the pouch of gold were first covered by the *New Orleans Daily Picayune* four days earlier, on November 24, 1848.

10. Bieber, "Mania," 3–48, 20.

11. John Haskell Kemble, *The Panama Route, 1848–1869* (Columbia: University of South Carolina Press, 1990). Thousands of goldrushers (one report was six thousand by mid-January 1849) were stranded on the Pacific side waiting for a ship up to California and had to pay for food and lodging during the wait. Many came back particularly when malaria and yellow fever began to take their toll. Part of the problem was the fact that ships that were expected to make repeated runs between Panama City and San Francisco were abandoned as their crews deserted to become goldminers.

12. These extras were published December 26, 1848, and January 8, 16, and 31, 1849. They have not been microfilmed, and there are few extant copies; only the Beinecke Library at Yale University has all four. The publication of supplements and extras was common by the larger newspapers of the period, but this is the only example in 1849 of which I am aware of an extra specifically concerning the California gold rush.

13. Carl I. Wheat, *Maps of the California Gold Region, 1848–1857: A Biblio-Cartography of an Important Decade* (San Francisco: Grabhorn, 1942), map 44, 27–28; and Carl Wheat, *Mapping the TransMisssssippi West, 1540–1857: A Preliminary Study,* vol. 3 (Worcester MA: American Antiquarian Society, 1954), map 565, 52. Although the notation "Avery Sc." appears on the legend, Carl Wheat guesses that this rare map was drawn by Lt. E. O. C. Ord, who drew similar maps for the military.

14. There is a large historiography concerning Greeley. See Suzanne Schulze, *Horace Greeley, a Bio-Bibliography* (New York: Greenwood, 1992).

15. One of Greeley's crusades was to find a "safety valve" for distressed New York laborers, and he chose the 1830–40s western United States as the ideal location for the East's urban poor (Illinois was his favorite). A recent book focusing on Greeley and the American West is Coy F. Cross, *Go West Young Man: Horace Greeley's Vision for America* (Albuquerque: University of New Mexico Press, 1995).

16. Paul Wermuth, *Bayard Taylor* (New York: Twayne Publishers, 1973). Taylor had published two books of poetry and a travel book before going to work for Greeley and eventually published nine travel books, four novels, an English translation of Goethe's *Faust*, as well as more poetry and other books.

17. An annotated reprinting of Taylor's *El Dorado* has been published with an introduction by James Houston, and an afterword by Roger Kahn (Santa Clara CA: Santa Clara University / Berkeley CA: Heyday Books, 2000).

18. See Richard B. Kielbowicz, *News in the Mail: The Press, Post Office, and Public Information, 1700–1860s* (New York: Greenwood, 1989), 145–51; and Richard R. John, *Spreading the News: The American Postal System from Franklin to Morse* (Cambridge MA: Harvard University Press, 1995), 30–37. Editors and readers accepted the fact that newspapers would copy extensively from one another.

19. Lee, *American Journalism*, 185–86.

20. *Boston Evening Transcript*, January 11, 1849.

21. *Boston Evening Transcript*, January 9, 1849.

22. *Boston Evening Transcript*, January 5, 1849.

23. Specialized studies of the religious press are Henry Stroupe, *The Religious Press in the South Atlantic States, 1802–1865* (Durham NC: Duke University Press, 1956) and Wesley Norton, *Religious Newspapers in the Old Northwest to 1861: A History, Bibliography, and Record of Opinion* (Athens: Ohio University Press, 1977).

24. There is not a large historiography about Abell or the *Baltimore Sun*, although the newspaper is usually mentioned in journalism histories (see Lee, *American Journalism*, 192; and Mott, *American Journalism*, 240–41). There is a family biography of Abell: William Abell, *Arunah Sheperdson Abell* (Chevy Chase MD: privately published, 1989); a centennial history of the Sunpapers, of which H. L. Mencken was a contributor: Gerald W. Johnson, *The Sunpapers of Baltimore* (New York: Knopf, 1937); and a recent commemorative history written for the 150th anniversary of the *Sun*, Harold A. Williams, *The Baltimore Sun: 1837–1987* (Baltimore: Johns Hopkins University Press, 1987).

25. *Louisville (KY) Daily Journal*, May 9, 1849; cited in Rohrbough, *Days of Gold*, 313n14.

26. Rudolph M. Lapp, *Blacks in Gold Rush California* (New Haven: Yale University Press, 1977), 50. See also Newell G. Bringhurst, "Slavery in the West," in *Dictionary of Afro-American Slavery*, ed. Randall M. Miller and John David Smith (Westport CT: Greenwood, 1988), 798–806.

27. Lee, *American Journalism*, 333. For a review of several of the major newspapers in the South in the nineteenth century, including the *Charleston (SC) Mercury*, see Carl R. Osthaus, *Partisans of the Southern Press: Editorial Spokesmen of the Nineteenth Century* (Lexington: University of Kentucky Press, 1994).

28. Osthaus, *Southern Press*, chap. 4.

29. *Charleston (SC) Mercury*, January 3, 1849.

30. A review of the California debate as part of sectional politics is in the classic David M. Potter, *The Impending Crisis, 1848–1861* (New York: Harper and Row, 1976), chaps. 4,

5. A more recent review of these issues is William W. Freehling, *The Road to Disunion: Secessionists at Bay, 1776–1854* (New York: Oxford University Press, 1990), chap. 27, 28. The story from California's point of view is probably still best told in the oldest California history, Herbert Howe Bancroft, *History of California, Vol. 6, 1848–1859* (San Francisco: History Company, 1888).

31. *Montgomery (AL) Tri-Weekly Flag and Advertiser,* January 20, and February 3, 10, and 13, 1849.

32. For a brief but good description of the *New Orleans Times-Picayune* during this time period, see Osthaus, *Southern Press,* chap. 3. A more thorough, though somewhat dated and very celebratory, history of the newspaper is Thomas Ewing Dabney, *One Hundred Great Years; The Story of the* Times-Picayune *from Its Founding to 1940,* (Baton Rouge: Louisiana State University Press, 1944).

33. A biography of Kendall is Fayette Copeland, *Kendall of the Picayune* (Norman OK: University of Oklahoma Press, 1943).

34. This express was set up and financed by Abell of the *Baltimore Sun.* Bennett of the *New York Herald* had previously established private expresses both from Canada (to get European news to New York faster by meeting ships as they approached Nova Scotia) and from New Orleans, and he participated in Abell's southern express during the Mexican War. See Harold A. Williams, *The Baltimore Sun, 1837–1987* (Baltimore: Johns Hopkins University Press, 1987), 28, for the *Sun*'s role in the expresses, and Crouthamel, *Bennett's Herald,* 46–47, for the *Herald*'s.

35. Circulation was given in a statement of the newspaper's carriers, December 28, 1848. The newspaper also advertised above the editorial column on the second page, as possessing the "Largest Circulation in America! . . . having not less than one-hundred thousand readers in town and country." This was wishful thinking but the *Cincinnati Daily Commercial* was a major newspaper in Cincinnati and the region.

36. John Unruh, *The Plains Across: The Overland Emigrants and the Trans-Mississippi West, 1840–60* (Urbana: University of Illinois Press, 1973), 69, 74; and Kate Gregg, "Missourians in the Gold Rush," *Missouri Historical Review* 39, no. 2 (January 1945): 143. William Gilpin was a well-known Missourian who traveled with Frémont in 1843. His letter was solicited by three businessmen in Independence as a way of drumming up business for their trailhead town.

37. The *Hamilton (OH) Intelligencer* article stated that it was copied from the *New York Advertiser*; this name, however, was not used by any of the major New York newspapers at that time. There was a newspaper, the *New York Daily Advertiser,* in the eighteenth century, edited by Francis Childs, but this was not publishing in 1849.

38. *Hamilton (OH) Intelligencer,* January 25, 1849. The D'Alvear ad appeared in many smaller newspapers in the current Midwest and was at various times made fun of and printed at apparently face value. See Jocelyn Maynard Ghent, "The Golden Dream and the Press: Illinois and the California Rush of '49," *Journal of the West* 17, no. 2 (1978): 17–27.

39. See Bernard Bailyn, T*he Ideological Origins of the American Revolution* (Cambridge MA: Harvard University Press, 1967) and Jeffrey Pasley, *The Tyranny of Printers* (Charlottesville: University of Virginia Press, 2001).

## 2. The Marketplaces for Information

1. The literature on the history of the book does not contain studies on the publication and distribution of guidebooks and maps. General overviews of the history of book markets and distribution in the mid-nineteenth century include John Tebbel, *Between Covers: The Rise and Transformation of Book Publishing in America* (New York: Oxford University Press, 1987); and his more comprehensive but less analytical *A History of Book Publishing in the United States, Vol. 1, The Creation of an Industry, 1630–1865* (New York: R. R. Bowker, 1972). See also Michael Hackenberg, ed., *Getting the Books Out: Papers of the Chicago Conference on the Book in 19th-Century America* (Washington DC: Center for the Book, Library of Congress, 1987). There are also several good recent studies of specific publishers, including Michael Winship, *American Literary Publishing in the Mid-Nineteenth Century: The Business of Ticknor and Fields* (Cambridge UK: Cambridge University Press, 1995) and Rosalind Remer, *Printers and Men of Capital: Philadelphia Book Publishers in the New Republic* (Philadelphia: University of Pennsylvania Press, 1996).

Guidebooks and maps are usually mentioned in histories of the western trails and the gold rush. For example, John Unruh, *The Plains Across: The Overland Emigrants and the Trans-Mississippi West, 1840–60* (Urbana: University of Illinois Press, 1973), 60, 72, 75, 108; Ferol Egan, *The El Dorado Trail* (New York: McGraw-Hill, 1968), 29–45; and John Caughey, *Gold Is the Cornerstone* (Berkeley: University of California Press, 1948), 47–54. These descriptions, however, are not comprehensive. The references that primarily discuss guidebooks are Ray Billington, "Books That Won the West," *American West* 4, no. 3 (1967): 25–32; Helen Kroll, "The Books that Enlightened the Emigrants," *Oregon Historical Quarterly* 45, no. 2 (1944): 103–23; Thomas Andrews, "The Controversial Hastings Overland Guide: A Reassessment," *Pacific Historical Review* 37, no. 1 (1968): 21–34; and Thomas Andrews, "Lansford Hastings and the Promotion of the Salt Lake Desert Cutoff: A Reappraisal," *Western Historical Quarterly* 4, no. 2 (1973): 133–50. Carl Wheat has thoroughly researched maps of western America, including maps of California and the gold rush: Carl Wheat, *Mapping the TransMissssippi West, 1540–1857: A Preliminary Study* (Worcester MA: American Antiquarian Society, 1954) and Carl Wheat, *The Maps of the California Gold Region: 1848–1857: A Biblio-Cartography of an Important Decade* (San Francisco: Grabhorn, 1942).

2. Gary Kurutz, *The California Gold Rush: A Descriptive Bibliography of Books and Pamphlets Covering the Years 1848–1853* (San Francisco: Book Club of California, 1997).

3. European publications in 1848–51 concerning California and the gold rush were extensive, especially in 1849. In that year there were eleven German, six English, three Dutch, one Norwegian, and two French guidebooks identified in Kurutz's bibliography (see appendix C).

4. The problem of readership is common to studies of information, reading, and the history of the book. Classic studies that discuss this problem are Ronald Zboray, *A Fictive People: Antebellum Economic Development and the American Reading Public* (New York: Oxford University Press, 1993); Cathy Davidson, *Revolution and the Word: The Rise of the Novel in America* (New York: Oxford University Press, 1986); and David Hall, *Cultures of Print: Essays in the History of the Book* (Amherst: University of Massachusetts Press, 1996). One study was able to gather evidence directly from readers: Janice A. Radway, *Reading the*

227

*Romance: Women, Patriarchy, and Popular Literature* (Chapel Hill: University of North Carolina Press, 1991).

5. In one study of a sample of thirty gold rush diaries, there were twenty-nine references to various guidebooks and republished western histories and geographies. David Potter, *Trail to California: The Overland Journal of Vincent Geiger and Wakeman Bryarly* (New Haven CT: Yale University Press, 1945), 21.

6. J. Goldsborough Bruff's surviving papers, sketches, and diary contain one of the most complete descriptions of an overland emigration company. Much of the material has been published in Georgia Willis Read and Ruth Gaines, *Gold Rush: The Journals, Drawings, and Other Papers of J. Goldsborough Bruff* (New York: Columbia University Press, 1949). The quotation is from a fragment of manuscript in his hand (Read and Gaines, *Gold Rush,* xviii). The original materials are at the Huntington Library in San Marino, California.

7. The dominance of New York in the book trade at this time is emphasized in most histories of the book. For example, see Tebbel, *Between the Covers* and Hackenberg, *Getting the Books Out.* The older centers of Boston and Philadelphia, however, still had a substantial number of publishers, and Cincinnati was becoming a regional book publishing center in the West. For the rise and relative fall of Philadelphia as a publishing center see Remer, *Printers and Men of Capital*; for Boston, see Winship, *Ticknor and Fields*; and for Cincinnati, see Walter Sutton, *The Western Book Trade: Cincinnati as a Nineteenth Century Publishing and Book-Trade Center* (Columbus: Ohio State University Press, 1961).

8. In his first issue, Greeley stated that his newspaper was to be "a new morning journal of politics, literature and general intelligence," thus contrasting it with Bennett's nonpolitical newspaper for the masses. *New York Tribune,* April 10, 1841. See also James Melvin Lee, *History of American Journalism* (Boston: Houghton Mifflin, 1917); and William E. Huntzicker, *The Popular Press, 1833–1865* (Westport CT: Greenwood, 1999). A good description of the advertisements and how they relate to the guidebooks and maps is Wheat, *TransMissssippi West,* 63–73.

9. Wheat, *TransMissssippi West,* 65–67. See also the relevant issues of the *New York Tribune.*

10. John Frémont, *Report of the Exploring Expedition to the Rocky Mountains in the Year 1842. To Oregon and North California in the Years 1843–44* (Washington: U.S. Senate, Gales and Seaton, printers) and (U.S. House of Representatives, Blair and Rives, printers, 1845). In addition to the twenty-thousand copies of this report ordered by each house of Congress and printed in Washington DC, in 1845, there were several private editions including one by Appleton in 1846.

11. John Frémont, *Geographical Memoir upon Upper California in Illustration of His Map of Oregon and California* (Washington DC: Wendell and Van Benthuysen, printers, 1848). The map contained for the first time the phrase "Golden Gate," referring to the San Francisco strait, and a small legend marked "El Dorado or Gold Region." For a description and assessment of the map ("the one great general map of 1848"), see Wheat, *TransMissssippi West,* 55–62.

12. John Frémont, *The California Guide Book; Comprising Col. Frémont's Geographical*

*Account of Upper California; Major Emory's Overland Journey from Fort Leavenworth in Missouri to San Diego, in California* (New York: D. Appleton, 1849).

13. Edwin Bryant, *What I Saw in California: Being the Journal of a Tour by the Emigrant Route and South Pass of the Rocky Mountains . . . in the Years 1846–47* (New York: D. Appleton, 1848).

14. "His [Bryant's] book probably played a greater part than any other single work in guiding the epic emigration of 1849," Potter, *Trail to California,* 21. The *St. Louis Weekly Reveille* stated on New Year's Day 1849 that the book was so much in demand that there was scarcely a copy for sale in the West. See Kate Gregg, "Missourians in the Gold Rush," *Missouri Historical Review* 39, no. 2 (1945): 143; and Unruh, *Plains Across,* 74.

15. Bryant, as did the Donner-Read party, traveled on a route explored by Frémont south of the Salt Lake and across part of the Great Basin south of the Humbolt River in present-day Nevada. The route south of the Salt Lake became known as the "Hastings Cutoff," from a guidebook written by Lansford Hastings and published in 1845. For further details of Bryant's life see Thomas D. Clark, "Edwin Bryant and the Opening of the Road to California," in, *Essays in Western History in Honor of Professor T. A. Larson,* ed. Roger Daniels (Laramie,: University of Wyoming Press, 1971), 29–43.

16. Bryant, *What I Saw,* 465. He was referring to the Donner Party. The last third of the book describes what happened to the Donner party and why.

17. G. G. Foster, *The Gold Regions of California* (New York: Dewitt and Davenport, 1848).

18. Foster, *Gold Regions,* vii.

19. *New York Tribune,* December 9, 1848.

20. Foster's range of books included an edition of Shelley's poems with a long and erudite introduction, the California guidebook, a romance novel entitled *Celio,* and his best known work, *New York by Gaslight,* which apparently sold some two hundred thousand copies. As in a typical nineteenth-century novel, however, he went from rags to riches to rags and died poor and just out of prison for forging a check. See Stuart Blumin's introduction to G. G. Foster, *New York by Gas-Light and Other Urban Sketches* (Berkeley: University of California Press, 1995), 27–45.

21. If this speculation is correct, then Foster must have completed the book, and Dewitt and Davenport printed it in two or three weeks. That is quick work which again shows newspaper training and maybe participation of the resources of the *Tribune.*

22. Foster, *Gold Regions,* iii.

23. Caughey traces the likely antecedents of Foster's research: Caughey, *Gold Is the Cornerstone,* 50.

24. Fayette Robinson, *California and Its Gold Regions* (New York: Stringer and Townsend, 1849).

25. *New York Tribune,* January 23, 1849.

26. Wheat, *TransMisssssippi West,* 75. The California sections of the map are reproduced in figure 7, chap. 4.

27. Robinson, *California and Its Gold Regions,* 88.

28. Robinson, *California and Its Gold Regions*, 89–90. Bryant actually began at Independence, Missouri, and took what became known as the California Trail hooking north to the Platte River before turning west (see map 1). The first few miles of this trail from Independence were along the Santa Fe Trail, and Bryant mentioned meeting three Santa Fe trading companies returning to Missouri (Bryant, *What I Saw*, 34). Robinson probably read that far in Bryant and wanted to use his name as an authority without bothering to actually learn the route taken by Bryant.

29. Robinson, *California and Its Gold Regions*, preface.

30. Henry Simpson, *Three Weeks in the Gold Mines, or Adventures with the Gold Diggers of California* (New York: Joyce, 1848). This book has been reprinted with a prologue and epilogue by Franz Dykstra (Haverford PA: Headframe Publishing, 1978).

31. Dykstra, epilog, Simpson, *Three Weeks*, 74. Dykstra surmises, "Presumably the publisher had the work 'ghosted', racing into print to serve this suddenly created market."

32. Simpson, *Three Weeks*, 37.

33. Simpson, *Three Weeks*, 67.

34. Dykstra, epilog, Simpson, *Three Weeks*, 75.

35. Dykstra, epilog, Simpson, *Three Weeks*, 74–75.

36. The ad in the *Tribune* stated that to buy the book one had to enclose twenty-five cents in a prepaid letter to Joyce and Company and that the book would be mailed to the purchaser, *New York Tribune*, December 20, 1848.

37. See appendix C. The early guidebooks published in Europe are a study in themselves, but in the first several months of the gold rush, they did not affect the market for information in the United States.

38. Wheat, *Mapping*, 92. According to Wheat, "T. H. Jefferson stands forth as the one truly great commercial production of the year. . . . [It] was a veritable tour de force in four sheets. . . . Jefferson used Frémont's 1845 and 1848 maps as a base, but he did his own cartography in the areas that he himself traversed."

39. W. P. Gregg, *American Emigrant's Preliminary Guide to the Gold Mines of California,* manuscript and typescript, 1849, California Papers Collection, American Antiquarian Society, Worcester MA.

40. T. H. Jefferson, *Accompaniment to the Map of the Emigrant Road from Independence Mo. to San Francisco, Californian* (New York: T. H. Jefferson, privately printed, 1849).

41. Wheat, *TransMisssssippi West*, 92.

42. If one compares the map notations, dates, and place names on the Jefferson map with diaries of other travelers in the various groups that split off from the original wagon train, it appears he was in the group ahead of the Donners but well in back of Bryant. None of the other diarists, however, mention Jefferson. See Rush Spedden, "Who Was T. H. Jefferson?" *Overland Journal* 8, no. 3 (1990): 2–16. There was only one other mention of Jefferson in 1846, in the *St. Louis Missouri Republican*, May 9, 1846, where he was in a list of names going to California.

43. In his journal entry on September 13, 1849, J. Goldsborough Bruff wrote, "Our camp ground is about the spot where a man named Jefferson, in 1846, had a fight with the Pauta Indians, who succeeded in carrying off the greater part of his stock. He has published a

small map, of the route through by 'Trucky Pass,'—a good Guide." Read and Gaines, *Gold Rush*, 137.

44. Jefferson, *Accompaniment to the Map*, 2.

45. The first edition of Foster's guidebook sold for 25 cents: by the 3rd edition it was 50 cents. Simpson's fraudulent guidebook sold for 15 cents; Robinson's book sold for 50 cents. Only Bryant's 4th edition with the guidebook-like appendix sold for over one dollar: it was advertised at $1.25.

46. Spedden, "T. H. Jefferson," 2. Spedden speculates that T. H. Jefferson may have been Thomas Hemings Jefferson, the son of Thomas Jefferson and Sally Hemings. The evidence is light but intriguing, especially that there is now DNA evidence that some Jefferson family member (not necessarily the president) fathered Sally's children, one of whom was a son named Tom Hemings, born 1790 (Fawn M. Brodie, "Thomas Jefferson's Unknown Grandchildren," *American Heritage*, October 1977). Spedden's speculation is that T. H. Jefferson was Tom Hemings, who left Monticello at about age fifteen, went to New York, and assumed another life there, possibly as a white. He then decided to make the 1846 trip across his father's Louisiana Purchase.

47. As in the case of the Jefferson map and guidebook, the value of these publications as information to overland travelers is a judgment made by historians and trail buffs based on hindsight. For the kind of information and advice that has been considered beneficial to travelers on the overland trail, see Andrews, "Controversial Hastings Guide," 21–34, and Andrews, "Lansford Hastings," 133–50.

48. Lansford W. Hastings, *The Emigrants' Guide to Oregon and California* (Cincinnati: George Conclin, 1845). There were subsequent editions in 1847, 1848, and 1849 under the title *The New History of Oregon and California* (all published by George Conclin of Cincinnati), and one in 1857 published by H. M. Rulison of Cincinnati. There is a reprint edition with an introduction by Mary Nance Spence (New York: Da Capo Press, 1969). For descriptions of Hastings's involvement in the Donner story, see George Stewart, *The California Trail: An Epic with Many Heroes* (Lincoln: University of Nebraska Press, 1962), 142–75; Bernard DeVoto, *The Year of Decision, 1846* (New York: St. Martin's Griffin, 2000), 307–15; and Andrews, "Controversial Hastings Guide," 133–50.

49. Andrews, "Controversial Hastings Guide," 135–36. Andrews points out that Hastings was only theorizing about such a route. When Hastings returned to California in 1845, after publication of his guidebook, he went the "old route," not attempting any trail south of the Salt Lake. This, Andrews claims, "sufficiently demonstrates that he did not have the Salt Lake Desert Cutoff—what became known as the Hastings Cutoff—in mind when he wrote that passage."

50. Andrews, "Lansford Hastings," 32.

51. William Clayton, *Latter-Day Saints Emigrants' Guide* (St. Louis: Chambers and Knapp, 1848). There is a reprint edition with an introduction by Stanley Kimball (Tucson AZ: Patrice, 1997). A roadometer was a device that counted the revolutions of the wagon wheel. The number of revolutions times the circumference gives the distance the wagon traveled.

52. *Missouri Republican*, October 3, 1849. Perhaps because of the excess demand for the book, it was not advertised in the newspaper (which was also printed by Chambers and

Knapp, the printers of the guide), nor in the Mormon newspaper, the *Kanesville Frontier Guardian.*

53. See Unruh, *Plains Across*, 18, 72–73; and Stewart, *California Trail*, 225.

54. Joseph E. Ware, *The Emigrants' Guide to California* (St. Louis: J. Halsall, 1849). There is a reprint edition with an introduction by John Caughey (Princeton NJ: Princeton University Press, 1932).

55. Caughey in his introduction says, "[Ware's Guide] was not only the first adequate guide-book but for several years continued to be the best in existence," Caughey, introduction, *Emigrants' Guide,* xiii. Wheat also praises Ware's guidebook: "To Joseph E. Ware must go the distinction of being the first to place before the gold-seeker a really practical guide book for those going overland to California." Wheat, *TransMissssippi West*, 88.

56. There is little biographical information about Ware. There is evidence, however, that he did leave for California in 1850 but never got there, a fact recorded in this poignant reference in a trail journal: "But the most lamentable case was that of the abandonment by his companions, of Joseph E. Ware. . . . He was taken sick east of Fort Laramie, and his company, instead of affording him that protection which they were now more than ever bound to do, by the ties of common humanity, barbarously laid him by the roadside, without water, provisions, covering or medicines, to die," Alonzo Delano, *Life on the Plains and among the Diggings* (Auburn and Buffalo NY: Miller, Orton and Mulligan, 1854), 162–63. See also Caughey, introduction, Ware, *Emigrants' Guide*, xix.

57. Solomon Sublette was the younger brother of William Sublette, who was one of the major figures in the American fur trade in the 1820s and 1830s. Solomon was also active in the western fur trade in the 1830s with his brother. See Robert Utley, *A Life Wild and Perilous: Mountain Men and the Paths to the Pacific* (New York: Henry Holt, 1997), 84–99, 146. One of the most-used cutoffs on the California Trail was named the Sublette Cutoff.

58. The mistakes were miscalculating the waterless stretch along the Sublette Cutoff in what is now western Wyoming and stating that there would be water and good grass along the Humboldt River in what is now Nevada. See Caughey, introduction, Ware, *Emigrants' Guide*, xv.

59. Ware reproduces word for word the final paragraph from the "Viator" letter of the December 26, 1848, issue of the *California Herald* (see chap. 1). Ware probably thought it was enough to deter anyone from that route.

60. Ware, *Emigrants' Guide*, xxiii.

61. At a 1984 conference on the need for research in the history of the book at the American Antiquarian Association, James Gilreath complained, "American historians seldom make book distribution the sole focus of their research. It is usually subsumed as a minor facet of another subject such as printing or publishing, although recently this situation has begun to change," James Gilreath, "American Book Distribution," in *Needs and Opportunities in the History of the Book: America, 1639–1876,* ed. John Hench and David Hall (Worcester MA: American Antiquarian Society, 1987), 103–86.

62. See Madeleine Stern, "Dissemination of Popular Books in the Midwest and Far West during the Nineteenth Century," in *Getting the Books Out: Papers of the Chicago Conference*

*on the Book in 19th-Century America,* ed. Michael Hackenberg, (Washington DC: The Center for the Book, Library of Congress, 1987), 76–97.

63. See Sutton, *Western Book Trade,* chap.s 8, 17. Sutton argues that the relative physical isolation of the current Midwest until the 1850s insulated their book markets from the East and allowed Cincinnati to develop as a regional publication center. See also Stern, "Dissemination of Popular Books," 75–87.

64. The best description of these elaborate auctions is in Tebbel, *Between the Covers,* chap. 3.

65. Michael Hackenberg describes the early development of the subscription book business in the 1840s in the East. Madeleine Stern describes the distribution of books through traveling salesmen (colporteurs) in the Midwest and West entirely as a method of distributing books published in the East. See Michael Hackenberg, "The Subscription Publishing Network in Nineteenth-Century America," in *Getting the Books Out: Papers of the Chicago Conference on the Book in 19th-Century America,* ed. Michael Hackenberg, (Washington DC: Center for the Book, Library of Congress, 1987), and Stern, "Dissemination of Popular Books."

66. The best collections of book-trade catalogs for this period are at the American Antiquarian Society and the Newberry Library. A discussion of various kinds of catalogs relevant to the history of the book is in Thomas Tanselle, *Guide to the Study of U.S. Imprints* vol. 1 (Cambridge MA: Belknap Press, 1995): xxxiii–xxxix.

67. This sample included all of the catalogs in the American Antiquarian Society and the Newberry from 1846–55 that might have listed the guidebooks, including those of individual publishers and bookstores and the large compendiums put out by Appleton, which not only listed its own publications but over twelve thousand listings of what was available in the mainstream book trade.

68. Archives of the St. Louis Mercantile Library, University of Missouri, St. Louis. The 1850 catalog is reprinted in John Neal Hoover, *Cultural Cornerstone, 1846–1998* (St. Louis: St. Louis Mercantile Library, 1998).

### 3. To the Trailheads

1. The South Pass route was the most traveled to California in 1849 and 1850 and carried about one-third to one-half of the entire emigration. The best summary of the sketchy statistics regarding the 1849 and 1850 emigrations is John D. Unruh, *The Plains Across: The Overland Emigrants and the Trans-Mississippi West, 1840–60* (Urbana: University of Illinois Press, 1973), 118–23. Unwilling to trust the numbers, Rohrbough simply states "by far the largest number of overland 49ers went by way of the California Trail," Malcolm Rohrbough, *Days of Gold: The California Gold Rush and the American Nation* (Berkeley: University of California Press, 1997), 62n16. See also George Stewart, *The California Trail: An Epic with Many Heroes* (Lincoln: University of Nebraska Press, 1962), chap. 9; and John Caughey, *Gold Is the Cornerstone* (Berkeley: University of California Press, 1948), chap. 6.

2. Rohrbough, *Days of Gold,* 63.

3. Swain diary, May, 3, 1849, J. S. Holliday, *The World Rushed In* (New York: Simon and Schuster, 1981), 95. (All of the diary entries in this chap. are for 1849 unless otherwise noted.)

4. Parke diary, May 3, James Davis, *Dreams to Dust: A Diary of the California Gold Rush* (Lincoln: University of Nebraska Press, 1989), 9.

5. A good example is I. S. Drake, cartographer, *Map of the State of Missouri* (Philadelphia: Thomas Cowperthwait, 1850). The Cowperthwait Company was a major publisher of books and maps in Philadelphia. In New York, J. H. Colton published both a large map of the United States and an atlas with separate maps of each state. In 1848 Colton also published a map of the western part of the continent including British Canada and Mexico (see figure 7, p. 129).

6. There are many detailed descriptions of this part of the Oregon-California Trail, probably the best of which is Merrill Mattes, *The Great Platte River Road: The Covered Wagon Mainline via Fort Kearny to Fort Laramie* (Lincoln: The Nebraska Historical Society, 1969). For the goldrushers, the following guidebooks covered this part of the trail well: T. H. Jefferson, *Accompaniment to the Map of the Emigrant Road from Independence Mo. to San Francisco, California* (New York: privately printed, 1849); John Frémont, *The California Guide Book: Comprising Col. Frémont's Geographical Account of Upper California*; (New York: D. Appleton, 1849); Edwin Bryant, *What I Saw in California: Being the Journal of a Tour by the Emigrant Route and South Pass of the Rocky Mountains . . . in the Years 1846–47,* (New York: D. Appleton, 1848); and Joseph Ware, *The Emigrants' Guide to California* (St. Louis: J. Halsall, 1849).

7. The history of western Missouri and each of the trailhead towns is summarized in Perry McCandless, *A History of Missouri, Vol. 2, 1820–1860* (Columbia: University of Missouri Press, 1972); Lew Larkin, *Vanguard of Empire: Missouri's Century of Expansion* (St. Louis: State, 1961); Merrill Mattes, "The Jumping-off Places on the Overland Trail," in *The Frontier Re-examined,* ed. John McDermott (Urbana: University of Illinois Press, 1967), 28–39; Walker Wyman, "The Outfitting Posts," *Pacific Historical Review* 38, no. 1 (1949): 14–23; and Walker Wyman, "The Missouri River Towns in the Westward Movement," *University of Iowa Studies, Abstracts in History III* 10, no. 4 (1964): 33–47. More specific histories of each of the towns include, for Independence, Eugene Wells, "The Growth of Independence, Missouri, 1827–1850," *The Bulletin of the Missouri Historical Society* 16, no. 1 (1959): 33–46; for Westport, William Bernard, "Westport and the Santa Fe Trade," *Transactions of the Kansas State Historical Society* 9, no. 2 (1905–6): 552–78; for Westport Landing and Kansas City, Charles Deatherage, *Early History of Greater Kansas City, Vol. 1: 1492–1870* (Kansas City MO: Interstate, 1927); for St. Joseph, Sheridan Logan, *Old Saint Jo: Gateway to the West, 1799–1932* (St. Joseph MO: John Sublett Logan Foundation, 1979); and for Kanesville and Council Bluffs, Charles Martin and Dustin Devereux, "The Omaha-Council Bluffs Area and the Westward Trails," *Overland Journal* 7, no. 4 (1989): 2–12.

8. Frank Popplewell, "St. Joseph, Missouri, as a Center of the Cattle Trade," *Missouri Historical Review* 32, no. 4 (July 1938): 443–57; and Clifford Carpenter, "The Early Cattle Industry in Missouri," *Missouri Historical Review* 47, no. 3 (April 1953): 201–5.

9. McCandless, *Missouri History,* chap. 5; and Louis C. Hunter, *Steamboats on the Western Rivers* (Cambridge MA: Harvard University Press, 1949).

10. McCandless, *Missouri History,* vol. 2, chap. 5; and Wyman, "The Outfitting Posts," 16–18."

11. Bernard, "Westport," 557–59. See also McCandless, *Missouri History;* and Lewis Atherton, "Business Techniques in the Santa Fe Trade," *Missouri Historical Review* 34, no. 3 (1940): 335–41. An example of successful merchandizing is shown in William Nester, *From Mountain Man to Millionaire* (Columbia: University of Missouri Press, 1999).

12. Wyman, "Independence," 14–23; Logan, *Old Saint Jo,* chap. 7; and Chris Rutt, *History of Buchanan County and the City of St. Joseph* (Chicago: Biographical Publishing, 1904), chap. 4.

13. A standard work on early Mormon history and the Mormon Trail is Wallace Stegner, *The Gathering of Zion: The Story of the Mormon Trail* (New York: McGraw Hill, 1964). A recent review of Mormon historiography is Ronald Walker, *Mormon History* (Urbana: University of Illinois Press, 2001).

14. Martin, "Omaha–Council Bluffs," 2–12; and Merrill Mattes, "The Northern Route of the Non-Mormons: Rediscovery of Nebraska's Forgotten Historic Trail," *Overland Journal* 8, no. 2 (1990): 2–14.

15. The most comprehensive catalog of Missouri newspapers is in William Taft, *Missouri Newspapers: When and Where, 1808–1963* (Columbia: State Historical Society of Missouri, 1964). Neither Westport nor Kansas City appeared to have had an active newspaper in 1849. The earliest Westport newspaper listed in Taft is the *Border Star,* which published from 1855 to 1868.

16. Minnie Organ, "History of the County Press of Missouri," *Missouri Historical Review* 4, no. 3 (1910): 149–66. Organ describes the *Lexington Express* as the "most noted paper established in 1840."

17. For example, James Gordon Bennett's specialized *California Herald* printed two exchange stories from the *St. Louis Republican* on December 26, 1848, and one in the January 16, 1849, issue; his *New York Herald* printed articles from the *St. Louis Republican* March 20 and 29, 1849, and April 10 and 19. Bennett printed exchange articles from the *St. Louis Union* December 26, 1848, and April 2, 1849.

18. Harmon Mothershead, "River Town Rivalry for the Overland Trade," *Overland Journal* 7, no. 2 (1989): 14–23, 16–17.

19. Jane Hamill Sommer, "Outfitting for the West, 1849," *Missouri Historical Society Bulletin* 24, no. 1 (1968): 344–46.

20. Sommer, "Outfitting," 340.

21. John Garraty and Mark Carnes, eds, *American National Biography* (New York: Oxford University Press, 1999), 72–73.

22. In addition to the individual newspaper issues, see Unruh, *Plains Across,* 69; and Mothershead, "River Town Rivalry," 14–23. The entire letter is reproduced in Sommer, "Outfitting," 340–44.

23. Josiah Gregg, *Commerce of the Prairies* (New York: Henry Langley, 1844). The book had five New York editions and a London edition in 1844–45.

24. *St. Joseph Gazette,* February 16, 1849. See also Unruh, *Plains Across,* 69. Stockton was known as an officer who fought in California; Kearny was lauded in the press in 1847 for his heroic trip to California through the Southwest; Moses Harris and Miles Goodyear were

mountain men in the 1820s and guided early emigrants to Oregon; and Joseph Meek became known because he returned from Oregon in 1848 with news of the Whitman massacre. For exploits of the mountain men, see Robert Utley, *A Life Wild and Perilous: Mountain Men and the Paths to the Pacific* (New York: Alfred Knopf, 1948). There is a reprint edition (New York: Henry Holt, 1997).

25. *St. Joseph Gazette*, March 1, 1849.

26. *St. Joseph Gazette*, May 4, 1849. See also Unruh, *Plains Across*, 70.

27. Daniel Robinson to his brother, James, in Bloomington, Illinois, May 3, 1849: California file, box 9, Huntington Library, San Marino CA.

28. Bruff journal, May 5, 1849. The journal is reprinted in Georgia Willis Read and Ruth Gaines, *Gold Rush: The Journals, Drawings, and Other Papers of J. Goldsborough Bruff,* 2nd ed. (New York: Columbia University Press, 1949), 5.

29. *St. Joseph Gazette*, May 4, 1849.

30. The old Fort Kearney was on the Missouri River just north of the Iowa border. In 1848, it was moved to Grand Island on the Platte River, where the various trails from the trailhead towns met.

31. *A Review of the Commerce of St. Louis for the Year 1849* (St. Louis: *St. Louis Republican,* 1850), 2: "As early as January, a few cases [of cholera] were reported in this city, but no serious apprehension was felt by the community at large until about the first of May, when the malady began to assume an epidemic form, and from the 7th to the 28th of the month, there were nearly 400 deaths." The "Review of Commerce" was a magazine published each year by the *St. Louis Republican.*

32. *St. Louis Republican*, April 10, 1849.

33. *St. Louis Republican,* May 5, 9, 1849: Mothershead, "River Town Rivalry," 14–23, 22.

34. Read and Gaines, *Gold Rush*, 5. In a later edition of his journal that he prepared for publication, he embellished this brief statement with "A steamer arrived to-day, from New Orleans,—starting with 500 emigrants, 47 of whom died on the passage [of cholera]." Read and Gaines, *Gold Rush,* 568n23. As noted in chap. 2, there are many differences between Bruff's original journals and the book manuscript he prepared years later, ostensibly from the journals; most likely the later manuscript was elaborated with information he learned after his trip but which he did not know at the time. See Read and Gaines, *Gold Rush,* liii–lxxii, for a discussion of the various Bruff documents.

35. Alonzo Delano, *Life on the Plains and among the Diggings* (Auburn and Buffalo NY: Miller, Orton, and Mulligan, 1854), 15.

36. Wyman, "River Towns," 33–47; and Unruh, *Plains Across*, 70.

37. *St. Joseph Gazette*, April 26, 1849.

38. Unruh, *Plains Across*, 75.

39. *St. Louis Missouri Republican*, February 14, 1849; and *St. Louis Daily Union*, February 15, 1849. See also Unruh, *Plains Across*, 75

40. Read and Gaines, *Gold Rush*, xvi–xviii.

41. Letter to Col. Peter Force, January 30, 1849, Read and Gaines, *Gold Rush,* xviii–xxxiii.

42. Bruff journal, April 2, Read and Gaines, *Gold Rush*, 4. There was no indication in the Bruff documents that stated why he decided to purchase outfits in Pittsburgh, but it made some sense in that it was the closest place to Washington from which they could ship by boat.

43. Bruff journal, May 7, Read and Gaines, *Gold Rush*, 7. This was the old Fort Kearny on the Iowa border with Missouri (see note 30 of this chap.).

44. Bruff journal, May 9–June 1, and 1853 book manuscript entry for May 31, Read and Gaines, *Gold Rush*, 8–14. The later manuscript mentions the guide but the original journals do not.

45. David Potter, *Trail to California: The Overland Journal of Vincent Geiger and Wakeman Bryarly* (New Haven CT: Yale University Press, 1945), 9. The organization and the constitution of the company was published in the *Charlestown Spirit of Jefferson*, February 20, 1849. David Potter, writing in 1945, asserts in his introduction to the Geiger and Bryerly journals that this company was unusual because of their "collectivist organization" and the fact that they published their constitution. Since 1945, however, gold rush research has uncovered a large number of documents from gold rush companies, particularly those that went overland, that published their constitutions and had a similar idea to pool resources and equally share profits. The large number of company prospectuses published in book or pamphlet form is shown in the Kurutz list, appendix C. There were many more company prospectuses published, like that of the Charlestown Company, in local newspapers.

46. Potter, *Trail to California*, 27.

47. Potter, *Trail to California*, 28–30. Edwin Bryant recommended packing on mules rather than using wagons for companies that did not include families (Bryant, *What I Saw*, 4th ed., 466). The company's original plans may have been based on this advice. They may have changed their plans in St. Louis where the purchasing committee may then have obtained a copy of Ware, who recommended lightly loaded wagons for all travelers.

48. Unlike the Washington and Charlestown companies, there are no published journals of the East Tennessee Gold Mining Company's trip. Their journey was documented in reports sent back to the *Knoxville TN Register* by Robert Williams, who was appointed to record the company's progress for the newspaper; letters sent by Wilberforce Ramsey to his family; and the unpublished reminiscences of David A. Deaderick, another member of the company. Ramsey letters MSS, Knoxville TN, Hoskins Library, University of Tennessee; and Deaderick Memoir, Typescript, Knoxville TN, Hoskins Library, University of Tennessee. Walter Durham summarizes the company's trip in *Volunteer Forty-Niners: Tennesseans and the California Gold Rush* (Nashville TN: Vanderbilt University Press, 1997), chap. 7. See also Neal O'Steen, "The East Tennessee Company: UT Gold Rush Adventurers," *Tennessee Alumnus* 23, no. 9 (Winter and Spring 1984): 23–25, 16–18.

49. Durham, *Volunteer Forty-Niners*, 85.

50. Deaderick Memoir, 86.

51. Ramsey letters, Wilberforce Ramsey to his brother Crozier in Knoxville TN, dated May 30, 1849.

52. Durham, *Volunteer Forty-Niners*, 85.

53. Ramsey letters, Wilberforce Ramsey to his father in Knoxville TN, dated July 14, 1849.

54. J. G. Hannon, *The Boston-Newton Company Venture: From Massachusetts to California in 1849* (Lincoln: University of Nebraska Press, 1969), 20–21. Other overland Massachusetts-based companies include the Congress and California Mutual Protection Association, the Sagamore and Sacramento Company, the Granite State and California Mining and Trading Company (organized in New Hampshire, but left from Boston), the Mount Washington Mining Company, and the Ophir Company.

55. The company and their trip are described and documented in Hannon, *Boston-Newton.*

56. Bryant, *What I Saw*, 4th ed., 1849, 466.

57. Their luggage included tents, air mattresses, rubber and woolen blankets, rain clothes, a stove, a collapsible rubber boat, saddles, harnesses, various tools, canned goods, and medicine. All of these items were advertised heavily in Boston newspapers. There is no record of what supplies were shipped to San Francisco, but they arrived safely September 14, 1849. Hannon, *Boston-Newton*, 32–35.

58. Hannon, *Boston-Newton*, 44. Both quotes from the Gould diary, April 17, 1849.

59. Hannon, *Boston-Newton*, 49. Staple's diary entry for April 23 states, "We also bought two wagons for our trip across the plains having satisfied ourselves we could transport more goods with the same number of mules than we could if we packed mules."

60. Hannon, *Boston-Newton*, 55.

61. Hannon, *Boston-Newton*, 58. Sweetzer had to go up to St. Joseph to collect their luggage and ship it back down river to Independence.

62. Swain's gold rush trip and experiences are thoroughly described and documented in one of the classics of modern gold rush literature, Holliday, *Rushed In*. The original Swain letters and journal are at the Beineke library at Yale.

63. William Swain to his wife Sabrina in Youngstown, New York, April, 14, 1849, Holliday, *Rushed In*, 66.

64. William Swain from St. Louis to his brother George, April 25, 1849, Holliday, *Rushed In*, 73.

65. Cholera killed twenty-six people the week of April 23, and by May 1 the epidemic was raging. The St. Louis "Review of the Commerce of St. Louis For the Year 1849" reported that during the month of May there were four hundred deaths from cholera. The quote from Gould is in Hannon, *Boston-Newton*, 55.

66. The trip of the Wolverine Rangers is documented in the letters Pratt and others wrote back to the newspaper, as well as in the Swain diaries and letters. Many of the letters to the *Statesman* have been republished in J. Cumming, *The Gold Rush: Letters from the Wolverine Rangers to the* Marshall, Michigan, Statesman *1849–1851* (Mount Pleasant MI: Cumming Press, 1974).

67. Pratt letter to the *Statesman* of May 5, printed May 23, 1849. Gilpin seems to have made the rounds talking to emigrants leaving from Independence. George Winslow of the Boston-Newton Company wrote to his wife that he had "conversed with Mr. Gilpin, a gentleman who lives nearby. . . . who crossed to the Pacific five times," Hannon, *Boston-Newton*, 68.

68. Pratt letter to *Marshall Statesman* from Independence, April 9, 1849. Pratt was prob-

ably right to feel proud of his shopping. "California" reported April 5 from Independence in the *St. Louis Republican*, "The supply of oxen is fair, and the demand good, at from $50 to 65 the yoke, as in quality and conditions." Walker Wyman, *California Emigrant Letters* (New York: Bookman, 1952), 36. Caughey indicates an average price of oxen in Independence in April was $60–$70 per yoke. Caughey, *Cornerstone*, 99.

69. Swain diary, May 3 and 4, Holliday, *Rushed In*, 94–96.

70. William Swain to his wife Sabrina in Youngstown NY, May 10, Holliday, *Rushed In*, 104.

71. William Swain to his brother George in Youngstown NY, May 15, Holliday, *Rushed In*, 110.

72. Delano, *Life on the Plains*, 19–20. Delano's original notes are not extant, and the only record we have of his trip is his 1854 book. Like Bruff's 1853 manuscript, this may be an embellished account of his actual trip.

73. Thomas D. Clark, *The Overland Journal of Charles Glass Gray* (San Marino CA: Huntington Library, 1976), Introduction.

74. The Buckeye Rovers' trip is well documented in the journals of Armstrong and Banks. See H. Lee Scamehorn, Edwin P. Banks, and Jamie Lytle-Webb, *The Buckeye Rovers in the Gold Rush* (Athens: Ohio University Press, 1989).

75. Parke's journal has been transcribed and published in Charles Parke, in *Dreams to Dust: A Diary of the California Gold Rush*, ed. James Davis (Lincoln: University of Nebraska Press, 1989).

76. The East Tennessee Gold Mining Company is not included in the table because they eventually took the Santa Fe Trail to California.

## 4. On the Trail

1. This part of the trip is very well documented in the Oregon and California trail literature. See, for instance, Merrill Mattes, *The Great Platte River Road: The Covered Wagon Mainline via Fort Kearny to Fort Laramie* (Lincoln: The Nebraska Historical Society, 1969); and Merrill Mattes, *Platte River Road Narratives* (Urbana: University of Illinois Press, 1988).

2. The geography of the trail has been extensively studied. See, for example, George Stewart, *The California Trail: An Epic with Many Heroes* (Lincoln: University of Nebraska Press, 1962); Mattes, *Great Platte River Road*; John Unruh, *The Plains Across: The Overland Emigrants and the Trans-Mississippi West, 1840–60* (Urbana: University of Illinois Press, 1973); Irene Paden, *The Wake of the Prairie Schooner* (New York: Macmillan, 1943); Irene Paden, *Prairie Schooner Detours* (New York: Macmillan, 1949); and Richard Brock and others, *Emigrant Trails West: A Guide to the California Trail* (Reno NV: Trails West, 2000).

3. In addition to the journals, diaries, and letters of the gold rush companies described in the previous chap., I used the writings of other goldrushers to supplement these sources when necessary to amplify a point or show a unique use of trail information.

4. The map shows the relative distances from the various trailheads to Fort Kearny. The longest route was from Independence and Westport, which was taken by Gray's Newark Overland Company and Gould's and Staples's Boston-Newton Company. Goldrushers leav-

ing from St. Joseph, including Geiger and Bryarly's Charlestown Company, saved about one week by starting farther north. Trailheads farther north, at Savannah Landing and Old Fort Kearny had the shortest route west of the Missouri River. If, however, a company traveled north from St. Joseph by land on the east side of the river, as did Bruff's Washington City Company, they saved very little in terms of distance, and it cost them in terms of time.

5. Swain diary, May 29, J. S. Holliday, *The World Rushed In* (New York: Simon and Schuster, 1981), 129. (As in the previous chap., all diary dates refer to 1849 unless otherwise noted.)

6. Vincent Geiger journal, May 12, 1849, David Potter, *Trail to California: The Overland Journal of Vincent Geiger and Wakeman Bryarly* (New Haven: Yale University Press, 1945), 77. Taming and branding mules was a trial for most of the neophyte travelers, usually done before leaving the trailheads. The Boston-Newton Company sensibly hired "four Mexicans" to break the mules (Charles Gould diary, May, 9, 1849, Jessie Hannon, *The Boston-Newton Company Venture: From Massachusetts to California in 1849* [Lincoln: University of Nebraska Press, 1969], 64). J. Goldsborough Bruff's company hired a William Stinson as a guide, who was in charge of breaking their mules (Georgia Willis Read and Ruth Gaines, *Gold Rush: The Journals, Drawings, and Other Papers of J. Goldsborough Bruff* [New York: Columbia University Press, 1949], 571). Swain and the Wolverine Rangers purchased oxen, which were much easier to break and harness, although he still called it "a mean job." (Swain journal, May 12, Holliday, *Rushed In*, 105).

7. For axle repair and the difficulties of crossing even small streams, see Geiger diary, May 14 and 15, Potter, *Trail to California*, 86; and Bruff diary, June 7 and 13, Read and Gaines, *Gold Rush*, 16, 20.

8. Swain diary, May 24, Holliday, *Rushed In*, 124. The goldrushers particularly feared the Pawnees, who had earned a reputation for fierceness from their harassing of early fur traders and Oregon emigrants. See Robert Utley, *A Life Wild and Perilous: Mountain Men and the Paths to the Pacific* (New York: Henry Holt, 1997), 61, 182. James Pratt wrote back to his newspaper, the *Marshall MI Statesman*, May 28: "Stories have been circulated here and elsewhere that emigrants have been attacked, plundered and slaughtered by them [Pawnees]" (Holliday, *Rushed In*, 127). The stories were false.

9. Holliday, *Rushed In*, 115.

10. Swain diary, Holliday, *Rushed In*, 126, 128.

11. Geiger diary, May 19, Potter, *Trail to California*, 80.

12. Edward Washington McIlhany, *Recollections of a '49er: A Quaint and Thrilling Narrative of a Trip across the Plains, and Life in the California Gold Fields during the Stirring Days Following the Discovery of Gold in the Far West* (Kansas City MO: Hailman, 1908), 21.

13. Swain, for instance wrote his wife June 14 from Fort Kearny, "we are doing first-rate business in the line of living and enjoying ourselves. I was unwell then but have picked up my crumbs greatly since" (Holliday, *Rushed In*, 135).

14. *Missouri Republican*, June 15, 1849, and the *St. Joseph Gazette* on the same day. See Unruh, *Plains Across*, 123, for examples of go-back rumors.

15. Horace Ladd letter of June 7, published in the *Marshall MI Statesman* July 11, Holliday, *Rushed In*, 131.

16. Alonzo Delano, *Life on the Plains and among the Diggings* (Auburn and Buffalo NY: Miller, Orton and Mulligan, 1854), 110.

17. Gray diary, May 9, 1849, Thomas D. Clark, *The Overland Journal of Charles Glass Gray* (San Marino CA: Huntington Library, 1976), 9.

18. William Johnston, *Experiences of a Forty-Niner* (Pittsburgh, 1892), cited in Holliday, *Rushed In*, 131.

19. Swain diary, Holliday, *Rushed In*, 124.

20. Charles Tinker, "Journal: A Trip to California," Eugene H. Roseboom, ed. *Ohio State Archeological and Historical Quarterly* 61 (1952), 64–85.

21. James Evans diary, June 30, Holliday, *Rushed In*, 127.

22. Bruff journal, June 11, Read and Gaines, *Gold Rush*, 18.

23. Banks diary, May 23, H. Lee Scamehorn, Edwin P. Banks, and Jamie Lytle-Webb, *The Buckeye Rovers in the Gold Rush* (Athens: Ohio University Press, 1989), 9.

24. Delano diary, May 23, Delano, *Life on the Plains*, 50.

25. *Missouri Republican*, May 23, 1849, and reprinted by the *New York Tribune*, June 14. The letters from "Pawnee" are frequently quoted in the trail historiography; see Stewart, *California Trail*, 233; Unruh, *Plains Across*, 412; Read and Gaines, *Gold Rush*, 587; and Walker Wyman, *California Emigrant Letters* (New York: Bookman Associates, 1952), 50–54.

26. These estimates are from Stewart, *California Trail*, 232–33, citing "Pawnee." There have been other reasonably authoritative estimates, all in this order of magnitude: 15,000, Unruh, *Plains Across*, 120; 30,000, Mattes, *Platte River Road*, 23; and 29,000, Holliday, *Rushed In*, 143.

27. Letter published in the *Missouri Republican*, June 16, 1849; Wyman, *Letters*, 49–50.

28. Geiger journal, May 28, 1849, Potter, *Trail to California*, 87.

29. Bruff journal, June 17, Read and Gaines, *Gold Rush*, 22.

30. E. D. Perkins diary, June 14, 1849, Holliday, *Rushed In*, 135.

31. George Gibbs diary, May 29, 1849; Holliday, *Rushed In*, 137.

32. Read and Gaines, *Gold Rush*, 578.

33. The best description of this part of the trail is Mattes, *Platte River Road*.

34. Unruh, *Plains Across*, 128–32, has an excellent discussion of intercompany communications.

35. At Fort Kearny, he left his company June 22 to visit with the commander of the fort, Colonel Bonneville; two days later he had dinner with a New York company, and following that a New Orleans ox train. He traveled with the New York company for two days and helped them ford the Platte. He did not rejoin his company until he received a note telling him to hurry up. Read and Gaines, *Gold Rush*, 21–27.

36. Bruff journal, June 29, Read and Gaines, *Gold Rush*, 27, 592.

37. Bruff journal, June 29, Read and Gaines, *Gold Rush*, 27.

38. Banks journal, August 14, 1849, Scamehorn, Banks, and Lytle-Webb, *Buckeye Rovers*, 65.

39. Unruh, *Plains Across*, 132.

40. Delano, *Life on the Plains*, 70.

41. Delano, *Life on the Plains*, 86. The death toll of oxen and cattle was frequently mentioned as one of the most unpleasant sights on the trail. P. F. Castleman described this alkaline area where he saw "more than one hundred dead oxen and two or three horses" (P. F. Castleman diary, July 10, Typescript, Bancroft Library, University of California, Berkeley) cited in Holliday, *Rushed In*, 191.

42. Potter, *Trail to California*, 116.

43. Swain letter, June 29, 1849, and Pratt letter printed in the *Marshall MI Statesman*, September 12, 1849, Holliday, *Rushed In*, 164–65.

44. Bruff journal, July 1, Read and Gaines, *Gold Rush*, 27.

45. Holliday, *Rushed In*, 178.

46. Delano, *Life on the Plains*, 70.

47. Gray diary, June 11, Clark, *Overland Journal*, 34.

48. Delano, *Life on the Plains*, 76.

49. Bruff journal, July 10, Read and Gaines, *Gold Rush*, 35.

50. The American Fur Company built Fort William in 1834 at the confluence of the Platte and Laramie rivers. The government purchased it in 1849 and renamed it Fort Laramie; it became part of the chain of forts built to protect emigrants. See Unruh, *Plains Across*, chap. 7.

51. Delano, *Life on the Plains*, 76. See also Bruff's journal, July 11 and his 1854 manuscript for good descriptions (Read and Gaines, *Gold Rush*, 36, 597).

52. Gray diary, June 11, Clark, *Overland Journal*, 35.

53. Geiger diary, June 14, Potter, *Trail to California*, 106; Swain diary, July 5, Holliday, *Rushed In*, 170; and Bruff journal, July 11, Read and Gaines, *Gold Rush*, 36.

54. Isaac Foster diary, June 16, Typescript, cited in Holliday, *Rushed In*, 170; and James Davis, *Dreams to Dust: A Diary of the California Gold Rush* (Lincoln: University of Nebraska Press, 1989), 188.

55. Bruff's Washington Company also made these repairs on July 10; Bruff journal, July 10, Read and Gaines, *Gold Rush*, 36.

56. Armstrong journal, July 3, Scamehorn, Banks, and Lytle-Webb, *Buckeye Rovers*, 30.

57. Banks diary, July 3, Scamehorn, Banks, and Lytle-Webb, *Buckeye Rovers*, 31.

58. Parke diary, July 2, Davis, *Dreams to Dust*, 45.

59. Joseph Warren Wood wrote of the event July 1, (Wood Diary MS, Huntington Library, San Marino CA); two days east of South Pass Sheldon Young mentioned it July 5 as a robbery and murder (Sheldon Young Log, Typescript, Huntington Library); and Henry Mann wrote a long story about it in his log July 4, and then on July 10 wrote, "I heard today that the man who had his trial near the South Pass for murder has been aquitted" (Henry Mann diary, Typescript, Bancroft Library, University of California, Berkeley).

60. Swain diary, August 1, Holliday, *Rushed In*, 205; Delano diary, June 29, Delano, *Life on the Plains*, 116; and Banks diary, July 6, Scamehorn, Banks, and Lytle-Webb, *Buckeye Rovers*, 36.

61. The cutoffs opened in 1848 and 1849 were the Hudspeth Cutoff, the Salt Lake Cutoff, the Lassen Cutoff, and the Carson Pass.

62. John Frémont, *Geographical Memoir upon Upper California in Illustration of his*

*Map of Oregon and California* (Washington DC: U.S. Senate, Wendell and Van Benthuysen, printers, 1848). Other maps giving an overview of the West were Mitchell, 1846, Colton, 1848, and Disturnell, 1848. Most of the emigrants carried Frémont's maps, but many may have carried only his very well-known 1846 strip map, which covered the Oregon Trail and did not include the route to California from Fort Hall.

63. Joseph Ware, *The Emigrants' Guide to California* (St. Louis: J. Halsall, 1849), 25–26. The Sublette Cutoff was named for William Sublette, an early mountain man.

64. Hannon, *Boston-Newton*, 148; Davis, *Dreams to Dust*, 50.

65. Clark, *Overland Journal*, 51, 53.

66. Ware, *Emigrants' Guide*, 25.

67. Armstrong diary, July 8, Scamehorn, Banks, and Lytle-Webb, *Buckeye Rovers*, 37–38. Recruiting cattle, and people, was a common term on the trail meaning to rest and gain strength.

68. Parke diary, July 8, Davis, *Dreams to Dust*, 50.

69. Delano journal, July 1; Delano, *Life on the Plains,* 121–23.

70. Davis, *Dreams to Dust*, 203.

71. Bruff journal, August 4, 1849, Read and Gaines, *Gold Rush*, 68. James Hutchings, later famous for his "Miners Ten Commandments" lettersheet and the *Hutchings California Magazine*, also got to the forks late (August 15) and noted the signboard: "A board fastened to a stick told us that this and that company had taken such a trail and recommended to their friend to follow them." James Mason Hutchings, *James Hutchings Diary* (Berkley: Bancroft Library, MSS 69/80).

72. Unruh, *Plains Across*, 305. Unruh's chap. 9 ("The Mormon 'Halfway House'") is a good discussion of the relationships between the Mormons and the emigrants.

73. Gray diary, July 2–14, Clark, *Overland Journal,* 51–64; and Staples journal, July 28–August 8, Hannon, *Boston-Newton*, 148–57.

74. William Clayton, *Latter-Day Saints Emigrants' Guide* (St. Louis: Chambers and Knapp, 1848), 19.

75. Bigler diary, August 27, 1848, cited in Irene Paden, "The Ira J. Willis Guide to the Gold Mines," *California Historical Society Quarterly* 32 (1953): 193–207, 197. The Thompson party was returning from the first big gold strike in California, which they named "Mormon Bar." The party included Henry Bigler, along with Azariah Smith, and the two Willis brothers, Ira and Sidney, each of whom played a role in the gold rush. They were each at Marshall's mill when gold was discovered in California.

76. In some good historical detective work by J. Roderic Korns, Irene Paden, and Will Bagley, this story was pieced together from the various diaries and the Willis guide. See: Korns, *West from Fort Bridger*, revised ed. by Will Bagley (Logan: Utah State University Press, 1994), 283–85; L. A. Flemming and A. R. Standing, "The Road to Fortune: The Salt Lake Cutoff," *Utah Historical Quarterly* 33, no. 3 (1965): 248–71; and Paden, "Willis Guide," 193–207. See also Unruh, *Plains Across*, 318–19.

77. Paden, "Willis Guide," 193–207, 200.

78. For example, Staples diary, August 19, Hannon, *Boston-Newton*, 167; Bruff journal,

August 29, Read and Gaines, *Gold Rush*, 630; and Castleman diary, August 15, Unruh, *Plains Across*, 498. In two cases I have seen, goldrushers who did not apparently purchase the guidebook copied it in back of their dairies: Hutchings, *Hutchings Diary* and William H. Bickford, *William H. Bickford Diary*, (Berkeley: Bancroft Library, MSS 78/83).

79. Staples diary, July 31, Hannon, *Boston-Newton*, 151. The "Mormon Express" may have been carrying mail from Salt Lake City back to Kanesville.

80. Staples journal, August 8, 1849, Hannon, *Boston-Newton*, 159.

81. Bigler diary, April 9, 1848, Stewart, *California Trail*, 198; and Paden, "Willis Guide," 193–207.

82. A brief but good discussion of the cutoff is Stewart, *California Trail*, 250–52.

83. Davis, *Dreams to Dust*, 56.

84. Niles Searls, *The Diary of a Pioneer* (San Francisco: Pernau-Walsh Printing, 1940). Citation from Holliday, *Rushed In*, 215.

85. E. D. Perkins diary, August 9, Thomas D. Clark, *Gold Rush Diary, Being the Journal of Elisha Douglass Perkins on the Overland Trail in the Spring and Summer of 1849* (Lexington: University of Kentucky Press, 1967). Citation in Holliday, *Rushed In*, 215. According to calculations made by Bruff, combined with mileage from the Ira J. Willis guide for the stretch south of the City of Rocks, the distance was about 230 miles.

86. Read and Gaines, *Gold Rush*, 94. The reason that the two mileages were similar when the cutoff really did eliminate a long northern loop to Fort Hall is that Meyers and Hudspeth had to pick their way carefully through several north-south mountain ranges in what is now southern Idaho, thus adding distance. George Stewart declares that Meyers and Hudspeth were bad at geography and engaged in wishful thinking (Stewart, *California Trail*, 252).

87. The Humboldt River is fed by a large number of springs in what is now northeastern Nevada and empties into the desert at what is called the Humboldt Sink. It has no outlet to the ocean, a fact that Frémont discovered in his travels of 1845–46. The Carson River, coming down from the east slopes of the Sierras empties into its own sink, about thirty miles south of the Humboldt Sink.

88. Bryant, *What I Saw*, 198.

89. Ware, *Emigrants' Guide*, 32.

90. Gould diary, September 9 and 10, Hannon, *Boston-Newton*, 182.

91. Ralph Bieber, "Diary of a Journey from Missouri to California in 1849 [diary of Bennett C. Clark]," *Missouri Historical Review* 23 (1928): 31; John Caughey, *Gold Is the Cornerstone* (Berkeley: University of California Press, 1948), 116.

92. Bryant, *What I Saw*, 217.

93. Gray of the Newark Overland Company most likely met this Mormon wagon train August 17 (Clark, *Overland Journal*, 82); The Boston-Newton Company definitely met them September 2, and "obtained some information from them respecting our road" (Hannon, *Boston-Newton*, 180); the Buckeye Rovers met them August 25 (Scamehorn, Banks, and Lytle-Webb, *Buckeye Rovers*, 71). Near the back of the pack, Swain's Wolverine Rangers and Bruff's Washington Company, traveling near to each other, met these Mormons September 8 (Swain), and September 9 (Bruff) near the headwaters of the Humboldt (Holliday, *Rushed In*, 235; and Read and Gaines, *Gold Rush*, 132).

94. The Great Meadow was about the location of the current town of Lovelock, Nevada, where the river spread out before flowing to its destination at the sink. Gould of the Boston-Newton Company found it "a beautiful camping ground of the most luxuriant grass surrounded by sand bluffs" (Hannon, *Boston-Newton*, 182).

95. Bryarly diary, August 9, Potter, *Trail to California*, 184.

96. The hardships of both the desert and the mountain crossing have been well described in many trail histories. See, for example, Stewart, *California Trail*, 264–70. Bryarly's journal for August 11–30 is a good description of the Charlestown Company's trip across the desert and over the Donner Pass, Potter, *Trail to California*, 188–211. Gould journal, September 16–27, describes the journey over the Carson Pass, Hannon, *Boston-Newton*, 186–92.

97. "Seeing the Elephant" was a common expression among gold rush travelers and miners that meant encountering great hardships. There has been much recent research on the Lassen trail, most of it not yet published. In the last few months of 2005 a lively discussion concerning Peter Lassen and the Lassen trail occurred on the Overland Trails listserv. I have benefited greatly from participating in this discussion and, in particular, from the contributions of Will Bagley, Wendell Huffman, Don Buck, Tom Hunt, Art Porter, and Stafford Hazelett.

98. Delano, *Life on the Plains*, 173–74. A week earlier, when Bryarly and Geiger passed that stretch of the river, they reported no such rumors, Potter, *Trail to California*, 176–78.

99. Delano, *Life on the Plains*, 174.

100. Stewart indicates Myers and Hudspeth probably left on the cutoff August 20. Stewart credits McGee for being the most influential in leading the initial crowds over the cutoff, although to later emigrants, the example of Myers and Hudspeth was probably the most important precedent. See Stewart, *California Trail*, 269–73; and Unruh, *Plains Across*, 353–55.

101. Delano, *Life on the Plains*, 178. This is a strange story since it was certainly not based on observation. One problem with Delano's account is that it was written for a book (presumably from his trail notes), which was published in 1854, and the account may have been embellished. By the time of his writing he knew much more about the Lassen trail than he did when he was there. Whether embellished or not, Delano gives a good and probably accurate feeling for the rumors and conversations that must have been swirling around wagon trains at the cutoff during the week around August 10.

102. Gray diary, August 18–21, Clark, *Overland Journal*, 82–84.

103. Banks diary, August 25, Scamehorn, Banks, and Lytle-Webb, *Buckeye Rovers*, 71–72.

104. Swain diary, September 14, Holliday, *Rushed In*, 239. The misspelling of Lassen's name as "Lawson," or "Lassin," as well as other variants, was common in the trail diaries during these weeks. The misspellings are an indication that most of the information was communicated orally.

105. Bruff journal, September 6, Read and Gaines, *Gold Rush*, 127.

106. Perkins diary, September 3, Thomas Clark, *Gold Rush Diary, Being the Journal of Elisha Douglass Perkins on the Overland Trail in the Spring and Summer of 1849* (Lexington KY: University of Kentucky Press, 1967), 116–17.

107. Banks diary, August 25, Scamehorn, Banks, and Lytle-Webb, *Buckeye Rovers*, 72.

245

108. Stewart, *California Trail*, 274.

109. Bruff journal, September 19, 1849, Read and Gaines, *Gold Rush*, 142.

110. Swain diary, September 17, Holliday, *Rushed In*, 240.

111. Swain diary, September 22, Holliday, *Rushed In*, 254–55.

112. This was Nobles Pass, opened in 1852 as a result of explorations by William Nobles, which connected the Lassen route at Black Rock with the new Shasta City; this is the current Highway 36 on the California side. See Stewart, *California Trail*, 305–6, and his map on page 300; also Unruh, *Plains Across*, 356. The "middle passage" has been a focus of the discussion of the Overland Trails Web site and research is ongoing. It is likely that McGee and Myers thought there was a shorter middle pasage and perhaps Myers and even Lassen had been looking—unsuccessfully—for such a pass from 1846 to 1847. In addition to Nobels Pass, a pass near the southern end of the Lassen trail is named for Jim Beckwourth; it was mentioned in the *Marysville Herald* of March 8, 1851. I am indebted to Don Buck, Tom Hunt, and Wendell Huffman for this information.

113. Gray diary, August 18, Clark, *Overland Journal*, 82.

114. The travelers would have had to guess the distance over the Donner Pass because the fork of the Lassen Cutoff was not specified on any map or guidebook of 1849; no reading of Ware, Bryant, T. H. Jefferson, or Frémont 1846, however, could put the distance much more than 200 miles. The Willis guide shows about 230 miles via the Carson route.

115. The story of the Oregon migrations and the Applegate Trail is summarized in Bernard DeVoto, *The Year of Decision, 1846* (New York: St. Martin's Griffin, 2000), 371–80. See also Unruh, *Plains Across*, 348–50.

116. *Oregon Spectator*, April 6, 1848.

117. There are two primary organizations that organize trips along the various emigrant trails, work to mark out the routes, and publish books and maps concerning the trails. They are Trails West, (http://www.emigranttrailswest.org/) and The Oregon California Trails Association (octa): http://www.ukans.edu/kansas/seneca/oregon/mainpage.html. For a detailed guide to the Applegate and Lassen trails, see Devere and Helen Helfrich and Thomas Hunt, *Emigrant Trails West: A Guide to Trail Markers Placed by Trails West, Inc.: Applegate, Lassen, and Nobles Emigrant Trails* (Reno: Trails West, 1984).

118. Delano, *Life on the Plains*, 178.

119. Oliver Goldsmith, *Overland in Forty-Nine: The Recollections of a Wolverine Ranger* (Detroit: published by the author, 1896).

120. Bruff journal, September 20, Read and Gaines, *Gold Rush*, 148.

121. Bruff journal, September 21, Read and Gaines, *Gold Rush*, 151.

122. Swain diary, September 23, Holliday, *Rushed In*, 256.

123. Swain diary, September 28, Holliday, *Rushed In*, 258.

124. Gray diary, October 1, Clark, *Overland Journal*, 114.

125. Joseph Middleton diary, October, 26, citation from Holliday, *Rushed In*, 282.

126. In late August, the military governor of California, Gen. Persifor Smith, authorized $100,000 for relief funds for the emigration, which was augmented by private donations of at least $12,000. Relief expeditions were sent to all three routes (Donner Pass, Carson Pass, and

Lassen's); the one to Lassen's was led by John H. Peoples, to whom Swain talked on October 12, followed by another led by Maj. D. H. Rucker. See Unruh, *Plains Across*, 368–50; and Stewart, *California Trail*, 282–85.

127. In August, 1849, General Smith sent Capt. William Warner to open "a sure and easy communication by land with the Atlantic States"; this must have been planned before Smith knew about the plight of the emigrants and authorized a relief party to roughly the same area. Warner's party was attacked by Indians September 26 north of Fandango Pass, and he was killed. Lieutenant Thompson, Warner's second in command, must have been traveling back to Sacramento after the attack when he posted the waybill found by Bruff. Read and Gaines, *Gold Rush*, 650.

128. Bruff journal, October 22, Read and Gaines, *Gold Rush*, 207–8.

129. Bruff journal, October 27, Read and Gaines, *Gold Rush*, 214–15.

130. Swain diary, October 13, Holliday, *Rushed In*, 276.

131. Swain letter to Sabrina, March 18, 1850, Holliday, *Rushed In*, 286. The last entry in Swain's diary was October 30, 1849. He described the rest of his journey to Lassen's ranch in letters to Sabrina and George the following spring.

132. These are the same people that we have met on various parts of the gold rush trail of 1849. It is not surprising that their names should show up since they were very much in demand by the goldrushers. A good narrative of Chiles's 1843 trip is in Stewart, *California Trail*, 36–47.

133. Lassen is an interesting character in California history, hated by many goldrushers but still considered a major figure in the state with many places named after him, including a mountain, a national park, and a national forest. The most recent article concerning Lassen is Andy Hammond, "Peter Lassen and His Trail," *Overland Journal* 4, no. 1 (Winter 1986): 33–41. There is no recent book-length biography of Lassen, and probably the best short biography is Ruby Johnson Swartzlow, "Peter Lassen: Norther California's Trail Blazer," *California Historical Society Quarterly* 18, no. 4 (1939): 291–314. Swartzlow revised and updated her article in *Lassen: His Life and Legacy* (Mineral CA: Loomis Museum Association, 1964). See also Geroge Kirov, *Peter Lassen: Highlights of His Life and Achievements* (Sacramento: California State Printing Office, 1940). I am indebted to Art Porter and Will Bagley for pointing out several of these citations.

134. The story of Frémont's excursion to the north, his return, and subsequent involvement in the Bear Flag revolt and the Mexican War in California has become lore in California history. See Neal Harlow, *California Conquered: The Annexation of a Mexican Province: 1846–1850* (Berkeley: University of California Press, 1982), chaps. 7, 8. A very anti-Frémont version of the story is in DeVoto, *Year of Decision*, 197–201.

135. Unruh writes that Lassen had no personal experience of the route: Unruh, *Plains Across*, 353. Stewart, on the other hand, writes, "Lassen had been one of the courier's escorts" but gives no evidence of this, Stewart, *California Trail*, 197. I would side with Unruh on this question because Frémont does not mention Lassen in his *Geographical Memoir* entry of May 25, when he returned from Klamath, although he had mentioned Lassen earlier in the *Memoirs*, when he visited Lassen's ranch, Frémont, *Geographical Memoir*, 26–27 (entries of April 9 and May 25).

136. This story is known primarily through Burnett's reminiscences, published in 1880. Peter Burnett, *Recollections and Opinions of an Old Pioneer* (New York: D. Appleton, 1880), 252–75. Burnett hired a guide, Thomas McKay, who claimed to have traveled the trail to California with pack trains, Burnett, *Recollections,* 255.

137. Burnett, *Recollections,* 265.

138. "We had from six to eight stout men to open the road, while the others were left to drive the teams," Burnett, *Recollections,* 266.

139. Stewart writes, without citation, that Lassen's "report" was "sent east, was printed in newspapers, and exercised a dangerous influence," Stewart, *California Trail,* 215. Unruh, citing Stewart, writes that the report "was rushed eastward to be printed in newspapers," Unruh, *Plains Across,* 353. This report was printed in the *Star and Californian* of November 18, 1848; in the *Oregon Spectator* of December 28, 1848; and in the *New York Herald* of February 12, 1849. I am indebted to Don Buck and Tom Hunt for pointing out the publication of Lassen's "report" in the *Star and Californian* and *Oregon Spectator.*

140. Unruh, *Plains Across,* 353, 504n37.

141. The letter is dated February 13, 1849, from Jackson County, Missouri. It is reprinted in an early edition of Read and Gaines's publication of Bruff's writing: Georgia Willis Read, and Ruth Gaines, *Gold Rush: The Journals, Drawings, and Other Papers of J. Goldsborough Bruff.* (New York: Columbia University Press, 1944), v. 2, 1201. This letter is not mentioned by any other gold rush diary that I have seen.

142. Israel Hale diary, 80 MSS, Titus Hale papers, Society of California Pioneers, San Francisco CA. Most of the diary was published in Israel Hale, "Diary of a Trip to California in 1849," *Quarterly of the Society of California Pioneers* 2, no. 2 (1925): 61–20. The entry for August 20 is on pages 113–14 of the article. There is a mistake in the transcription of the Hale diary in the article that affects the interpretation of Hale's remark about "Childs" discovering the route. The manuscript reads "a Mr. Childs" instead of "Mr. Childs," indicating a less definite knowledge about the information. Hale also copied parts of both the Willis guide and the Applegate waybill (including the advice about sending parties in advance to dig out wells at Rabbit Hole Springs) at the back of his diary. The guides are in the manuscript but not in the printed version of the diary.

### 5. Information and Communications in California

1. Travelers who came over the Donner Pass would first reach habitation in California at Johnson's ranch; if they came over the Carson Pass, they headed for Coloma, and if they came over the Lassen Cutoff, they arrived first at Lassen's ranch.

2. Richard R. John, *Spreading the News: The American Postal System from Franklin to Morse* (Cambridge MA: Harvard University Press, 1995), 148.

3. David Potter, *Trail to California: The Overland Journal of Vincent Geiger and Wakeman Bryarly* (New Haven CT: Yale University Press, 1945), 62–69.

4. Charles Parke, *Dreams to Dust: A Diary of the California Gold Rush,* ed. James Davis (Lincoln: University of Nebraska Press, 1989), 86–88, 99–103.

5. Jessie Hannon, *The Boston-Newton Company Venture: From Massachusetts to California*

*in 1849* (Lincoln: University of Nebraska Press, 1969), 194. Different goldrushers referred to Sutter's Fort and Sacramento City, which in the fall of 1849 were distinct. Sutter's Fort was on high ground away from the American River, while Sacramento City was a tent city primarily of stores and boarding houses along the levies of the river.

6. Hannon, *Boston-Newton*, 197, 203–7, 214–15.

7. H. Lee Scamehorn, Edwin P. Banks, and Jamie Lytle-Webb, *The Buckeye Rovers in the Gold Rush* (Athens: Ohio University Press, 1989), introduction, and chap. 5.

8. Alonzo Delano, *Life on the Plains and among the Diggings* (Auburn and Buffalo NY: Miller, Orton and Mulligan, 1854), 1243–48.

9. Thomas D. Clark, *The Overland Journal of Charles Glass Gray* (San Marino CA: Huntington Library, 1976), 121–27.

10. Swain letter to his brother George, January 6, 1850, J. S. Holliday, *The World Rushed In* (New York: Simon and Schuster, 1981), 312.

11. Horace Ladd letter to his wife, November 20, 1849, printed in the *Marshall MI Statesman*, January 23, 1850; See John Cumming, *The Gold Rush: Letters from the Wolverine Rangers to the* Marshall, Michigan, Statesman *1849–1851* (Mount Pleasant MI: Cumming, 1974), 68.

12. Georgia Willis Read and Ruth Gaines, *Gold Rush: The Journals, Drawings, and Other Papers of J. Goldsborough Bruff*, 2nd ed. (New York: Columbia University Press, 1949), l–lii. Neither Bruff's journal nor Read and Gaines's research adequately explain the actions of the rest of the Washington Company's members, or Bruff himself at his camp. It was a common practice, particularly in the desert crossings, for a company to separate with one or more remaining with wagons and animals and others forging ahead for water and returning to rescue those left behind. Why did at least some members of the company not come back for Bruff—he was only about thirty-five miles from Lassen's ranch? Also, Bruff passed up many opportunities to leave the camp in November with various groups that visited him before his health broke but after it must have been obvious that his company had deserted him. For the story of Bruff's camp, see Bruff journal, November 6, 1848–March 16, 1849, Read and Gaines, *Gold Rush*, 233–53.

13. Delano, *Life on the Plains*, 233.

14. Letter published in Honolulu newspaper the *Friend*, which Damon edited. Reprinted in Carl Wheat, *The Maps of the California Gold Region, 1848–1857* (San Francisco: Grabhorn, 1942), ix.

15. John Frémont, *Geographical Memoir upon Upper California in Illustration of his Map of Oregon and California* (Washington DC: U.S. Senate; Wendell and Van Benthuysen, printers, 1848). The map along with Frémont's commentary and Emory's description of the southern trails were also published commercially in 1849 by D. Appleton in New York as a guidebook (see chap. 2).

16. Wheat, *Maps of the Gold Region*, x.

17. Wheat, *Maps of the Gold Region*, x.

18. Edward Buffum, one of the New York Volunteers, who wrote of his experiences in the gold mines in a popular book published in 1850, described his first trip into the northern mining region as the idea of starting into the mountains on foot, without a guide . . . [where]

there was no road": "[W]e knew not whither we were going, only that we were in the right direction." Edward Gould Buffum, *Six Months in the Gold Mines* (Philadelphia: Lea and Blanchard, 1850), 41.

19. In mid-1849 there were probably four printing presses in California: three in San Francisco, two of which were used to print newspapers, and the third used to print the first book published in California. There was another press in Sacramento used to print the first issues of the *Sacramento Placer Times*. See Edward C. Kemble, *A History of California Newspapers* (New York: Plandome Press, 1927), 88–100, 133–40. There are no known maps printed in California in 1849.

20. Neal Harlow, *California Conquered: The Annexation of Mexican Province: 1846–1850* (Berkeley: University of California Press, 1982), 323–31.

21. Wheat, *Maps of the Gold Region*, xxviii.

22. This early printing press was until 1846 used for letterheads, circulars, official documents such as notices of regulations and proclamations and small books. Zamorano has become a well-known figure in California history in large part because of his role as California's first printer. See G. L. Harding, *Don Augustin Zamorano: Statesman, Soldier, Craftsman, and California's First Printer* (Los Angeles: The Zamorano Club, 1934).

23. The first and probably still the best history of early newspapers in California is by Edward Kemble in a supplement to the *Sacramento Union*, December 25, 1858. Kemble purchased the *Californian* and the old Zamorano printing press in 1848 and remained a major figure in California newspapers for most of his life (he died in 1886). His history has been republished several times, the most recent being Edward C. Kemble, *A History of California Newspapers, 1846–1858* (Los Gatos CA: Talisman, 1962).

24. Kemble, *History of California Newspapers*, 90. (Subsequent references refer to the 1962 reprint.)

25. Letter signed "E. S.," printed in the *New York Tribune,* November 21, 1849.

26. Kemble, *History of California Newspapers*, 90. King was a Georgia congressman, and was sent to California by President Taylor to report on the gold rush and to represent the U.S. government at the constitutional convention in September 1849 (although he was too ill to attend). His report to Congress was influential and republished in 1850 (Thomas Butler King, *California: The Wonder of the Age; A Book for Every One Going to or Having an Interest in That Golden Region* [New York: W. Gowans, 1850]), but his proslavery views made him unpopular in California. See Harlow, *California Conquered*, 328–29.

27. *Sacramento Placer Times*, May 19, 1849. See Kemble, *History of California Newspapers*, 137–42, for a description of the founding and first months of the newspaper.

28. Kemble, *History of California Newspapers*, 143–45. The *Transcript* became a Democratic spokesman and the *Settlers' and Miners' Tribune* was established in part to give voice to the squatter community in Sacramento after the squatter riots in August 1850.

29. In early 1849, eastern newspapers advertised lectures on gold mining using a very different credibility marker, that of "professor"; see chap. 1.

30. Swain letter to his wife, Sabrina, from the South Fork of the Feather River, February 17, 1850, Holliday, *Rushed In*, 330. The *California Tribune* was a special edition of Horace

Greeley's *New York Tribune* sent by steamer every month to California. It was a kind of inverse of Bennett's *California Herald* in that it emphasized eastern news for Californian readers, whereas the *Herald* specials emphasized California news for eastern readers (see chap. 1).

31. See Kemble, *History of California Newspapers*, 168–71, 175–76. A much more detailed description of newspapers in the northern mines is Chester B. Kennedy, "Newspapers of the California Northern Mines, 1850–1860: A Record of Life, Letters and Culture" (PhD diss., Stanford University, 1950).

32. Franklin Langworthy, *Scenery of the Plains, Mountains and Mines*. (Princeton: Princeton University Press, 1932), 119, cited in Gary Kurutz, "You Have Mail: Reading and Writing during the Golden Era," *The Book Club of California Quarterly News-Letter* 61, no. 3 (Summer 1999): 5.

33. Bayard Taylor, *El Dorado: Adventures in the Path of Empire* (New York: George Putnam, 1850), 27, cited in Kurutz, "Mail," 9. Bayard Taylor was the reporter from the *New York Tribune* who Horace Greeley sent to California to write about the gold rush (see chap. 1).

34. Kurutz, "Mail," 8, gives examples of sick miners finding a "curative effect" in reading books.

35. There are many descriptions of the gambling houses both in San Francisco and in the mining camps; for a summary see Malcolm Rohrbough, *Days of Gold: The California Gold Rush and the American Nation* (Berkeley: University of California Press, 1997), 146–48.

36. Delano, *Life on the Plains*, 289.

37. F. P. Wierzbicki, *California as It is and as It May Be* (San Francisco: Bartlett, printer, 1849).

38. Wierzbicki, *California*, (1849; repr. with an introduction by George Lyman, New York: Burt Franklin, 1970), 40–41.

39. Lyman, introduction, Wierzbicki, *California*, xxix.

40. Wierzbicki, *California*, preface to the first edition, September 30, 1849.

41. Wierzbicki, *California*, 32–34.

42. Lyman, introduction, Wierzbicki, *California*, xxix–xxx. The sales figures imply that about four to five thousand copies were sold; the number of people who read the book must have been several times those numbers.

43. Douglas C. McMurtrie, *A Check List of California Non-Documentary Imprints, 1833–1855* (San Francisco: Work Projects Administration, 1942). The Works Projects Administration in 1938 organized an extensive survey of books by place of printing and date, made as part of the "American Imprints Inventory." This included an exhaustive search for California imprints under the direction of Douglas McMurtrie, a historian of California printing. Wierzbicki was the only book on the list for 1849.

44. Robert Ernest Cowan, *Booksellers of Early San Francisco* (Los Angeles: Ward Ritchie Press, 1953), 3.

45. Cowan, *Booksellers*, 3–4; for the history of bookselling in Sacramento, see C. Wenzel, "The Booksellers of Sacramento in the early 1850s," *Quarterly News Letter of the Book Club of California* 23, no. 4 (Fall 1958): 79–84.

46. D. W. Bryant, "Charles P. Kimball: San Francisco's 'Noisy Carrier,'" *California Historical Society Quarterly* 28, no. 4 (December 1939): 4.

47. A day-by-day description of Kimball's life as a peddler and letter carrier along the Sacramento River and in the northern mines is given in his journal: C. P. Kimball, *Diary of Charles P. Kimball,* Charles P. Kimball Papers MS, Society of California Pioneers, San Francisco.

48. *San Francisco Mercantile Library Catalog* (San Francisco: 1854). The Mercantile Library issued its first catalog in 1854 with three thousand entries.

49. Letter printed in the *St. Joseph Adventure,* August 17, 1849. See Walker Wyman, *California Emigrant Letters* (New York: Bookman, 1952), 144.

50. Buffum, *Six Months,* 63.

51. Walter Colton, *Three Years in California* (New York: A. S. Barnes, 1850), 202.

52. A classic study of rumor defines the difference between news and rumor as news having some form of secondary verification: Gordon Alport and L. Postman, *The Psychology of Rumor* (New York: Henry Holt, 1947). In a more recent sociological study of rumor, Jean-Noel Kapferer argues that this definition creates a problem because of the difficulty of defining verification: Jean Noel Kapferer, *Rumors: Uses, Interpretations, and Images* (New Brunswick NJ: Transaction, 1990).

53. Parke, *Dreams to Dust,* 98. The "lake of gold" was an oft-told myth in the mines, a variant of the "mother lode" stories. Miners were frequently searching for the original source of the gold that they found in the river beds, and they reasoned it had leached down from some higher source in the mountains. Neither the fabled lake of gold nor a mother lode was ever found.

54. Bruff journal, June 29, 1850, Read and Gaines, *Gold Rush,* 362.

55. Bruff journal, June 29, 1850, Read and Gaines, *Gold Rush,* 366.

56. Wierzbicki, *California,* 41.

57. Louise Clappe, *The Shirley Letters from the California Mines, 1851–1952,* ed. Marlene Smith-Baranzini (Berkeley CA: Heyday Books, 1998), 108–9. Clappe was writing to her sister from Rich's Bar under the pen name of Dame Shirley. Her letters, probably written for publication, were published in 1854 in San Francisco's first literary magazine, *The Pioneer.*

58. The use of the lottery metaphor was very common and easily understood. There were many instances of miners digging within yards of each another with one striking it rich and the other getting nothing. A good description of miners' attitudes with respect to the luck of gold mining is Holliday, *Rushed In,* chap. 11.

59. Luther Melancthon Schaeffer, *Sketches of Travels in South America, Mexico and California* (New York: James Egbert, 1860), 188, cited in Kurutz, "Mail," 5.

60. Holliday, *Rushed In,* 330.

61. Holliday, *Rushed In,* 334. The twenty-nine letters sent to Swain as well as his journal and the letters that he wrote home are in the Coe Collection at the Beineke Library at Yale.

62. D. Robinson to Sister from Sacramento City, October 3, 1849, California File, Huntington Library, San Marino CA.

63. A. Hyde to Parents, from Southern Mines, California File, Huntington Library, San Marino CA.

64. J. F. Stacey to Clarinda (his wife), from Los Angeles, October 27, 1850, California File, Huntington Library, San Marino CA.

65. *Sacramento Placer Times*, September 1, 1849.

66. John, *Spreading the News*, chap. 2. For the early history of the postal service to California see also Le Roy Hafen, *The Overland Mail* (Glendale CA: Arthur H. Clark, 1926), 37–49.

67. Voorhies's instructions are reproduced in E. Wiltsee. *The Pioneer Miner and the Pack Mule Express* (San Francisco: California Historical Society, 1931), 19–21. See also Harlow, *California Conquered*, 321–22.

68. Harlow, *California Conquered*, 323, 415n32.

69. Theron Wierenga, *The Gold Rush Mail Agents to California and Their Postal Markings, 1849–1852* (Muskegon CA: self-published, 1987). Chapter 3, "The California Mail Agents," discusses the legislation and early history of the mail service to California. Also see Hafen, *Overland Mail*.

70. John Caughey, *Gold Is the Cornerstone* (Berkeley: University of California Press, 1948), 55–68; and J. H. Kemble, *The Panama Route, 1848–1869* (Columbia: University of South Carolina Press, 1990).

71. Wierenga, *Mail Agents*, 50–51.

72. In 1851 B. F. Butler in San Francisco published a map of postal routes with a listing of sixty-one post offices, most of them in the mining regions. Butler was located in the Post Office building in San Francisco, suggesting at least that his list of Post Offices was official. B. F. Butler, "Map of the State of California, Gold Region, Post Office Routes &C.," 1851, Huntington Library, San Marino CA.

73. Wiltsee, *Pioneer Miner*, 18.

74. *Sacramento Placer Times*, December 29, 1849.

75. Weld and Company advertised in October 1849 an "inland express" between San Francisco, Benicia, and Sacramento, which was bought out by one of its partners, J. R. Hawley, who also bought out Young and Company in 1850. Wiltsee, *Pioneer Miner*, 56–57.

76. Kimball, *Diary*, October 1, 1849.

77. Wiltsee, *Pioneer Miner*, 33–37. Wiltsee related that Todd's story was told through an "interview," probably given to Hubert Bancroft.

78. Wiltsee, *Pioneer Miner*, 35.

79. Wiltsee, *Pioneer Miner*, 40–43. Wiltsee reprinted the Tolles diary for December 1849–February 1850.

80. Wiltsee, *Pioneer Miner*, 44–45.

81. Wiltsee, *Pioneer Miner*, 41–42.

82. Wiltsee, *Pioneer Miner*, 44. Most of the one-man expresses sold out first to partners and, eventually, to the larger express companies. Todd was unusual in that he grew from a one-man operation to compete with the national companies, but he also sold out in October 1851 to agents of Adams Express. He formed another express in April 1852, which he called "Todd's Express," but then sold that to Wells, Fargo and Company in September 1853.

83. Wiltsee, *Pioneer Miner*, 47–57.

84. *Sacramento Placer Times*, August 18, 1849.

85. Irving McKee, *Alonzo Delano's California Correspondence: Being Letters Hitherto Uncollected from the* Ottawa (Illinois) Free Trader *and the* New Orleans True Delta, *1849–1852*.

(Sacramento: Sacramento Book Collectors, 1952). The *True Delta* published the letter on August 1, 1852.

86. William Murray to his wife, from San Francisco, September 27, 1849, William H. Murray letters, Society of California Pioneers.

87. William Murray to his wife, from Sacramento, January 19, 1850.

88. Letter from J. Collamer, postmaster general, November 15, 1849, cited in Wierenga, *Mail Agents*, 45.

89. Swain letter to his brother George, June 15, 1850, Holliday, *Rushed In*, 370–71.

90. The historiography of the early express businesses in America is thin and is centered around the histories of individual companies. The earliest is Alexander Stimson, *History of the Express Companies and the Origins of the American Railroads* (New York: Published by the author, 1858), which is still a good reference. There is a reprint edition, New York: Alfred A. Knopf, 1948. For Adams Express, see M. C. Nathan, *Adams and Co., First Large Organized Western Express Co., and Its Successors* (San Francisco: Book Club of California, 1960); and A. Shumate, *The Notorious I. C. Woods of the Adams Express* (Glendale CA: Arthur H. Clark, 1986). Much has been written about Wells Fargo, including histories sponsored by the company, beginning with one written by Henry Wells, a founder of the company: H. Wells. *Sketch of the Rise, Progress and Present Condition of the Express System* (Albany NY: Van Benthuysen's Steam Printing House, 1864). See also company histories, Robert Chandler, *Wells Fargo in Sacramento Since 1852* (San Francisco: Wells Fargo Bank History Department, 1992); and F. C. Wells, *Wells Fargo Since 1852* (Los Angeles: Wells Fargo Bank, 1988). A recent history of the company is Philip Fradkin, *Stagecoach: Wells Fargo and the American West* (New York: Free Press, 2001). For the history of the current American Express Company, see Alden Hatch, *American Express: A Century of Service* (Garden City NJ: Doubleday, 1950); and Ralph Thomas Reed, *American Express, Its Origin and Growth* (New York: Newcomen Society in North America, 1952). Although not an academic history, an interesting publication with great reproductions of early art about the express business is the Time-Life book, D. Nevin, *The Expressmen* (New York: Time-Life, 1974). For express companies that were stage coach lines and overland mail carriers, see Hafen, *Overland Mail* and Roscoe P. Conkling, *The Butterfield Overland Mail, 1857–1869* (Glendale CA: Arthur H. Clark, 1947).

91. W. F. Harnden began operating a package-carrying service between Boston and New York in 1839. It was so successful that within three years he had expanded to the current Midwest and to the South and Europe. See Stimson, *History of the Express Companies.*

92. Todd advertised that he would carry gold to San Francisco and deliver it to a bank or an international express. On some trips, he claimed, "my express matter was pretty heavy. I supposed I had at least two hundred thousand dollars worth of dust with me," Wiltsee, *Pioneer Miner*, 34.

93. The Francis Post story related in this paragraph has been pieced together from documents in the California file, American Antiquarian Society (AAS), Worcester MA.

94. We do not know the resolution of the complaint, if any, because there is no further correspondence about the matter in the AAS files.

95. Wiltsee, *Pioneer Miner*, 60.

96. See Richard Brown, *Knowledge Is Power: The Diffusion of Information in Early America, 1700–1865,* (New York: Oxford University Press, 1989).

## 6. The Gold Rush in 1850

1. Bayard Taylor went to California specifically to report on the gold rush for Greeley's *New York Herald* and did not participate at all in the mining. Theodore Johnson was another reporter who went to California primarily to return and publish a book about his trip. See Theodore Johnson, *Sights in the Gold Region and Scenes by the Way* (New York: Baker and Scribner, 1849). James Pratt of the Wolverine Rangers, went to mine, but an important part of his trip was reporting back to his newspaper, the *Marshall (Michigan) Statesman*, about the overland travel and the mining. Others, such as Alonzo Delano, had contracts with newspapers (in his case the *New Orleans True Delta* and the *Ottawa [Illinois] Free Trader*); see Irving McKee, *Alonzo Delano's California Correspondence: Being Letters Hitherto Uncollected from the* Ottawa (Illinois) Free Trader *and the* New Orleans True Delta, *1849–1952* (Sacramento: Sacramento Book Collectors, 1952).

2. Georgia Willis Read and Ruth Gaines, *Gold Rush: The Journals, Drawings, and Other Papers of J. Goldsborough Bruff* (New York: Columbia University Press, 1949), lxv. At the time (1869), Bruff was trying to get the Society of California Pioneers to publish his book after several eastern publishers rejected it. The statement, therefore, might have been a sales pitch rather than what actually happened.

3. Read and Gaines, *Gold Rush*, lxvi–lxxii. There are many inconsistencies among Bruff's various editions, and one of the great advantages of Read and Gaines's work is that one can compare the various versions.

4. Alonzo Delano, *Life on the Plains and among the Diggings* (Auburn and Buffalo NY: Miller, Orton and Mulligan, 1854; New York: Arno, 1973).

5. Edward Gould Buffum, *Six Months in the Gold Mines* (Philadelphia: Lea and Blanchard, 1850); Walter Colton, *Three Years in California* (New York: A. S. Barnes, 1850). Other books written by goldrushers are listed in the bibliography in appendix C.

6. John Cumming, *The Gold Rush: Letters from the Wolverine Rangers to the* Marshall, Michigan, Statesman, *1849–1851* (Mount Pleasant MI: Cumming, 1974), introduction.

7. Pratt to the *Marshall (MI) Statesman* from Chicago, March 8, 1849, printed by the newspaper March 14, Cumming, *Wolverine Rangers*, 6–7.

8. Pratt letters to the *Marshall (MI) Statesman,* from Chauneen and Ottowa, Illinois, March 10 and 13, 1849; from St. Louis, March 20, 1849, and Independence, April 3, 1849, Cumming, *Wolverine Rangers*, 8–14.

9. Horace Ladd to the brother of Charles Palmer, from Independence MO, May 14, 1849, printed in the *Marshall (MI) Statesman*, May 30, 1849, Cumming, *Wolverine Rangers*, 24–25.

10. Cumming, *Wolverine Rangers*, 27.

11. Herman Camp to "Mary Edna and Others," from fifty miles west of Ft. Laramie, July 8, 1849, published by the *Marshall (MI) Statesman*, September 5, 1849, Cumming, *Wolverine Rangers*, 49–55.

12. It is possible to tell from the names who was in the community and who was not because

the names of all the original members of the company, mostly from Marshall and nearby towns, were published by the Marshall, Michigan, *Statesman,* April 11, 1849.

13. As described in chap. 4, the company struggled in the West, particularly over the Lassen Cutoff, and arrived at Lassen's ranch November 8, 1849. Except for the one letter from Ladd described in this paragraph, which he got out through the government relief team, it was not possible to send letters until mid-November, and they would not reach Michigan until late January 1850.

14. Horace Ladd to Ann, October 18, 1849, printed by the *Marshall (MI) Statesman* January 9, 1850, Cummings, *Wolverine Rangers,* 67–68.

15. Horace Ladd to Ann, November 20, 1849, from Feather River Mine, printed by the *Marshall (MI) Statesman,* January 23, 1850, Cummings, *Wolverine Rangers,* 68–69.

16. James Pratt to George Wright from San Francisco, December 20, 1849, printed in the *Marshall (MI) Statesman,* February 20, 1850, Cummings, *Wolverine Rangers,* 69. The newspaper printed excerpts of the letter which they received from Wright, presumably Pratt's law partner in Marshall.

17. James Pratt to George Wright from San Francisco, January 7, 1850, printed in the *Marshall (MI) Statesman,* March 20, 1850, Cummings, *Wolverine Rangers,* 79–82.

18. James Pratt to George Wright from San Francisco, January 12, 1850, printed in the *Marshall (MI) Statesman,* March 20, 1850, Cummings, *Wolverine Rangers,* 85.

19. Horace Ladd to "My Dear Ann," from the Feather River mines, January 9, 1850, printed in the *Marshall (MI) Statesman,* March 20,1850, Cummings, *Wolverine Rangers,* 86–90.

20. Horace Ladd to "My Dear Ann," Cummings, *Wolverine Rangers,* 89.

21. E. S. Camp to "My Dear Molly," from the Feather River Mines, January 9, 1850, printed in the *Marshall (MI) Statesman,* March 20, 1850, Cummings, *Wolverine Rangers,* 92.

22. E. S. Camp to "My Dear Molly," Cummings, *Wolverine Rangers,* 92.

23. John Caughey, *Gold Is the Cornerstone* (Berkeley: University of California Press, 1948), 168–71. For wage rates, see appendix B.

24. Horace Ladd to his father from Feather River, February 6, 1850, printed by the *Marshall (MI) Statesman,* April 10, 1850, Cummings, *Wolverine Rangers,* 97.

25. The appeal of making money through hard work and perseverance was strong for the middle-class Protestants who formed the majority of goldrushers. Many may have made the kind of calculations shown in appendix B, and these letters from goldrushers would have reinforced the conclusions of that arithmetic. For the importance of middle-class culture in the gold rush, see Brian Roberts, *American Alchemy: The California Gold Rush and Middle-Class Culture* (Chapel Hill: University of North Carolina Press, 2000).

26. "M. M." to Chambers and Knapp from Sutters Fort, January 24, 1850, published by the *Missouri Republican,* March 22, 1850, Walker Wyman, *California Emigrant Letters* (New York: Bookman Associates, 1952), 89–90.

27. John Crigler to this father, printed in the *Missouri Republican,* February 15, 1850, Wyman, *Letters,* 92.

28. Simeon Switzler to his son from "Dry Diggings," October 12, 1849, printed by the *Missouri Statesman,* January 25, 1850, Wyman, *Letters,* 90–91.

29. A "mess" was the name given to a group that traveled and ate together, usually with one wagon and the animals necessary for pulling, as well as the equipment and provisions carried in the wagon. A wagon train was made up of messes.

30. "M. M." to Chambers and Knapp, from Sutter's Fort, January 24, 1850, printed by the *Missouri Republican,* March 22, 1850, Wyman, *Letters,* 92–95.

31. Taylor to his brother, J. P. Taylor from Weaverville CA, November 21, 1849, printed by the *Missouri Republican,* February 15, 1850, Wyman, *Letters,* 91–92.

32. *Boston Transcript,* February 12, 1850.

33. *New York Tribune,* November 15, 1849.

34. *New York Tribune,* November 20, 1849.

35. In addition to Taylor's letters, see the following letters from late 1849 in the *New York Tribune,* November 16 (Theodore Johnson), November 23 ("J.W.M."), December 5 (no by-line), and several December 8 ("by our correspondent"–no name); in the *New York Herald,* see issues of November 12 ("RWM)," "S.Z.F.C," "J. Williams," and several letters without names or initials under the heading "Our California Correspondence"), November 13 (three letters designated "private correspondence"), and December 8, (several letters from "Our San Francisco Correspondence").

36. Daniel Robinson to his sister and brother from Sacramento City, October 3, 1849, MS, California File (HM 19771), Huntington Library, San Marino CA. The file contains many letters from Robinson to his sister and brother, both from the trail and from California.

37. David Jackson, *Direct Your Letters to San Jose: The California Gold Rush Letters and Diary of James and David Lee Campbell, 1849–1852* (Kansas City MO: Orderly Pack Rat, 2000), 40.

38. J. S. Holliday, *The World Rushed In* (New York: Simon and Schuster, 1981), chap. 11.

39. John Ingalls to "Bro Trum" [Ingall's brother, Trumble] from the steamer "Senator," December 13, 1849 MS, American Antiquarian Society, Worcester MA.

40. "McK" from San Francisco, March 13, 1849, printed in the *Missouri Republican,* June 22, 1849, Wyman, *Letters,* 160.

41. A. D. McDonald to his brother from Marysville CA, published in the *St. Joseph Adventure,* July 5, 1850, Wyman, *Letters,* 148.

42. William B. Royall from Dry Digginsville, October 16, 1849, published in the *Missouri Statesman,* January 4, 1850, Wyman, *Letters,* 158.

43. "V. J. F." from San Francisco, April 6, 1849, printed in the *Missouri Republican,* June 22, 1849, Wyman, *Letters,* 161.

44. Letter published in the *New York Herald,* and reprinted in the *St. Joseph Adventure,* July 27, 1849, Wyman, *Letters,* 159–60.

45. Franklin Street, *California in 1850 Compared with What It Was in 1849* (Cincinnati OH: R. E. Edwards, 1851), 48.

46. Sweetzer letters MSS, California File, Huntington Library, San Marino CA.

47. Sweetzer to Littlefield and Blood from Sacramento, April 4, 1850, California File, Huntington Library, San Marino CA.

48. Sweetzer to Littlefield and Blood from Sacramento, May 24, 1850, California File, Huntington Library, San Marino CA.

49. Sweetzer to Littlefield and Blood from Sacramento, June 16, 1850, California File, Huntington Library, San Marino CA.

50. Sweetzer to Littlefield and Blood from Sacramento, September 25, 1850, California File, Huntington Library, San Marino CA.

51. Sweetzer to Littlefield and Blood from Sacramento, October 28, 1850, California File, Huntington Library, San Marino CA.

52. Sweetzer to Littlefield and Blood from Sacramento, November 13, 1850, California File, Huntington Library, San Marino CA.

53. Littlefield to Sweetzer from San Francisco, January 14, 1851, California File, Huntington Library, San Marino CA. Letterheads were very popular stationery that showed lithographed views of California on one side of the page. See Roger and Nancy Olmsted, "Letters of Gold," *America West* 13, no. 3 (1976): 13–19.

54. Sweetzer was honored in February 1908 as one of the last ten living California pioneers who were members of the Society of California Pioneers, and he was the only one living in California. His obituary was entitled "The Passing of the Pioneer." *Sacramento Grizzly Bear,* October 1910.

55. The classification of American gold rush publications in Kurutz's bibliography shown in appendix C lists four titles for guidebooks published in 1848 and fifteen such books in 1849; there are only three listed for 1850 and three for 1851.

56. Bayard Taylor, *El Dorado: Adventures in the Path of Empire* (New York: George Putnam, 1850); Colton, *Three Years*; and Thomas Butler King, *California: The Wonder of the Age; A Book for Every One Going to or Having an Interest in That Golden Region* (New York: W. Gowans, 1850).

57. For instance Riley Root, *Journal of Travels from St. Joseph to Oregon* (Galesburg MO: Gazetteer and Intelligencer, 1850) and J. A. Taylor, *A Journal of the Route from Ft. Smith, Arkansas, to California in the Year 1849* (Bowling Green MO: job office printer, 1850).

58. Leonard Kip, *California Sketches, with Recollections of the Gold Mines* (Albany NY: Erastus H. Pease, 1850); William M'Ilvaine Jr., *Sketches of Scenery and Notes of Personal Adventure in California and Mexico* (Philadelphia: Privately printed by Smith and Peters, 1850); John Frost, *Frost's Pictorial History of California* (Auburn NY: Erastus H. Pense, 1850); and William M'Collum, *California as I Saw It* (Buffalo NY: George Derby, 1850).

59. Kip, *California Sketches,* preface, dated February 1850.

60. M'Ilvaine, *Sketches of Scenery,* 7.

61. Edward Gould Buffum, *Six Months in the Gold Mines,* (Philadelphia: Lea and Blanchard, 1850). A short biography of Buffum, and a publishing history of his book is in Doyce B. Nunis, "Edward Gould Buffum: Early California Journalist," *California History* 73, no. 2 (1994): 114–29.

62. Buffum stayed in California and joined the staff of the *San Francisco Alta California* in 1850. He was elected to the San Francisco legislative assembly in 1854 and then to the state legislature from the Know-Nothing Party.

63. Buffum, *Six Months*, 132.

64. Walter Colton, *Three Years in California* (New York: A. S. Barnes, 1850).

65. Colton, *Three Years*, 1.

66. For example, a Thanksgiving sermon by the Rev. J. A. Benton from Sacramento was reprinted by the *Sacramento Placer Times*, perhaps because it took this topic for its theme: J. A. R. Benton, *California as She Was, As She Is, As She Is to Be* (Sacramento: Placer Times Press, 1850). An English guidebook, with no named author, based its pitch on California's nonmining future: *California: Its Past History; Its Present Position; Its Future Prospects* (London: published for the proprietors, 1850). See also Jessie Quin Thornton, *Oregon and California in 1848* (New York: Harper and Bros., 1849).

67. J. S. Holliday, *Rush for Riches: Gold Fever and the Making of California* (Berkeley: The Oakland Museum and the University of California Press, 1999), 91. Porter advertised his "Aerial Transport—the Best Route to California" in several eastern newspapers.

68. James Alexander Read, *Journey to the Gold Diggings by Jeremiah Saddlebags* (New York: Stringer and Townsend, 1849).

69. See Roberts, *American Alchemy*, 3–4, for a brief analysis of the Saddlebags cartoon. The middle-class urbanite going to California and dropping, temporarily, his middle-class repressions is a major theme of the book, and the lithograph shown in figure 9, "An Independent Gold Hunter on His Way to California," is on the cover.

70. The role of California in the election of 1848 and the 30th and 31st Congresses has a rich historiography. Good summaries include David Potter, *The Impending Crisis, 1848–1861* (New York: Harper and Row, 1976), chap. 5; and William Freeling, *The Road to Disunion: Secessionists at Bay, 1776–1854* (New York: Oxford University Press, 1990), chap. 28.

71. Bancroft describes King as a "northern man with southern views," the opposite of Taylor, who was a southern Whig who proslavery southerners thought was a traitor to their section's cause. Bancroft's view of King is summed up in his statement "King made an ass of himself, generally," Herbert Howe Bancroft, *History of California, Vol. VI, 1848–1859* (San Francisco: History Company, 1888), 283. For a more generous view of King, see Neal Harlow, *California Conquered: The Annexation of a Mexican Province: 1846–1850* (Berkeley: University of California Press, 1982), 327–29.

72. Estimates of the 1850 overland travel to California center around forty-five thousand in that year compared to about twenty-five to thirty thousand in 1849. Estimates for travel to Oregon and Utah are eighty-five hundred for 1850 compared to about two thousand in 1849. See John Unruh, *The Plains Across: The Overland Emigrants and the Trans-Mississippi West, 1840–60* (Urbana: University of Illinois Press, 1973), 120; and George Stewart, *The California Trail: An Epic with Many Heroes* (Lincoln: University of Nebraska Press, 1962), 296.

73. Unruh estimates that at least two thousand travelers died of cholera in 1850, about 4 percent of the travelers in that year; Mattes estimates about five thousand deaths in 1850, about 6 percent of the travelers. See Unruh, *Plains Across*, 408–9, 516n75, for a review of estimates of deaths by various trail historians.

74. Stewart, *California Trail*, 296–306, is the best discussion of the changes between 1849 and 1850.

75. Kanesville took advantage of the good reputation of the Clayton guidebook, which showed the route from Mormon Landing, near Kanesville. In 1851 the trail on the north side of the Platte River was called the Council Bluffs Road instead of the Mormon Road. By 1854, when the Kansas-Nebraska Act opened the Indian territory, Council Bluffs (about eight miles north of Kanesville), became the premier trailhead to California and Oregon as well as to Utah. Charles Martin and Dorothy Devereux, "The Omaha-Council Bluffs Area and the Westward Trails," *Overland Journal* 7, no. 4 (1989): 2-12; and Merrill Mattes, "The Northern Route of the Non-Mormons: Rediscovery of Nebraska's Forgotten Historic Trail," *Overland Journal* 8, no. 2 (1990), 2-14.

76. Walker Wyman, "The Outfitting Posts," *Pacific Historical Review* 28, no. 1 (1949): 14-23, 20; and Sheridan Logan, *Old Saint Jo: Gateway to the West, 1799-1932* (St. Joseph MO: John Sublett Logan Foundation, 1979), 50-52.

77. Charles Deatherage, *Early History of Greater Kansas City, Vol I: 1492-1870* (Kansas City MO Interstate, 1927), 267-68.

78. Unruh, *Plains Across*, 253-60.

79. Stewart, *California Trail*, 301.

80. Unruh wrote that in 1850, "possibly 600 or more men still struggled across the Hastings Cutoff." Unruh, *Plains Across*, 319. Three goldrushers that took the Hastings Cutoff are well documented. They were Madison Moorman (Irene Paden, *The Journal of Madison Berryman Moorman* [San Francisco: California Historical Society, 1948]); Sarah Royce (Sarah Bayliss and Ralph Gabriel Royce, ed., *A Frontier Lady: Recollections of the Gold Rush and Early California* [Lincoln: University of Nebraska Press, 1977]); and Lorenzo Sawyer (Lorenzo Sawyer, *Way Sketches; Containing Incidents of Travel Across the Plains from St. Joseph to California in 1850* [New York: E. Eberstadt, 1926]).

81. Royce, *Frontier Lady*, 34.

82. Paden, *Moorman*, 116n110. Paden, who edited the Moorman journal and wrote about the Willis guide, does not resolve the difficulty of why the Willis guide would have been sold on the Hastings Cutoff. Other Mormon guides were sold describing different routes west of Salt Lake City; for example, William Coleman wrote of his trip in 1849, "We were provided with a mormon [*sic*] guide-book published by one who had become familiar with the overland routes during the Mexican war, and later by a trip to and from California."

83. Goldrushers who wintered over in Salt Lake City were termed "Winter Mormons," or "Winter Saints"; there were several hundred in the winter of 1849-50 and perhaps as many as nine hundred in the winter of 1850-51. Unruh provides a good description and analysis of the interactions among the Winter Mormons and the permanent residents, Unruh, *Plains Across*, 323-33.

84. Unruh estimates about 1,000 goldrushers traveled the Mormon Corridor in each of 1849 and 1850; Unruh, *Plains Across*, 319. See also John Caughey, "Southwest from Salt Lake in 1849," *Pacific Historical Review* 6 (1937): 143-64.

85. Riley Senter to cousin Ordelia from Salt Lake City, October 1849, and February 1850 MS, Bancroft Library, University of California, Berkeley CA.

86. Unruh, *Plains Across*, 319. The Hunt company reached California before Christmas.

**Conclusion**

1. The best recent historical work on information and its dissemination is Richard Brown, *Knowledge Is Power: The Diffusion of Information in Early America, 1700–1865* (New York: Oxford University Press, 1989). The book is a series of case studies that illustrate the importance of information marketplaces and diffusion in a variety of situations from the colonial period to the mid-nineteenth century. Brown's introduction traces the historiography of information dissemination in various subfields of social and cultural history.

**Appendix B**

1. Robert A. Margo, *Wages and Labor Markets in the United States, 1820–1860* (Chicago: University of Chicago Press, 2000), appendix tables 3A.5, 3A.6, 3A.7).

2. Rodman W. Paul, *California Gold: The Beginning of Mining in the Far West* (Cambridge MA: Harvard University Press, 1947), 120–21.

3. Margo, *Wages and Labor Markets*, appendix table 6C.2.

4. Edward Buffum, *Six Months in the Gold Mines* (Philadelphia: Lea and Blanchard, 1850), 69.

# Index

Johnson, Theodore, 166, 173
Johnson, William, 89
Johnson's ranch. *See* Coloma (Culloma) CA
*A Journey of the Voyages and Travels of a Corps of Discovery* (Gass), 220n12
*Journey to the Gold Diggings by Jeremiah Saddlebags* (Stringer and Townsend), 174–76
Joyce and Company (publisher), 45–46

Kanesville IA, 62, 64–66, 70, 177, 260n75
*Kanesville Frontier Guardian*, 66
Kansas City MO, 235n15. *See also* Westport/ Westport Landing MO
Kansas-Nebraska Act, 260n75
Kansas River. *See* overland route trailheads
Kearny, Stephen, 8, 50, 67, 69, 235n24
Kemble, Edward C., 131–32, 136, 250n23
Kendall, Wendall, 37
Kimball, Charles P., 137, 145
King, Thomas Butler, 131, 171–72, 176–77, 250n26, 259n71
*Knowledge Is Power* (Brown), 13, 261n1
*Knoxville (Tennessee) Register*, 237n48
Kurutz, Gary, 44, 135

Ladd, Horace, 88, 157–58, 160–61
Langworthy, Franklin, 135
Laramie Mountains, 92
Larkin, Thomas O., 15, 23, 27
Lassen, Peter, 102, 115–16, 120, 245n97, 247n133, 247n135
Las Vegas NV, 180
Latter-Day Saints. *See* Mormons
*Latter-Day Saints' Emigrants' Guide* (Clayton), 55–57, 102–4, 216
Lea and Blanchard (publishers), 156, 173
letters and private communications: as guidebook-like advice, 162–66; impact of unpublished, 166–67; and role in business communications, 167–71; as source of information, 153–56; of the Wolverine Rangers, 156–62
Lewis and Clark expedition, 6–8, 220n12, 222n22

Lexington MO, 81
*Lexington Democratic Journal*, 66
*Lexington Express*, 66
Littlefield, Edwin, 169–71
livestock and draft animals: company selection of, 75, 91; horses vs. mules as, 54, 76; Indian predation of, 10, 114, 230n43; mules as, 79, 87, 240n6; on-the-trail deaths of, 94, 103, 113, 115, 242n41; oxen as, 80–81, 163, 238n68; and pack animals vs. wagons, 52, 78, 237n47, 238n59; personal experience recommendations on, 163–64; scarcity of feed for, 77, 108–9; theft of, 94. *See also* supplies and equipment
Locke, Richard, 155
Loeser, Lucien, 16, 21
Long, Stephen H., 8, 221n15
Louisiana Purchase, 231n46
*Louisville Examiner*, 68
*Louisville Journal and Courier*, 47
*Louisville (Kentucky) Morning Courier*, 47
Lucas, Samuel D., 67

mail and freight delivery: business communications for, 155, 167–69; via "Mormon Express," 105, 244n79; problems encountered with, 169–71; and sea shipments to California, 78, 119, 121. *See also* private express companies; transportation routes; U.S. Post Office Department
Manser, Tom, 160
maps: Bruff creation of, 73; by Derby, 125, 126f, 128–30; early gold rush sources of, 43–45, 50, 52–55; by Frémont-Preuss, 47, 50, 58, 99f, 123, 128, 243n62; information assessment and, 3–5; by Jackson, 125, 127f, 130; by Jarvis, 124f, 125, 128; by Jefferson, 53–54, 214; military expeditions and, 8; newspaper advertising for, 26–27; newspaper credibility from, 19–21, 23; by Ord, 125, 224n13; publishers of, 50, 52, 125, 129f, 130. *See also* publishers and booksellers

Breinigsville, PA USA
30 November 2010
250309BV00001B/5/P